Primary Teaching Assistants:
Learners and Learning

D1324607

This book is one of two readers for the Open University course E111, 'Supporting learning in primary schools'. This is a 60 point (600 hours) part-time course for teaching assistants, learning support staff and adult volunteers working with primary-aged children and their teachers.

The companion book for the course is *Primary Teaching Assistants: Curriculum in Context* edited by Carrie Cable and Ian Eyres.

How to apply:
If you would like to register for this course, or find out about other Open University courses, you should call: +44 (0)1908 653231 or visit the website at www.open.ac.uk.

Primary
Teaching Assistants:
Learners and Learning

Roger Hancock and Janet Collins

 David Fulton Publishers   in association with

David Fulton Publishers Ltd
The Chiswick Centre, 414 Chiswick High Road, London W4 5TF

www.fultonpublishers.co.uk

First published in Great Britain by David Fulton Publishers 2005

10 9 8 7 6 5 4 3 2 1

David Fulton Publishers is a division of Granada Learning Ltd, part of ITV plc.

Note: The right of the individual contributors to be identified as the authors of this work has been asserted by them in accordance with the Copyright, Designs and Patents Act 1988.

British Library Cataloguing in Publication Data
A catalogue record for this book is available from the British Library.

ISBN 1–85346–977–7

Typeset by FiSH Books, London
Printed and bound in Great Britain

Contents

Acknowledgements

We wish to thank those who have written chapters for this Reader or who have given their permission for us to edit and reprint writing from other publications. A special thanks to Kathy Simms for her invaluable secretarial and administrative support, and to Kathryn Creber and Julia Rodney for their preparation of the final manuscript for handover to the publishers. Thanks to Carrie Cable for her involvement in Section 4. Grateful acknowledgement is made to the following sources for permission to reproduce material in this book. Those chapters not listed, ten in all, have been specially commissioned.

Chapter 2: Schlapp, U. and Davidson, J. (2001) 'Classroom assistants in Scottish primary schools', *Spotlights* 85. Reproduced by kind permission of the Scottish Council for Research in Education, Glasgow/Edinburgh.

Chapter 4: Mason, L. (1998) 'My history of helpers', *The Inclusion Assistant*. Reproduced by kind permission of the Alliance for Inclusive Education, London.

Chapter 5: Wedell, K. (2001) 'Klaus' story: the experience of a retired professor of special needs education', in: T. O'Brien and P. Garner (eds), *Untold Stories: Learning Support Assistants and Their Work*. Reproduced by kind permission of Trentham Books Ltd, Stoke on Trent.

Chapter 9: Claxton, G. (2002) *Building Learning Power*. Reproduced by kind permission of TLO Limited, Bristol.

Chapter 10: Burke, C. and Grosvenor, I. (2003) 'Learning: "Let us out...!"', in: *The School I'd Like*. Reproduced by kind permission of Routledge, London.

Chapter 11: Thomas, A. (1998) 'Informal learning', in: *Educating Children at Home*, London: Cassell. Reproduced by kind permission of Continuum, London.

Chapter 13: Dhillon, A. (2003) 'Net gains for slum children', *The Times*, 17 July 2003. © Amrit Dhillon/News International Syndication, London (17 July 2003).

Chapter 14: Crowley, S. and Richardson, M. (2004) 'Raising the bar: improving children's performance through information and communication technology', in: C. Bold (ed), *Supporting Learning and Teaching*. Reproduced by kind permission of David Fulton Publishers, London.

Chapter 15: Kay, J. (2002) 'Assessment and recording', in: *Teaching Assistant's Handbook*, chapter 6, pages 103–118. Reproduced by kind permission of Continuum, London.

Chapter 17: Stern, J. (2003) 'Homework and holidays', in: *Involving Parents*, chapter 6, pages 54–62. Reproduced by kind permission of Continuum, London.

Chapter 18: Alderson, P. (2003) *Institutional Rites and Rights: A Century of Childhood.* Reproduced by kind permission of the Institute of Education, University of London.

Chapter 20: Collins, J. (1998) 'Hearing the silence in a classroom full of noise: empowering quiet pupils', originally published in *TOPIC,* issue 20, Autumn 1998. Reproduced by kind permission of the National Foundation for Educational Research, Slough.

Chapter 21: Royal College of Psychiatrists (2004) *Eating Disorders in Young People: Factsheet for Parents and Teachers.* Reproduced by kind permission of the Royal College of Psychiatrists, London.

Chapter 23: Eaude, T. and Egan, J. (2001) 'Looked after children', *Primary Practice (Journal of the National Primary Trust),* number 27, January 2001, pages 31–35. Reproduced by kind permission of the National Primary Trust.

Chapter 24: Oliver, C. and Candappa, M. (2003) *Tackling Bullying: Listening to the Views of Children and Young People,* Summary Report RB400, pages 5–11. Reproduced by kind permission of HMSO/Department for Education and Skills.

Chapter 25: Taylor, H. (2003) 'Primary school bullying and the issue of gender differences', *Education 3–13,* **31** (3), 11–14. Reproduced by kind permission of Trentham Books Ltd, Stoke on Trent.

Chapter 26: Johnson, P. (2004) 'Boys don't cry', *Education Guardian,* 16 January 2004. Reproduced by kind permission of the author.

Chapter 28: Kay, J. (2002) 'Supporting children's learning and behaviour in school', in: *Teaching Assistant's Handbook,* chapter 7,   pages 119–139. Reproduced by kind permission of Continuum, London.

Chapter 29: Reay, D. (2000) 'A useful extension of Bourdieu's conceptual framework? Emotional capital as a way of understanding mothers' involvement in their children's education', *The Sociological Review,* **48** (4), 568–585. Reproduced by kind permission of Blackwell Publishing Ltd, www.blackwell-synergy.com. (The chapter in this book is based on the edited version republished as Reay, D. (2002) 'Family capital, schooling and social class', in: A. Pollard (ed), *Readings for Reflective Teaching,* London: Continuum, pages 57–59.)

Chapter 30: Plummer, G. (2000) *Failing Girls,* chapter 6, pages 97–117. Reproduced by kind permission of Trentham Books Ltd, Stoke on Trent.

Chapter 31: Jameson, G. (1994) 'Three Billy Goats: six children and race, language and class', *Primary Teaching Studies,* volume 8, number 2, Summer 1994, pages 27–31. Reproduced by kind permission of the University of North London (now part of London Metropolitan University).

Chapter 33: Gardiner, G. (2001) 'Life as a disabled head', *Primary Practice (Journal of the National Primary Trust),* number 29, Autumn 2001, pages 20–22. Reproduced by kind permission of the National Primary Trust.

Chapter 34: Pearce, S. (2003) 'Compiling the white inventory: the practice of whiteness in a British primary school', *Cambridge Journal of Education,* **33** (2), 273–288. Reproduced by kind permission of Taylor & Francis Ltd, www.tandf.co.uk/journals.

Chapter 35: Kenner, C. (2003) 'An interactive pedagogy for bilingual children', in: E. Bearne, H. Dombey and T. Grainger (eds), *Classroom Interactions in Literacy,* pages 90–102. Reproduced by kind permission of Open University Press/McGraw-Hill Publishing Company, Maidenhead.

Chapter 36: Cooley, R. (2003) 'Beyond pink and blue', *Rethinking Schools,* volume 18, number 2 – Winter 2003. Reproduced by kind permission of Rethinking Schools, Milwaukee.

Chapter 37: Reay, D. (2003) 'Troubling, troubled and troublesome? Working with boys in the primary classroom', in: C. Skelton and B. Francis (eds), *Boys and Girls in the Primary Classroom,* pages 151–166. Reproduced by kind permission of Open University Press/McGraw-Hill Publishing Company, Maidenhead.

Introduction

Roger Hancock and Janet Collins

In choosing chapters for this edited collection, *Primary Teaching Assistants: Learners and Learning*, two principles have been uppermost in our minds. First, the chapters have been chosen for their relevance to the understandings and practices of teaching assistants in primary schools today. Second, the chapters need to meet the study needs of students registered for The Open University course E111 *Supporting Learning in Primary Schools*. This is a 60 point (600 hours) part-time course for teaching assistants, learning support staff and adult volunteers working in primary schools. (The companion book *Primary Teaching Assistants: Curriculum in Context* is the second reader supporting the course.)

The book's sub-title *Learners and Learning* provides a further focus for its content. Our selections aim to bring together understandings about all learners in schools and this arises from the notion that a school contains a 'community of engaged learners' (Eckert *et al.* 1989). Children tend to be seen as the only learners in schools but we would argue that adults – teachers, teaching assistants and parents – are learners too. Adults need to learn about learning and its content, but also need to learn from children if they are effectively to support them in their learning. We believe education is an interactive process and feel uneasy with the idea of a curriculum being 'delivered' to children. This implies they are passive recipients of knowledge with little opportunity to impact upon it or make it their own. By comparison, in this book, we aim to reinforce the view that learners are active participants in their own learning. Our chapter selections also shed light on 'learning' as a whole school and life-wide process. There's a sense in which we are all experts on our own learning processes – whether we are adults or children.

Following their entry into classrooms in the 1960s as 'aides', 'helpers' and 'auxiliaries', teaching assistants have become essential to teachers and children. For many teachers it would be hard to contemplate running a classroom without the support of teaching assistants. Teaching assistant work ranges from classroom maintenance tasks, through to teaching-related activities and specialised learning support for children who 'provide the greatest challenge to the routine confidence and competence of teachers' (Nind and Cochrane 2002: 1). Given the way teaching assistants have increasingly taken on responsibilities that hitherto would only have been done by a qualified teacher, there is now a great deal of overlap between the training and study interests of teaching assistants and those of teachers.

Teaching assistants are immersed in the same professional world as teachers and they stand to benefit from reading what teachers read. However, teaching assistants have their own distinctive contribution to make to school life and children's learning. This arises from the way they are, to a large extent, positioned between teachers and children. This increases their opportunities for close contact with groups of children and with individuals. Their working 'place' gives them openings for shared, personalised exchanges with pupils, flexibility for moment-by-moment adaptations to learning tasks, and chances to gather 'inside understandings' about children's learning and to share these with teachers.

Until relatively recently, teaching assistants were dependent upon an educational literature written mainly for teachers. The last five years, however, has witnessed a growing number of publications aimed specifically at teaching assistants themselves – particularly with regard to the practice of learning support. This is a welcome development because it does teaching assistants a disservice to see them simply as 'assistants' and an adjunct to a teacher's practice. However, in 2001, O'Brien and Garner (2001: 2) expressed concern that the views, expectations, aspirations, beliefs and values of learning support assistants themselves were poorly represented in the available literature. This remains an issue as we go to press.

In this book we aim to compensate for this lack of published knowledge from those well placed to describe learning support practice and analyse it. We have chosen pieces that we feel are authored in such a way as to communicate central ideas about learners and learning to a wide readership. We have therefore included pieces written by teaching assistants, teachers, academics, researchers and others which reflect a broad-based understanding of learning, its many elements and the abundant contexts in which learners can engage with learning. We have also included chapters written by a parent and a pupil. Ideally, we would have liked to have included more 'insider' teaching assistant accounts than we have. We hope others will take this on as their work becomes better understood and theorised, and teaching assistants themselves become more confident at explaining and researching their own practice.

There's a sense, however, in which teaching assistants might now inherit a difficulty that teachers have yet to resolve – how to find the time and energy to write about classroom practice when the daily job is all consuming. Despite a 'teacher as researcher' movement dating back some 30 years, most published work for teachers comes from those who have left the classroom as their main place of work, and, it needs to be said, from those who have no direct experience of it at all – apart from when they were children. Just as teachers need collaborative support to become writers and researchers, so it is true for teaching assistants. In order to further our understanding of school learning, and learning more generally, it is essential that all perspectives are heard in the educational literature (see, for instance, Collins *et al.* 2001; O'Brien and Garner 2001; Hancock 1997). In producing this book, it has been our aim to shed light on learning support in primary schools through bringing together a number of distinct voices which have significant things to say about learning and learners.

A note on titles

We are aware of the many titles that are used to describe adults, other than qualified teachers, who provide learning support to children in schools. As the UK government has expressed its preference for the term 'teaching assistants' we have used this in the book's title. However, a variety of titles will be found within the selected chapters and, as Chapter 1 suggests, this is important because it reflects the diversity of learning support roles that can be found throughout the UK and beyond.

References

Collins, J., Insley, K. and Soler, J. (2001) *Developing Pedagogy: researching practice.* London: Paul Chapman.

Eckert, P., Goldman, S. and Wenger, E. (1989) *Jocks and Burnouts: social identity in the high school.* New York: Teachers College Press.

Hancock, R. (1997) 'Why are class teachers reluctant to become researchers?' *British Journal of In-Service Education*, **23** (1), 85–99.

Nind, M. and Cochrane, S. (2002) 'Inclusive curricula? Pupils on the margins of special schools', *International Journal of Inclusive Education*, **6** (2), 185–98.

O'Brien, T. and Garner, P. (eds) (2001) *Untold Stories: learning support assistants and their work.* Stoke on Trent: Trentham Books.

Section 1
Learning support

Roger Hancock and Janet Collins

The practice of learning support as carried out by teaching assistants has developed considerably in recent times and has doubtless run ahead of conceptual and theoretical understanding. The eight chapters in this section have been selected because we feel they all contribute towards an understanding of the nature of support. Five of these are commissioned pieces and this reflects the shortage of published writing that captures, in detail, learning support practice.

In Chapter 1, through a review of eight learning supporters across the UK, Roger Hancock and Jennifer Colloby examine the variety of titles and roles and attribute significance to these differences. An overview of Scottish support practice is provided in Chapter 2 by Ursula Schlapp and Julia Davidson. There have been a number of large-scale surveys of teaching assistants and evaluations of their practice in England but this chapter usefully provides a view from Scotland where 'classroom assistant' is the preferred term, and where professional boundaries seem more clearly defined than they are south of the border.

In Chapter 3, Linda Shaw recalls significant support events in her life and sets the receiving and giving of support within a human rights framework. We need to know much more about how children experience learning support and particularly the inter-personal dimension of being supported. Lucy Mason, in Chapter 4, provides candid suggestions to supporters with regard to what may help and what may hinder. Chapter 5 provides an insider's view of providing support. Here, among other reflections on the practice of support, Klaus Wedell highlights the opportunities that learning supporters have for tuning into individual children's feelings.

In Chapter 6, Sally Wallace describes her duties as a SENCO's assistant, particularly with regard to her growing involvement in ICT. Currently, in England and Wales, there is the intention that 'higher level' teaching assistants take on a variety of administrative duties and it is likely that ICT competence will be an important area of skill for those who take on these responsibilities.

Chapter 7 was originally a conference presentation to a large audience of learning supporters at Manchester Metropolitan University by Katie Clarke and

Pat Rangeley. Theirs is a first-hand account of inclusion in action during one day in the life of Nadia, Katie's daughter. It highlights the centrality of the contribution of Pat (and her learning support colleague Kath Williams) as Nadia's co-supporters. The final chapter in this Section is a close description of the role of one teaching assistant as she works with a group of children in a mathematics lesson. In this chapter, Jennifer Colloby provides an insight into the way in which Caroline Higham shapes her 'intermediary' role, working directly with a small group of children, but also being very aware of the teacher's practice and wider developments within the classroom.

Chapter 1

Eight titles and roles

Roger Hancock and Jennifer Colloby

The roles and responsibilities of teaching assistants have become increasingly defined. In this chapter, Roger Hancock and Jennifer Colloby, from the Open University, examine the wide ranging work of eight learning supporters across the United Kingdom and consider why there are significant variations in their duties.

Learning support staff in the United Kingdom have many titles and many types of responsibilities. Preferences for job titles are to be found at both regional and local levels. Generic titles like 'classroom assistant', 'learning support assistant' and 'teaching assistant' are commonly used but there are many other terms by which support staff are known. Also, given the possible range of duties, staff can find themselves doing significantly different work with varying levels of responsibility.

Job titles are important. Titles can be closely related to our sense of worth and status at work. Ideally, they should accurately describe the nature of work as an employer defines it, but also as employees themselves experience it. Titles that achieve this balance help people to feel good about themselves and the work they do. 'Non teaching staff' was once commonly used in schools to refer to staff not qualified as teachers. Marland (2001) suggests this title is offensive. The use of the term 'assistant' can be questioned too, given that support staff are often doing much more than 'just' assisting a teacher or a child.

In order to explore titles and roles, we obtained thumbnail sketches from eight classroom support staff from around the UK. Eight schools were selected with a degree of randomness through LEA website lists. Telephone contact was established with headteachers who helped with the identification of a support staff member from their school. The eight staff then collaborated with us to construct short accounts to capture what they saw as the main purpose of their work.

We make no claims for the representativeness of our findings. However, through the words of support staff themselves, we feel the eight accounts give a good sense of the nature of the work that is often termed 'learning support', and an indication of the variety of titles and roles that can be found across the UK.

A learning support assistant (LSA)

I give support in the classroom – especially with literacy and numeracy. I personally do a lot of craft, design technology and art. In fact, I run a lunchtime art club. I organise the staffroom, and when we have visitors I look after them. I'm the first-aider and I keep an eye on health and safety. I also stock-take art and the general use materials, as well as having an involvement with our Book Fairs. I am team-leader for the other LSAs and I do any ad hoc jobs and quite a lot of clerical jobs. I accompany children and teachers when they go out on trips. I work the ICT equipment. I set up televisions, do photocopying and ensure the copier is running properly. I set up the overhead projectors and the listening centres. I have to make sure these machines are ready and available. I also take money and liaise with parents. I work with Years 1 and 2 but I'm all encompassing. We have LSAs who are actually attached to classes. However I divide my time between Years 1 and 2. This means I work with four teachers. I don't work in Reception. I'm therefore more wide-ranging than some colleagues who are based in single classrooms. I do a lot of display throughout the school as well as in classrooms. I'm there for the children but I support the staff as well. Everywhere in the school that I can be used, I'm used.

Jane Powell, St Francis RC Infant School, Cardiff, South Wales

A classroom assistant

As a classroom assistant at Alexandra Parade Primary School I have lots of different duties assigned to me. I have responsibility for running the school tuck shop and children come to buy their tuck as school starts. I have to keep a check on stock levels and order more items, as they are needed. Four days a week all the children receive a piece of fruit and it is my responsibility to distribute it throughout the school. After this is done I help out in the classrooms as needed. I work with small groups of children to develop their reading skills or help them with their writing. It depends on what the teacher asks me to do. I help to create displays by selecting and mounting children's work. Each day I work to a different timetable but I always undertake any administrative duties such as photocopying and filing for the teachers in Primary 4 to Primary 7 (8–12 years). I tidy up after art sessions and I particularly enjoy my work with individual children who are struggling with some aspect of mathematics. Every day I do playground duty and I share the role of first-aider with other assistants in the school. My husband runs the school football team and my duties include 1 hour each week to help organise the team and their equipment and transport them to away matches. At the moment there are just two girls in the football team and I hope that eventually more girls will want to play.

Margaret Verrecchie, Alexandra Parade Primary School, Glasgow, Scotland

A nursery assistant

I work in the pre-school with children who are 3 and 4 years of age. My main duties as a nursery assistant are to assist the teacher in both the planning of activities and the work with the children. I help to develop the yearly plan and, from this, the monthly plan which is then broken down into the daily plan. When I arrive at school I help to set out the resources that are first needed. The children arrive at 9.15 am and I settle them to various activities and help those who are painting to put on aprons and make sure names are written on paper so I can easily identify children's work. I am responsible for 'brek' for all the pre-school children. Brek is a healthy eating snack, which consists of milk, some fruit, and often toast. The supervision of this takes 1 hour as children come in groups of 6 at a time. After this I supervise class activities but if it is PE that day I go and set out the equipment in the hall. Some kind of physical activity takes place each day and I help the children with this. When we return to the classroom I help children change back into their shoes. The final 30 minutes of the morning is spent on reading or puzzle activities and making sure the children have all their belongings when parents collect them at 12 o'clock. After this I clear and tidy the classroom and update the teacher with any information I have been given by parents. Together we also evaluate the morning's activities and consider our next day's plan.

Sheila McKnight, Strabane Primary School, County Tyrone, Northern Ireland

A nursery nurse

As a nursery nurse my main role is to assist the Nursery and Reception teachers with children in the early years, but I also help out generally throughout the school when necessary. I have a lot of direct involvement with children but I also oversee the classroom resources – I keep the art and craft areas running smoothly, for instance. I get involved in all parts of the curriculum, particularly supporting children's learning in literacy, numeracy, music, art, and IT. I am involved in planning learning activities with the teachers. At the moment, in the afternoon, we are taking steps to integrate the Nursery and Reception children and I find this enjoyable. I am a first aider, I assist children with toileting and washing, I take them to lunch and out into the playground, and I drive the school's minibus. I work with all children when in the classroom and I particularly enjoy working with those who sometimes struggle with their learning. I find it very satisfying to succeed with them, although I do have to work concertedly at achieving this success with some children.

I frequently attend one-day courses which I find very important for my development and knowledge. For instance, I recently went on an 'improving the classroom' workshop with the Reception teacher and an early years conference to hear Peter Clarke, the children's commissioner for Wales. I feel very fortunate to be employed as a nursery nurse because posts are not that easy to find in North Wales. When qualified nursery nurses get a nursery nurse post here they tend to stick with it.

Dawn Jones, Ysgol Cynfran Llysfaen, Colwyn Bay, North Wales

A learning mentor

I work with individual children who have barriers to learning. The overall aim is to improve attendance, reduce permanent and fixed term exclusions, and improve behaviour. I'm currently based in the Infants right through to Years 3 and 4. As the learning mentor, I observe them in the class to see how they are getting on. They might have targets they need to meet – for instance, to arrive on time or finish a task without being distracted. I liaise with parents early in the morning and they know that I am available at that time. Parents also know that they can ring me or ask to see me at other times. We run a breakfast club and that provides a good opportunity for me to talk informally to parents and children. There may be something that's on a child's mind – something that's troubling them. I have a room with resources where I can talk to children who are upset. I have regular planning meetings with teachers every Monday. I was a nursery nurse in the school for 15 years before I took on my current role. I had therefore developed relationships with most parents which are essential for my new role.

It's quite hard for me to draw the line between a classroom support role and a learning mentor's role, especially when you've done the former job for so many years. I am working with 13 children at the moment – the maximum is 15. When I'm in a class helping one of my children, if another child needs help of some kind and the teacher's busy I usually help out.

Alison Cundy, Alt Primary School, Oldham, England

A bilingual assistant and home–school link worker

I have two jobs – the first is a bilingual classroom assistant and the second a home–school link worker. In the first I work mainly with Turkish children, most of whom are new arrivals from Turkey. The post is funded by an Ethnic Minority Achievement Grant and I am employed for thirteen hours a week. I usually work within the classroom with small groups, but sometimes I take one or two children outside the room. I also run a small class myself when I teach Turkish to Year 4 children. I find 8–9 years is the best age to teach Turkish because children have learnt to read and write English and this can be used to support their progress in another language. At this age they also seem to particularly enjoy learning Turkish – they appear 'ready'.

My second job arose out of the liaison work with parents that I did as part of the bilingual classroom assistant role. For this, I am employed for six hours a week. I work entirely with parents, supporting them as and when necessary. I help them with a range of tasks related to their children's schooling. I liaise with teachers, get involved in translations, help them with written English when, for instance, they need to register their children or fill out a school meals application form, take phone calls when parents find it hard to express themselves in English, and try to resolve any communication difficulties that may arise. I find I'm needed in many ways and that six hours is not enough time to meet the needs that parents have so I often give time that is voluntary.

Didem Celik, Whitmore Primary School, London, England

A parent helper (now classroom assistant)

When I was a teenager, I worked in a children's clothes shop, 'A and V Fashions', Lerwick, where there were always children coming in with parents. Some could have their tantrums and whatever else when they couldn't get things, but I'm a very patient person. Working in a clothes shop prepared me for working in schools. I kept a toy box and books in the corner. If the parents were looking a bit stressed then I would say to their children, 'Oh come and see this', and read them a story.

When my children went to school I started going on their school trips. I also volunteered to do the youth club as well as being a parent helper. It inspired me to do more. I just love working with children. As a parent volunteer I was flexible and would help with sale tables and raising money for charity. I would donate things to be sold. I'd go on school trips, any sort of trips with any age. I would get involved whenever I had the opportunity. I helped out for five years and it was fine because I could still be home for my three children.

At one time, I wasn't sure whether to work with children or old folk, so I decided to go for K100 ('Understanding Health and Social Care') with the Open University. I got my certificate and ended up applying for a job here. My three children are fine about me getting involved. When I see them in school, two call me 'mam' and the other one calls me 'Louise'. I just treat them the same as the other bairns. They know I'm now a member of staff.

Louise Dix, Aith Junior High School, Shetland, Scotland

A teaching assistant

I work with small groups of pupils outside the classroom in a resource room. My work is part of the school's performance management programme and I am regularly observed by the head teacher. The majority of my working week is spent supporting a Year 4 class but for 30 minutes a day I withdraw a small group of Year 2 children as part of the Early Learning Strategy Programme. I assess and support their phonic awareness. I also withdraw a group of Year 4 children as part of the Additional Literacy Programme. I discuss and co-plan my input with the class teacher. We all return to the Year 4 classroom for the second half of the literacy hour. During the numeracy lesson, I ensure my group are working well and offer support across the class.

I spend my lunchtimes preparing materials. In the afternoon I offer general support and thus build relationships with all the children. The school has a reading intervention programme and I spend the final 30 minutes of each school day working with Year 2 children who need this additional help. The school sent me on a 12-week training course for this. I also help children with their reading and each Tuesday afternoon I undertake pupil assessments. I liaise with parents and we work together to help children with their reading. I write reports for the SENCO and help create IEPs. As a school governor, I have responsibility for SEN provision.

I am the school's PE co-ordinator. I organise both PE lessons and the after-school sports clubs. As a qualified football and athletics coach, I run the football (for both boys and girls), run athletics clubs and assist with the clubs for skating and gymnastics.

Keith Eddyshaw, Warren Primary School, Nottingham, England

Discussion and conclusion

The eight roles and titles featured in this chapter are learning support assistant, classroom assistant, nursery assistant, nursery nurse, learning mentor, bilingual assistant, parent helper and teaching assistant, respectively. Analysis of these thumbnail accounts reveals the following main categories of involvement for the eight people collectively:

1. clerical and administrative duties (e.g. stock checking, photocopying and filing)
2. out-of-class involvements (e.g. liaising with parents, art club, support on trips)
3. setting up and maintaining equipment (e.g. IT support, reprographic maintenance)
4. health and safety (e.g. distributing fruit, overseeing children's snack time, first aid)
5. curriculum and learning support (e.g. literacy and numeracy, art, teaching Turkish)
6. management (e.g. leading other TAs)
7. servicing (e.g. staffroom maintenance, tidying the classroom).

We note the wide-ranging nature of the duties highlighted in the above analysis but also the rich mix of involvements within each individual thumbnail sketch. We believe, however, that if we talked to the same group of staff in a year's time we would pick up significant shifts in their duties and responsibilities. Moreover, if we had selected a different group of eight people with exactly the same titles, we would have found a slightly different set of duties being carried out. Lee (2003), in a review of the existing literature on learning support staff, suggests there is 'no common pattern to teaching assistants' work' (p. 25).

Although we identify seven types of work, Category 5 (direct support for children's curriculum learning) took, by far, the highest proportion of respondents' time. It is important to remember too, that other categories of work can result in support for children's curriculum-related learning – for instance, liaising with parents (Category 2) or distributing fruit (Category 4).

We suggest that the variation in titles, roles and responsibilities of learning support staff in this small study arises because there is a great deal of negotiation about their roles and related deployment at the level of individual schools and, even, individual classrooms. Variation is also explained by the way in which support staff and teachers are working in locally negotiated 'interdependent ways' rather than clearly designated hierarchical relationships with watertight role boundaries (see Hancock *et al.* 2002).

Teachers and learning support staff, we believe, are involved in an on-the-spot process of decision-making whereby the totality of the work to be done is, in certain ways, shared. This means that learning support staff in this study are taking on some duties that once were done only by a qualified teacher. Clearly this poses questions about where teacher professional boundaries should be drawn, but also what is to be done about the remuneration of support staff who are now involved in teaching-related duties. However, that said, the variation in learning support staff roles seems to be a desirable workforce development. It offers a localised, creative way of utilising adult skills thus maximising support for teachers and for children's learning.

References

Hancock, R., Swann, W., Marr, A., Turner, J. and Cable, C. (2002) *Classroom Assistants in Primary Schools: employment and deployment*, ESRC project dissemination report, Faculty of Education and Language Studies, The Open University. Available from: w.r.hancock@open.ac.uk.

Lee, B. (2003) 'Teaching assistants in schools', *Education Journal*, **68**, 25–7.

Marland, M. (2001) 'Unsung heroes', *Report* (October), Magazine of the Association of Teachers and Lecturers, London.

Chapter 2

Classroom assistants in Scottish primary schools

Ursula Schlapp and Julia Davidson

In recent years there have been a number of surveys highlighting the work of learning support staff in schools, particularly in England. In this chapter, Ursula Schlapp and Julia Davidson, researchers based at the University of Glasgow, report on the interim findings of a national evaluation of the Classroom Assistants Initiative in Scotland.

Introduction

The Classroom Assistants Initiative is one of a package of Excellence Fund initiatives launched in Scotland in 1999 by the Scottish Executive Education Department (SEED), which aims to raise standards throughout Scotland's schools. Over 2000 assistants have already been appointed, and the aim is to increase this provision to 5000 by March 2002.

The Initiative seeks to 'free up' teachers' time for teaching through the deployment of classroom assistants. These assistants carry out a range of practical and administrative tasks, and work under the direction of the class teacher in the supervision and support of pupils' learning. A national evaluation of this Initiative is currently being undertaken by the Scottish Council for Research in Education for the SEED. The evaluation began in January 2000 with an analysis of education authorities' reports of their pilot programmes. This gave a national picture of the Initiative at the end of the pilot phase.

Evaluation of the main phase of the initiative began in Autumn 2000 when information was collected, by postal survey and classroom observation, from a national sample of education authorities and schools.

This addresses three main questions:

- How are classroom assistants deployed?
- What do classroom assistants do?
- What is the impact on teachers and pupils?

It is findings from this stage of the research that are reported here.

How are classroom assistants deployed?

The evaluation found that the majority of schools allocate their classroom assistants to more than one teacher, although some assistants, particularly in small schools, may work with a single teacher. Some schools also allocate time for tasks, such as photocopying or playground supervision, which support staff and pupils across the school.

Decisions about allocation of classroom assistants depend, among other things, on the size of the schools and the number of assistants. The following examples from two schools participating in the evaluation illustrate different approaches.

Working with all classes

In one school, where there was only one assistant, rigorous timetabling was used to enable all classes to have a share of her time. The classroom assistant explained her schedule as follows:

> I have a timetable: three quarters of an hour twice a week, for each class...because I have a timetable the teachers know when to expect me. The class teacher has a small notebook into which they write the things for me to do.

A class teacher in this school commented that their main opportunity to talk with their assistants is at lunchtime. And pupils were aware that their class only received support for two sessions per week, but appreciated the help. One P3 girl reported that:

> She is not in class that often...twice a week. She helps us when we get stuck...In case you don't get it...Today she helped me with the Stile game. She helped me with knowing what to do. She said do the opposites...say it said 'up' you had to look for 'down'...

Working with one stage

A headteacher who allocated a classroom assistant to each stage for the duration of the school year explained the approach thus:

> ...long periods of time being settled, and getting to know the children and children knowing them well and respecting them, is making a difference in what can be achieved...The concept is that they will stay there, though there may be an opportunity to move around if they wish, rather than always be Pl/2 assistants, for example.

Until recently this school had only one classroom assistant and the headteacher had found it much harder to allocate the assistant's time, or to see what difference she had made, 'except against the teachers' stress level!'

As the example above suggests, there is some evidence that the nature of the classroom assistants' contribution changes as the amount of time spent with particular teachers and classes increases. In autumn 2000 teachers who were receiving classroom assistant support were timetabled for amounts ranging from 30 to 40 minutes to more than 25 hours per week.

What do classroom assistants do?

Classroom assistants are undertaking a wide range of tasks, many within the classroom, but also elsewhere in the school. Out-of-class tasks may include those with an emphasis on care, such as playground supervision and first aid, and those with a more administrative emphasis, such as taking responsibility for a library or other resource area. Individual schools determine the balance of tasks, but the following example illustrates a typical range.

A typical range

This classroom assistant is timetabled to work in seven different classes. Teachers complete planning sheets, which indicate lesson type, activity and resources required. The assistant has time to prepare resources on Monday mornings, and on Thursday afternoons uses time not allocated for classwork for administration and preparing displays. She saw her role as being to:

- keep children on task
- consolidate learning
- read with small groups
- support activities in literacy and numeracy with an emphasis on practical application
- support ICT.

As she put it:

> I seem to have been nominated computer expert. All the IT problems come to me. If computers fail I can fix about 60% myself, otherwise I send them off to IT.

She was also helping to organise a Book Evening, and took children in the minibus to play football with other schools.

Supporting learning as the major role

A clear finding at this stage of the evaluation was that the largest amount of classroom assistant time is directed to supporting learning within the classroom. There seems to be an expectation on the part of the majority of teachers, headteachers and classroom assistants that this is the main function of the post.

Despite, or perhaps because of, this shared expectation regarding the classroom assistant's role, a number of difficulties were reported. These were broadly concerned with time management, and the boundaries between teaching and support.

Need for planning time

With this emphasis on supporting learning it is understandable that many teachers and classroom assistants would like more time together to plan. In many cases the assistant's contract hours did not allow for discussion before or after school. Some teachers describe 'snatched moments at break time', but other duties such as playground supervision may mean even this is not possible. Some schools have been experimenting with other approaches to making time available during the school day, using assembly times for meeting, or asking senior staff to cover for colleagues. One headteacher explained that:

> [Time for meetings] has to be timetabled and by using DHT to cover classes eats into DHT's timetable, however benefits outweigh difficulties.

A number of teachers and classroom assistants noted concern over the effects of conflicting demands on the classroom assistants' time, and in particular, the classroom assistant being repeatedly called away at short notice from timetabled sessions. As one teacher explained:

> My classroom assistant is frequently accompanying other classes on trips etc in my allocated slot. Therefore, tasks I had for him to do can't go ahead as planned.

Boundaries of the remit

It was evident from the survey that, at this stage of the Initiative, the role of 'classroom assistant' is still evolving. While most respondents thought their job descriptions for remits were clear, some teachers and some assistants expressed uncertainty, particularly about the boundary between supporting and teaching.

One headteacher explained that it could be easier to set out clear boundaries for the classroom assistant's role with a relatively untrained person, whereas there may be a shadowy divide for those with prior experience, for example as nursery nurses. The classroom assistants at this school were described as not being afraid to ask 'Is this within my remit?' One had a background working in industry and had a different perspective on being trained than is perhaps usual in education. She expected clear guidelines on what she should be doing, whereas the headteacher felt that:

> Schools, I think, tend to fudge some of that stuff [job description]. Don't make it too explicit and too clear and 'don't ask and I won't tell' kind of stuff, if it's going over the boundary. And sometimes it is a very difficult boundary, between teaching and supporting.

What is the impact on teachers and pupils?

Teachers perceived that the biggest impact classroom assistants had on their use of time resulted from delegating to the assistants the preparation of classroom materials and resources. However, as mentioned above, this activity did not occupy the major part of classroom assistants' time. In this area therefore, a small input – 'an extra pair of hands' – appears to make a substantial difference to teachers' perceptions of their workload.

Within the class, most classroom assistants work with groups of pupils or individuals, supporting them in a variety of reinforcement tasks and games. Their presence also frees teachers to give more attention to teaching individuals and groups while the assistant helps to keep others on task and resolve minor difficulties, Some teachers report that they therefore expect more from pupils and have increased enthusiasm for teaching.

There are, nonetheless, challenges to working together, among them the already mentioned lack of planning time, the extra work required to plan, and demands placed on the abilities of particular assistants.

However, teachers and headteachers believe that the Classroom Assistants Initiative has led to an improvement in pupils' participation in activities, in the range of learning experiences offered to them, and to a lesser extent in their motivation and behaviour. The following example illustrates one classroom assistant's impact on practical mathematics activities.

Supporting practical activities

The class teacher and the classroom assistant in one of the primary schools studied have been working together for two years. The classroom assistant supervises practical activities in mathematics with mixed ability groups. She rotates from group to group so that all have an opportunity to work with her. The classroom assistant is able to keep a group on task in a way that would be hard in a whole-class context. As the teacher explains:

> We are timetabled for two consecutive days each week. When I work on practical work it is more rushed and not much time. Our classroom assistant can take her time on practical work and talk them through it more.

During the observation of a P5/6 class, the classroom assistant was working on weight with a small mixed ability group of three girls and one boy. Each child took a turn to estimate the weight of a different parcel and record this. They then checked the object's weight on the scales. Pupils said:

> ...we were enjoying it. We were weighing...Weighing boxes...a little surprised [at the weights]...Had to see if we got the exact weight of box...on testing we were just about right.

Attainment

Many respondents think that the Classroom Assistants Initiative is already contributing to raising attainment, as one teacher's remarks illustrate:

> I get more 'quality time' with individuals and groups...She [the classroom assistant] certainly helps our time to flow...I can say definitely, that because I am getting more

time with individuals and groups, that we are getting through more, and in more depth, particularly with the poorer ability groups...I'm certainly expecting the attainment targets to be met more quickly and perhaps more easily and comfortably...

However, concrete evidence of the impact of the Initiative on pupil attainment was hard to find at this early stage of the Initiative, and may continue to be in a climate of multiple policy initiatives all aimed at improving pupils' attainment.

Emerging issues

Different issues emerged from the schools with classroom assistants and those who had not yet been allocated assistants. In the latter case, schools were concerned that pupils were missing out. Schools with assistants, on the other hand, experienced a number of specific difficulties. In particular, finding space for assistants, adjusting to the requirements of team working, and the training and support available for classroom assistants.

Finding space for classroom assistants

Despite the general success of the Initiative, some schools experienced practical difficulties in accommodating classroom assistants. Headteachers commented on difficulties arising from small classrooms and lack of space for working with groups, let alone finding 'a work area they can call their own'. The use of staggered breaktimes, as a way to manage staffroom overcrowding and provide playground cover, may isolate assistants from the other staff, with consequent effects on planning and teamworking. As one classroom assistant explained:

> Due to playground duties I feel I miss a lot by not being in [the] staffroom with other members of staff. You don't know what is going on.

On the other hand, playground duty was an opportunity for classroom assistants to develop their relationships with pupils.

Teamworking

Remarkably few problems in teamworking have emerged, despite the fact that headteachers and teachers have, to date, received limited support and advice on how to manage the Initiative, or how to involve classroom assistants in whole-school activities. The majority of class teachers with classroom assistants found it easy to work with them and appreciated their flexibility, competence and initiative. Classroom assistants were equally positive: good relationships with teaching staff were characterised by mutual respect, good communication, being made to feel a valued part of the team, and supportive teachers and headteachers.

However these good relationships sometimes took time to develop, as one classroom assistant explained:

I feel teachers are gradually seeing the classroom assistant as an 'assistant'. At first they were embarrassed being helped, but now it is like a team.

Training and development

The amount of training available to classroom assistants seems to vary considerably. Most had received induction training from the school and/or authority, but many had received little subsequent support. Only about half of the assistants participated in planning meetings with teachers, and few were involved in whole-school development activities on a regular basis. The expectation that most classroom assistants will spend a substantial proportion of their time supporting learning in class increases the need for them to have appropriate qualifications and training. The delay in providing support material for teachers may also mean that some have had unrealistic expectations of what a classroom assistant can be expected to undertake.

Conclusions

Classroom assistants are relieving teachers of routine tasks and providing extra support for pupils. Together these contributions are believed by many to have the potential to help raise pupil attainment. However, tensions exist because of the wide remit and competing demands on classroom assistant time. Also those schools and teachers not yet benefiting from classroom assistant support are concerned that their pupils are missing out. These factors need to be addressed in order to make the Initiative more effective. In addition the findings at this stage of the evaluation suggest that in striving to find a balanced approach, authorities and schools may in particular wish to consider the following:

- prioritising and limiting the range of tasks that individual assistants undertake
- ensuring adequate time for teachers and assistants to plan and discuss activities
- providing continuing training and support for assistants and those working with them.

Chapter 3

Supporting human rights

Linda Shaw

Linda Shaw, co-director of the Centre for Studies on Inclusive Education has a long-standing commitment to human rights. Using memories from her childhood and previous work, she considers, in a heartfelt way, the nature of support and its potential to contribute towards a truly inclusive society.

Support has many aspects. I want to focus on the aspect often known as personal, emotional and spiritual support. To a greater or lesser extent, like fish in water, this kind of support is one of those funny things we are not aware of until it drains away or comes to revive us when our lives feels dry and barren. Support in this sense is not about money, or other material sustenance, but about how we human beings can help each other achieve what I can only call 'our hearts' desires' – to be the very best we can possibly be. Support in this sense is about helping people become their true selves. It is absolutely certain that, one way or another, giving and receiving support makes a difference.

Ironically, like many people, I like to think I don't need support. Independence is highly valued in our competitive, individualistic, consumerist culture and needing support exposes our vulnerabilities. Yet support, its nature, how to get it, how to give it, and why and how it's sought and given have been recurring considerations in my experience of growing up, education, work, and relationships.

The sick room: seeking support as a child

As a young girl, I felt unsafe when I started school having moved homes around the same time because of the sudden death of my mother. I remember it being a cause of great consternation that I couldn't learn to read and I was taken out of the classroom to have separate instruction in a room known as the 'sick room'. It was the room where children were taken when they were ill and contained various medical-looking materials. It was cold in there. I did not get better at reading in that sick room which only increased the consternation people expressed about me.

Then what seemed like a miracle happened. During the school week I sometimes stayed with my Nana. To me her house was a wonderful place, particularly the kitchen which had a cosy corner where the sofa met the open fire range. Here I was allowed to curl up at a little table and look at women's magazines. This is where I learned to read. Somewhere between looking at the magazines, talking with my Nana, and combing out her long grey hair, which I did whenever I stayed with her, I found I could read. I suppose my Nana was my first learning supporter and what a great job she did. I never forget it.

Support from my school teachers

Three teachers come to mind when thinking about support and education – all from my secondary school days where I had unpredictable swings in achievement, finishing very much on a down swing. I suppose I still felt unsafe at school and used to try and hide away at the back of the classroom. Mainly I got away with it, except in the classes run by Mrs Summer the English teacher. She would call me up to the front and ask me to tell the class what I had been reading and what I made of it (I was a vociferous reader by now). This I found easy because I loved books and because she made me feel good talking about them. English language and English literature were two of the four subjects where I got a GCE qualification. The other was art and the fourth was chemistry.

The physics teacher along with the music teacher were two people I remember for their distinct lack of support in the terms I am discussing it. The physics teacher did not like to talk and made us learn from books, which I was able to do. But one day I got stuck and asked a question and kept asking it because I so much wanted to understand, even though he kept referring me back to the book. This 'cheeky' act merited me a staff detention. As for the music teacher, his habit of flicking chalk at students who sang 'wrong' notes silenced the melody in many – permanently I fear. After all these years I am still practising my music and finding my voice with a wonderful singing teacher, conductor, pianist and choir, where everybody is made welcome.

Supporting human rights

Looking back, some events seem significant in arriving at my current understanding of supporting human rights.

I keenly remember Maureen, a woman of my age, whom I have not met since our school years. My last memory of her was as teenagers when occasionally, on my way to what was then a grammar school, I used to find her at the gate of her house with her mother. I used to say hello to her but she did not answer. Only her mother acknowledged me.

It was my feeling that Maureen did not use words. At that time she was no longer at school with us. It was when we were very young that I remember us being together in the classroom and it was then that an incident took place which had a profound effect on me. Something had happened to Maureen which I feared might happen to me. She had wet herself, and her shame was being made a target for bullying by a number of pupils. To my horror they forced her to sit down and stand up in ritualistic fashion along the length of an unvarnished wooden bench, leaving a trail of wet marks behind her. I remember feeling an absolute conviction that something was happening that should not be happening and I tried to stop it. I don't remember whether I had any effect but the overwhelming feeling that I felt then and which stays with me now is that this kind of behaviour, which I now recognise as stigmatising, is a threat to humanity and somebody must do something about it. It is what I now under-stand as part of a cycle of behaviours and attitudes which, if left unchallenged, perpetuate human rights abuse.

Supporting people with disabilities

I left school as soon as I could at 16 to begin a secretarial course. It was about this time that I had my first experience of disability. I was part of a youth group of disabled and able-bodied young people that held its meetings at a residential home for disabled people known as 'The Home for Incurables'. Here I met people who were not allowed out in the evening because the Home would be locked by the time they returned and no staff would be available to provide personal assistance. This was as much a pivotal experience for me as the experience of Maureen's personal torment in my early years.

Some of these people introduced me to the concepts of discrimination, social justice and civil rights for disabled people. I already knew that people can hurt others, although they might not mean to, and the disabled people I met taught me about the damage that social systems can do as well, also often unintentionally.

Media support for social justice

These issues of social justice came to play an increasingly important part in my working life, which began on a local newspaper. Although I trained as a secretary, I did not want to be one and I managed to persuade the editor of the local newspaper to give me a job. This was mainly because of a joint interest in the adventure books of John Buchan, and because being able to type and do shorthand meant I could be put to work immediately. This led to work on a regional newspaper and later on to a job on a radio station in Hong Kong where I arrived like many 'Westerners' before me after a year's travel in search of 'The East'.

During my time on newspapers it was customary for stories about disabled people to be directed to the Women's Page and for pictures of people with learning difficulties to be censored, although stories about them might also be allowed in that same section of the newspaper. Since I was for a period the only young woman on the local newspaper, it was often seen as one of my jobs, along with writing up the weddings, to provide material for the Women's Page. I took this as an opportunity to develop my understanding of disability as a human rights issue which I had been introduced to through my youth club and investigate and report on disability from that aspect. By the time I was working for the regional newspaper and on radio, 'care in the community' was increasingly being suggested as the preferred social policy for disabled people rather than institutional care. The human rights understanding of disability I provided was relevant to these developments and attracted a new status as important material for leading features and stories rather than Women's Page 'fillers'.

Although my work in radio in Hong Kong was different in many ways from that on newspapers in the UK, I still tried to bring human rights considerations to the fore in the stories I covered there in my role as a 'social welfare correspondent'. Ironically it was a matter of human rights which played a part in my eventually leaving journalism after more than 20 years. I felt I had to challenge an editor's approach to a story on human rights grounds. So, I returned to England and took up a job as a support worker for two women moving out of a long-stay mental handicap hospital to a home of their own.

Support, inclusion and human rights

The job as a support worker led me to my current work at the Centre for Studies on Inclusive Education (CSIE) where I have been a co-director since 1988. CSIE is an independent education centre promoting inclusive education and challenging segregated schooling. We are part of a growing movement which wants to see the phasing out of segregated 'special' schools.

I remember a question at the interview about how being a support worker in community care was connected to what was then called integration in education. I said it was all part of the same human rights campaign. In many ways working at CSIE has been an ideal job for me combining writing, organising and lobbying about issues I care about. It has been a worthwhile job and that is what I have always wanted from work. I can honestly say I have rarely felt bored or alienated in the work I have done. To me work is a foremost expression of who you are and of your relationship with life. To me it is a serious matter for a person to be made miserable at work and I resist it.

Supporting from the heart

Support work is a work of the heart and it is a work of relationships. It is an enduring concern of mine how the ground rules might be worked out to sustain a respectful, enabling and enhancing partnership all-round. This is something I find very complex when I am in a supporting role. Some of the complexity seems to me to be about how to resolve what feel like conflicting ideas. These are: support is about care and love and therefore should be 'free'. Most supporters, however, would not be able to support without pay. Supporters need to be held accountable, particularly regarding the way they handle differentials in status and power. Supporters deserve to be treated with respect and not as somebody's 'dogsbody'.

I would have been happy to remain a support worker. I still keep in contact with the women but found the pay and conditions were not compatible with my personal life, especially financing a part share in a home of my own. The low status and recognition given to support work generally by society has changed little since then. It remains the general approach to career progression that managerial and specialist skills are rewarded more highly, and that the more expert and well-paid a person becomes the more distanced they are from giving personal support in the organisations where they work.

Another element in relationships of support that causes tension is that people in the supporting role are not immune from the tendency to do more harm than good in taking action. The tendency to 'do something no matter what' is very strong in the Western tradition of individualism and independence (in Buddhist culture, for example, there are positive concepts of 'non-action' and 'no-thing'). We may forge ahead with changes without properly taking into account the wishes of those we seek to help or failing to envisage the possibility of unexpected consequences. 'The road to hell is paved with good intentions' is a saying which has been used to describe how the development of segregated services for disabled people proved counter-productive for many in terms of quality of life. It is a sobering reminder of how being well-intentioned is no guarantee of being helpful.

Supporting self worth and inclusion

In many ways support work in education is a new profession, a profession in the making with many issues to be addressed. The work of learning supporters, as I prefer to call them, or teaching assistants, which is the official term, to a large extent has been born of necessity. Mainstream schools, required to become more inclusive, are finding they need varied input from a team of adults with a wide range of skills and experiences in order to respond to the full diversity of pupils, whatever their needs and abilities. In short, teachers cannot do it alone.

It matters a lot to me that as supporters work out their new professional role, and their contribution to inclusive development, they can hold on to an understanding of support as being fundamentally connected with pupils' personal, emotional and spiritual development, and with justice and equality. Without a sense of dignity and self worth it's widely acknowledged that learning becomes more difficult and that if learning is difficult, dignity and self worth can be hurt. Supporters – as an integral part of schools and classrooms – can ease the way and help children and young people become the best possible learners they can be in the differing and often challenging circumstances in which they find themselves.

Chapter 4
My history of helpers

Lucy Mason

> Given the power of adults, pupils' voices are often at risk of not being heard. Pupils can provide valuable feedback so we do need to invite them to tell us what they think. In this chapter, Lucy Mason, who has considerable experience of receiving support, reflects on the helpers who have provided it.

Tracy

My first helper, as far as I can remember, was called Tracy. She was quite nice. She was the 'motherly' type but she wasn't OTT. She had a daughter at my school who was asthmatic. I think that gave her an understanding of how frustrating it was for young people when they couldn't always join in. She was my helper from nursery until Year 1, when she left because she hurt her back and could no longer lift me. Tracy always coped well when I hurt myself. She never seemed to feel guilty which was nice for me because so often when I'd hurt myself I spent more time reassuring helpers and calming them down than I did thinking about myself.

Mrs Marny

My next helper was Mrs Marny. She was much older and I can't remember ever liking her. She was strict and took it upon herself to scold me whenever she felt it necessary. So this meant all the little mischievous things young kids do had much bigger repercussions for me. She was a great believer that all children told lies (all the time in my case). I remember once I'd told Mrs Marny you could buy goats milk at a shop near my house. Indeed this was a fib but the next day when Mrs Marny was unable to buy the milk she completely blew her lid. She wheeled me into the disabled toilet and locked the door. This was not unusual, this was Mrs Marny's favourite place to yell at me.'You're a liar aren't you Lucy?', 'You tell porkie pies don't you Lucy?', 'It's a sin isn't it Lucy?', she yelled, her face inches away from mine. She paced up and down the toilet, 'blah blah blah blah blah', her face grew redder. This, a scene I was used to, was somewhat comical to me. 'Are you laughing at me?' she roared. I shook my head. Unfortunately I do not have an inconspicuous laugh. My whole body tends to shake which in turn makes my chair squeak. Mrs Marny's belief that I never told the truth was to have horrible effects later on. On a school trip to the Thames Barrier Mrs Marny placed me on a flip-up seat, which was a bad idea as I am little and my feet did not touch the floor. Of course the seat fulfilled its design and flipped, sending me flying. Myself being brittle I ended up with a badly broken leg and a broken arm. Did she believe me? No. Was I over-reacting? Yes. Would she phone my mum? No. Was I just to carry on as normal? Yes. Did she plonk me back in my wheelchair? Yes. Did I get shouted at for crying? Yes. Did my mum go mad? Yes. Was I in hospital for a month? Yes. Did Mrs Marny make it worse? Yes. Did she lose her job? No. Did the hospital have to treat her for shock? Yes. Was I fed up? You bet!

Mrs Marny was not only good at making large mistakes but little ones too. She was so nervous about leaving me that I had to accompany her to the loo! And when I first took my powered wheelchair to school in order to be more independent in the playground, she insisted on running along beside me, shooing away any friend who tried to come and play with me. She justified this by saying that it was to make sure I didn't injure any of their feet by rolling over them, because their mothers would come and blame her. She was prejudiced too. One of the only black kids in my class was called Ayesha and was always getting into trouble. Ayesha was my mate and Mrs Marny hated her. I can remember so many incidents when Mrs Marny reported that Ayesha had done dangerous things to me that were complete mistellings of the truth. By the age of 7 my mum and I were so fed up of Mrs Marny that we decided to leave the school. We had already tried numerous times to complain about her, but the head teacher saw nothing wrong with her routines and described her as the 'Salt of the Earth'. When I joined my next school Mrs Marny expected to transfer with me. She saw no reason why we had advertised the job at all and questioned it strongly when she applied for it. Luckily at my new school my headteacher was himself disabled, and he had already agreed that me and my mum could be part of the interview panel. There were three applicants – Flo, Mrs Pen, and Mrs Marny. At first glance Flo seemed to be quite nice but lost several Brownie Points by pinching me on the cheek and saying 'Aah, ain't she sweet'. Mrs Marny was a tyrant and in mid-interview blurted out 'She's a terrible liar you know!' Funnily enough she was not reinstated.

Mrs Pen

Mrs Pen was great. Everyone picked her as their first choice. She didn't seem strict, but at the same time wasn't patronising. She had a son in my class who later came to be one of my good friends. Mum says she remembers the time he came to my house to teach me chess, a 'nice, quiet, civilised pastime', but instead we re-enacted World War Two. Mrs Pen seemed to have a good understanding of the oppression of disabled people. She was the most adventurous of all my helpers. So many of my helpers are so scared of 'Health and Safety' rules they do not let me do anything in the least bit risky, but Mrs Pen realised I had to learn for myself what was safe and what wasn't. I remember once I managed to climb two bars up a ladder by myself in P.E. which is something most of my helpers would never have let me have a go at. Unfortunately, two years on, Mrs Pen had to leave the job as she fell over a badly installed paving stone whilst chasing her cat and hurt her back. Indeed there were a few times I hurt myself whilst with Mrs Pen, like when on a school journey I broke my leg splashing around in the sea, but I would much rather have a few broken bones and an independent life than no broken bones and a sheltered life.

Flo

Funnily enough, my next helper was Flo. She had a job working in the school already, so we decided to give her a chance. I can't think of a better way to describe Flo than 'Fluffy'. She was the kind of person whose house you'd imagine to be pink and frilly and covered in posters of kittens and bunny rabbits. I always liked Flo. She never once shouted at me and we could have a good laugh. But Flo was not the kind of person you could call 'good in a crisis'. Mum told me that once she was called to the school because I had hurt my arm and when she asked 'Where's Flo?' I replied 'I don't know. She always gets upset when I hurt myself, so I didn't bother to tell her'. Flo stayed with me until I finished primary school. She could not transfer with me because my secondary school was too far, and she stayed on at my primary school to help another disabled child who had joined.

Ali

My first helper at secondary school was called Ali. She was only temporary which was a shame because we really got on. Ali was young and naughty and we had a great laugh. She had her nose pierced, which was a great ambition of mine, and was great around all my friends.

Rachel

My next helper was called Rachel. I liked her at first but found her a bit bossy. She was young and got scared if she didn't know exactly where I was. She showed this by getting angry at me. Rachel left because she was only temporary too.

Lauren

My next helper was Lauren. She started off quite timid but her confidence grew and so did her temper. Our friendship did not. Luckily Lauren was also temporary and left after three weeks.

Jade

After Lauren left, myself and the Head of the Inclusion Support Service decided to try a new set-up. I was to have two helpers, one for four days a week, one for one day a week. This meant I'd get to know two helpers so, theoretically, there'd be back-up if one was away. My main helper was Jade. She was great. All my friends liked her and she was a real laugh. There were times when we had problems with each other, but we sorted them out at fortnightly reviews with a mediator from learning support. Jade used to encourage me, especially in P.E. I remember doing badminton with her. It was not something I expected to be able to do, but we devised our own methods and it worked. I used to go swimming with her, the P.E. teacher and a friend. Jade and I used to do races and Jade would set me and my friends to do crazy things, like underwater ballet. With her help and the P.E. teachers, I managed my lifesavers badge, my survival badge, my 800 metres and my bronze. Jade and me were similar. We both hated insects. Once a huge cockroach crawled into the changing room. Jade picked me up, climbed up onto the changing bench and we both waited there scream-ing until a lifeguard came in and killed it. Jade left after 18 months because she was offered the same job in another borough, which paid over £2 an hour more. I found this hard because LSA work is so underpaid in some boroughs that you hardly can find someone who can do the job for a long time, which is disruptive to my education and my own personal feelings.

Clover

My other helper was called Clover. We never got on. I thought she was crazy. She never quite got the gist of the job. At first she wouldn't let my friends push me. When my mum had words with her she took them too literally and the next day at school she asked anyone who walked past, even if I'd never met them before, if they would like to push me! Something that really offended me about Clover was when one day in the corridor when it was very crowded, to make people aware that I needed room, she yelled 'Cripple coming through, cripple coming through!' I was not amused. Something that really embarrassed me about Clover was one day, when walking down the corridor we met Mr Tucker, a senior teacher whom Clover had never even seen before who happened to be eating a chocolate bar. Clover marched straight up to him and said, 'Ooh, can I have a bite?', and bit the end off his Twix! A little shocked,

Mr Tucker looked down at his half-eaten Twix and gave it to Clover. It no longer looked so appetising. Clover not only lacked common sense, but was a bit of a religious freak too. I myself have nothing against Christians, I mean, I believe in God, but Clover went well over the top. Day after day she told me that if I went to church then God might cure me and make me walk. She told me that if I let Jesus into my life then I would go to Heaven. One day I replied, 'I won't go to Heaven'. 'Why?', she asked. 'Because as far as I know there are stairs up to Heaven and I haven't read anything in the Bible about a lift.' Clover did not see that I was being comical and told me not to worry, once I'd died God would raise me from my imperfect body and give me one like hers. She did not understand why I was not joyously relieved. Clover not only got on my nerves, but the nerves of all my friends too. Once, in a really important French exam she went round to everyone individually and introduced herself. 'Hello! I'm Clover, as in the butter, how do you do...' Clover was asked to leave four weeks later.

Karen

My next helper was called Karen. She was nice. We had a few arguments but got on most of the time. Karen was really helpful and my friends liked her. Karen was easy to talk to. She had two children of her own who she used to talk about a lot. After working with me for four months, Karen fell over playing Volleyball and hurt her ankle. This meant she could not lift me for several months. Several people in my LEA started to question whether anyone should be lifting me at all. This would have caused great problems for me and other students, as our ability to cope in mainstream schools would have been jeopardised. I remember one thing which really upset me was when the whole of my year and the year below me went on a school trip to Chessington and I could not go because there was no one to lift me on and off the coach, and the school had forgotten about me. When I found out about this I was really angry and upset, feelings which often make me become stubborn. So in the following lesson I went on strike. My point was the school expected me to behave like everyone else in the sense that I had to do what they said, but they didn't offer me the same privileges. Unfortunately my science teacher was not very sympathetic and threatened to put me on 'red report'. For the same financial reasons as Jade, Karen had to leave after eighteen months.

Mary

My next (short-term) helper was called Mary. She was claustrophobic and therefore would not go in the lift with me. Nor could she lift me as she had a bad arm. Mary spent most of her time working in a special school and talked to me like I was about three. In her time with me she decided that one of my friends was a schizophrenic and almost wrote to the school suggesting that she had counselling.

Sarah

My next helper was also short-term. She was called Sarah. She was nice a lot of the time and at the beginning I even recommended that she be given a full-time job at my school. But Sarah suffered from severe mood swings which put a heavy strain on our relationship.

Dotty

My current helper is called Dotty and her name says it all. The school seems to love her but I do not. She is clumsy and can often be rude. She is rarely on time to collect me for lessons and can appear to be quite selfish at times, e.g. my helpers are meant to buy lunch for me but unless I buy mine when she says, my friends have to buy it for me as she does not like to wait for her food. I could put up with Dotty's physical incapabilities but something which deeply offends me is that Dotty has said to me twice that I would not have a helper if I could make my own decisions, which I think is the biggest possible misunderstanding of the job.

I do not know where my 'history of helpers' will end as I cannot see into the future, but the stream of helpers will inevitably flow on and will never run smooth until the system is changed and LSAs are trained and paid properly.

(All names have been changed apart from the author's.)

Chapter 5

Klaus' Story

Klaus Wedell

Klaus Wedell, emeritus professor at the Institute of Education, London, has made a major contribution to understanding and practice in the area of learning difficulties. His working week involves him as a volunteer helper in a small local school. In this chapter, he analyses the role that he has taken on and his approach to supporting children and communicating with teachers.

It seems to me that support basically takes two forms. There is help, firstly, designed to enable children to take part in the normal curricular activity in the classroom – which already covers a range of levels – so that every child benefits from the teaching and learning going on in their group. This support is geared to help children to understand and respond, and so to bypass their particular learning difficulties as far as possible.

Secondly, help is aimed specifically at supporting children to overcome particular difficulties. Clearly, there is no hard and fast separation between these two forms of support. Even in our classes, which incorporate such diverse learning levels, however, there are a few children who teachers feel need additional help targeted specifically at their particular learning needs. There is considerable controversy about whether this kind of help should be given in the normal class group or by withdrawing children. In our school, children already experience a variety of subgroup and whole group learning, and so 'withdrawal' becomes a relative concept in terms of numbers, particularly as the school design is part open-plan.

Working with individuals

I've usually been allocated to individual children whom the teaching staff feel need specifically targeted help. When I first started at the school, I was assigned children from one of the larger age cohorts at the upper infant level. Most only needed help for a year or less, until the teachers felt that they could continue to make progress with their age peers. In the last two years I have been assigned a couple of children in the top year who are still having difficulties. I've emphasised to the teachers that I'm working to them, and where relevant, also to our SENCO.

When I'm asked to work with a child, I ask the teacher to tell me as specifically as possible whatever he or she would like me to help the child achieve, which the child is not currently achieving. Similarly, with the SENCO, the question is how I can support a specific need as set out in the individual education plan (IEP). The SENCO and I share a notebook in which I write down each week what I have been trying to work on with the children, and the idea is that the teacher also reads this. In a small school like ours, it is usually possible also to talk briefly with the teacher during the course of the morning. My aim is to ensure that the children are not handed to me to carry out some supposedly beneficial activity which is not a part of the teacher's own day-to-day plans for the children.

I've been very concerned that working once a week with children lacks the intensity required to achieve an appropriate rate of progress. It has always struck me that it is unreasonable to suppose that, in most instances, this kind of drip-feed can be an effective way of helping children to progress. And yet it is probably still one of the most common ways in which help is offered, largely because of limitations in staffing. I've tried to devise arrangements by which this problem can be overcome – with greater or lesser success. One of the main ways of achieving some continuity is to devise activities which the child can continue in the current classwork. In my work with the two children in the leaving class (Year 6), the teacher has asked me to support them in developing their narrative writing for SATS, so it has been relatively easy to link what they write with me with their writing in the classroom. Work with children in the infants class has usually involved me in devising activities which can be carried on as part of the current classroom work, which the children can share with other children. I've also tried to organise work children can do at home with their parents for a short period on three or four nights a week. This too has met with variable success.

Focusing on strengths and needs

All through my work, initially as an educational psychologist, and later in university posts, I've been trying to find ways to focus teaching on children's particular strengths and needs. I've tried to work out how one can achieve a progressive understanding of these by starting with activities which are as near as possible to the day-to-day learning problem. If teaching in this way doesn't work, I regard this as an indication for focusing more on underlying difficulties. Not surprisingly, I've sometimes been told a child I'm working with has indications of dyslexia. I've not found such descriptions more helpful than detailed information about exactly what difficulties the child is having in the classroom. When you are an LSA it can be quite hard to get specific information about what the teacher finds a child can and cannot do – and under what conditions. It is usually more difficult to obtain information about what a child can do than about where the child is failing. There is a similar problem about discovering the particular situations in which a child performs better than in others, so as to get an idea about likely teaching approaches. These values are a subject of the initial – and ongoing – conversations with the teachers and the other LSAs.

Two main strategies for support

There seem to me to be two main strategies for working with children who have particular learning difficulties. One is to start working at the level at which the children are achieving and work up from there. This usually seems to be effective with younger children. For older children, where building up self-esteem and confidence is crucial, such a strategy can seem rather demeaning. So it is better to find a way of enabling them to achieve as near as possible to the expected level, but providing all the cuing and support this requires. Progress then takes the form of systematically removing each of the forms of support, so marking steps in the children's progress.

One ten-year-old I was asked to help was one of those children who have difficulty in setting ideas down in writing. He also had some difficulties in sorting his ideas out. However, he was highly knowledgeable about sheep, and so we decided to write a booklet about what happened in the life-span of a sheep. He dictated this account into a tape recorder over several sessions and then played it back to both of us. Not surprisingly, the syntax and vocabulary of his oral account was infinitely more sophisticated than in his usual written work. We discussed the structure of his account stage by stage, making changes where necessary to improve the sense of what he was saying. He then wrote it out section by section, partly in the sessions and partly at home. I learned a great deal about sheep – for instance that barren sheep were termed 'empties', and that when you take your sheep to a show, you bring them in the night before to 'calm them down and tart them up'. The boy became increasingly impressed with his own account, so we were able gradually to omit the tape recording stage and proceed straight to writing. The complete account was finally printed out as a booklet and the headteacher helped him to incorporate pictures of sheep, so he could present it to his parents for Christmas.

The younger children I was asked to see were frequently those at the upper end of the infants class who were having difficulty in catching on to phonics. One problem was finding out exactly which spellings they were having difficulty with. It became apparent that we needed to derive a spelling progression from the Literacy Strategy and use it to check both which aspects they had already mastered and which might be appropriate to learn as a next step. The errors the children made were usually of the plausible phonic alternative (PPA) type –

which typically became apparent when they tried to spell words with vowel digraphs such as 'ou', 'ai'. Planning help for these difficulties pointed up an interesting difference of view between the teacher and myself. She thought it best to teach children digraphs by grouping words according to the various ways of spelling the same sound. My view was that the children's errors were already PPAs, and that one needed to start by teaching contrasting sounds. The contrasts needed to be highlighted by focusing attention on what the words looked like and also linking the spelling with the meaning of the words. So with respect to these particular children we agreed to differ.

Work on spelling at this level lent itself well to having children work in small groups or pairs so they could play phonics games. I had to devise tailor-made activities, adapting Happy Families games so that the families consisted of sets of relevant words with contrasting vowel digraphs the children had found difficult. The children could take these sets of cards back into their classroom, where they could teach others to play the game, and so gain kudos. I also used the computer so they could build up words with the relevant digraphs, and complete sentences using the words.

Checking progress

A crucial aspect of the 'building up skills' approach is recording progress over the short-term. The children – let alone I myself – needed to know that these approaches were in fact meeting their learning needs. Checking the accuracy of spelling words is relatively straightforward within the activities of giving individual or group help. Getting feedback about the children's performance in the classroom can be less precise – another instance where close collaboration with the teacher pays dividends. Checking progress on the work in the narrative writing task with the older children also has its problems. In one sense, the 'reducing cues' method can be self-validating. If the children can maintain the performance level when the cues and help are progressively withdrawn, there is reasonable evidence that learning has taken place. However, agreeing, for example, whether children have demarcated sentences appropriately, is more subjective. I worked with a boy and a girl who also still had limited spelling competence. We decided that the SENCO would tackle the spelling. The boy had difficulty using the given SAT title as a stimulus to start writing, but the girl wrote endlessly and with little relevance to the set title. We again used a cuing approach, largely to bypass the spelling limitations of the task. In this instance we used the Clicker software, which also spoke the written text back so the children could listen for where sentences might end. Because this work was closely geared to the work the children were doing in the classroom, the progress monitoring was largely taken on by the teacher, in the context of the assessments in the class. One could not fail to reflect on the fact that the national curriculum assessment procedure was pushing teaching into the SAT task as an end in itself.

Tuning in to children

The account of my work as an LSA shows what many of us find – that LSAs have the opportunity to tune in to individual children's feelings and attitudes to an extent which is often not open to teachers. Some children open up in conversation about their personal problems and about their family issues. Children's story writing also often reveals their preoccupations and concerns, so that one cannot help but become aware of the background to their problems. The dilemma then is in deciding how far one should allow these topics to open up, and when to make it clear that this kind of communication needs to be channelled back to the teacher. As an LSA, one at least has the opportunity to try to tune one's interaction and relationship with the children in a way which matches their needs. In some instances, children try to test the limits in terms of control; in others, one is faced with the task of defining the limits of personal interaction. Both situations can prove quite demanding for both male and female LSAs, and it is interesting to note how the perceptions of the relative roles of child and LSA gradually come to be established over time. This was brought home to me in a tangential way when it was decided one year to decorate the annual governors' report to parents with the infant children's pictures of the staff. My depiction featured me peering intently at a computer through my half-moon glasses.

Continuing to learn

During my jobs at universities, I also tried to keep my feet on the ground by learning from the experience of the teachers on our advanced courses and working with them on their assignments in schools. I used these opportunities to match the strategies for special needs teaching with the more theoretical issues which underpin one's actions. However, I feel the recent years of work as an LSA have taught me as much again – and I am continuing to learn. The experience has also brought home to me, even more, the superhuman intellectual demands made on individual teachers and LSAs faced with meeting the diversity of learning needs in class groups of children. It really is time we moved away from the rigidity which this organisation imposes on the education of our children. The contribution LSAs can make is slowly becoming recognised as part of the way in which the nature and levels of learning needs can be served by the nature and levels of expertise that a range of professional approaches can offer in schools. But as recent research into the function of LSAs has shown, it seems there is still a long way to go in many schools before the resource LSAs represent will be fully realised. Perhaps paradoxically, small village schools faced with finding ways to respond to the complex learning demands of their multi-age classes may well be indicating the way ahead.

Chapter 6

Being a SENCO's assistant

Sally Wallace

Sally Wallace, a learning support assistant (LSA), describes and reflects upon her role as an assistant to a teacher who is a special educational needs co-ordinator (SENCO). Sally's extended role requires that she draws on her previous experience as a learning supporter, but also utilises her administrative background. The way she complements the work and professionalism of a part-time teacher SENCO seems to link her into being a 'higher level' teaching assistant (DfES 2003).

Introduction

I have worked in primary schools for about nine years as a general support assistant and also as a special needs assistant. During that time I have built up my qualifications and, because of staff changes, I'm probably the most qualified of the teaching assistants in our school. In 2003, I was approached by the headteacher of my current primary school to take on the special educational needs administration because of my learning support skills, my ICT knowledge and my secretarial background.

I work part-time for 21 hours a week. I have just decreased my hours in order to have one day off a week. My timetable comprises ten hours of class time with Year 4 (9-year-olds), and five hours for additional literacy support where I work with a small group each day on their literacy programme. The other six hours are with the Special Educational Needs Co-ordinator (SENCO). I therefore have three support roles. I have been working as a SENCO's assistant for about four months so my role is still developing. The SENCO herself is in school for two days a week so sometimes I find I am the only source of contact when someone wants to know where something is. We keep a joint diary and communications book so that I can keep track of the SENCO's whereabouts when, for instance, she has to attend a conference. We're finding the communication book is vital as sometimes this can be the only contact we have if she's particularly busy.

My experience in previous schools has been that the SENCO also holds a full-time or part-time teaching post and I have always been amazed at how they have managed to cope with this range of duties. I am aware too that SENCO workloads have increased greatly, given changes in assessment procedures and SEN legislation. Also the delegation of funding to schools and a policy of reducing the number of statements for children have led to a greater requirement for in-school support and administration. Originally most of the SEN administration tasks were carried out by the office staff but their workload has increased in other ways. For instance, one additional task they now have is children's admissions and this is one of the reasons why I was asked to take on the SENCO's assistant role.

Assisting the SENCO

Currently, my formal list of duties includes:

- continual updating of children on the SEN register, extracting and updating SEN audit information, and filing
- sending internal memos and e-mails, and letters to parents
- accessing the internet for particular information
- making diary entries – in both mine and the SENCO's diaries
- operating 'SIMS' (Schools' Information Management Support), a computer systems programme, operating IEP (Individual Educational Plan) Writer, and various other computer programmes like Microsoft Excel and Word
- liaising with teachers, school helpers, and other LSAs regarding resources and meetings
- storing, sorting and filing SEN information from journals, publications, circulars and conference notes.

The SENCO is a very approachable person and we have a good relationship. As well as sorting out all the files and various information, she has asked me to fill in 'at a glance' forms to go inside all the SEN files on the children. This is a detailed task in which I look through three different types of data to gather all the information required – and we have approximately 140 children on the SEN register. However, it's good to have an ongoing task which I can do independently when the SENCO might be at a meeting. When I first started I actually wondered if I would have enough to do but now I am getting into the role I think I might need some extra hours.

When outside agencies meet with the SENCO I am often working where they meet. I have already established that if they want me to work elsewhere it's no problem but they seem happy for me to be there. I find that as a SENCO's assistant I am now more informed about many more school issues. Details of staff meetings often come up in conversation and TAs would not normally be informed about these unless they directly affected our duties. I am taken into confidence about staff changes before they have officially been announced and other matters which might concern the school as a whole. The SENCO has also consulted me about the best use of teaching assistants for extra hours that might have been offered to us when a new child arrives.

One drawback for me can be that teachers almost see me as an additional SENCO rather than an assistant. One teacher had an expectation that as I worked with the SENCO and knew all the resources (which I don't) I would be able to work out a programme of support for the group I would be working with from that class. I also get asked other questions about specific SEN computer programmes and I have to reply that I'm still in a 'learning mode'.

We are about to introduce 'peer mediation' into the school and I have made the various resources that go into this, such as forms for the children to use, a special box, a dry-wipe information board, and certificates – again, liaising between SENCO, deputy head and staff. Because we were up against time to introduce this, it resulted in my working part of my lunch time and early in the morning but, from my experience, that is what LSAs increasingly find themselves doing.

Already my SENCO assistant's role has developed since the beginning of this school year and I feel that there is much more to come. A slight disadvantage is that I have hours assigned early in the morning and also over two afternoons. It would work better if all my hours were together so that I could have a good 'run at things' but they were set to suit teachers' requirements regarding my other support assistant related roles.

It can be frustrating sometimes to have to leave jobs half done, and having to switch from one role to another certainly keeps you on the ball. I'm grateful for the last course I undertook (the Advanced Diploma in Child Care and Education) as some of the modules specifically covered aspects such as disability and SENs and the early years curriculum. To have background knowledge of the 2001 SEN Code of Practice, IEPs and Statements has helped a lot and now I have an increased understanding of how the assessment system works.

Using ICT

We were due an SEN audit just as I started at the school so things were a bit frantic. This involved learning SIMS, which incorporates 'STAR' (an IT database), and this holds all the SEN records. I went through all the records and updated the SEN codes after the stages of assessment changed from five to three – thus 'SA' (for School Action), 'SA+' (for School Action Plus) and 'S' for Statement. This meant the SENCO could extract certain information to give to the LEA audit team. It was necessary to put in extra hours during that time as it was important to get it finished. Unfortunately the SIMS software only operates in the main school office so I have to go there to access it. Otherwise I am normally situated outside the staffroom, where the SENCO has her work area. This is an open-plan space, which isn't ideal for security reasons as people have to walk past the working area to go into the staffroom, but at least the SENCO and SEN resources are easily accessed by staff and pupils. At times the SENCO feels that it would be preferable to have access to a more private area.

Another computer programme, 'IEP Writer', has now been installed, which I have also needed to learn. This holds all the current IEPs of the children and can be accessed by the teaching staff. All IEPs and SEN records need to be updated regularly so it can be a big task. IEP Writer is a relatively recent piece of software that both the SENCO and myself have needed to learn about. It greatly supports the writing of IEPs and therefore is a good aid for the teachers. It helps a lot with regard to target setting and establishing links with the National Literacy and Numeracy Strategy and the National Curriculum. We do lack the time, however, to explore the real potential of this software. We have the facility to use IEP Writer 2 but, again, we need time to learn how to use it.

Much of my learning has been school based and most of my ICT learning has been done in school. My own study of a small number of LSAs in Dorset found them to be keen to learn more about schools and the work of supporting children in order to be more effective. They expressed a need for more training opportunities (Wallace 2001). From my experience, LSAs have used ICT much more in the last two years. However, ICT training has not been a high priority for the LEA or the school. Most training that is available is skewed towards literacy, numeracy and special needs.

The need for statistical analyses of children's attainments has created a need for more ICT understanding by teachers and LSAs. All LSAs have had to learn things such as mail merge and internet searching, for instance. Art displays now require ICT skills. The requirement to use digital cameras and camcorders is increasing and the operating of these has fallen mostly to teaching assistants. This requires us to know how to use the equipment, download it to a file on the computer and also be able to use the scanner if we want to reproduce pictures for displays. Recently, when the Year 4 children were studying famous artists, it was important to surf the net for images and information. We sometimes find ourselves doing our ICT learning alongside the children.

A further development that I may be able to assist with is the school's website when this is eventually developed. The British Educational Communications and Technology Agency (BECTA) has highlighted the need for schools to open up this channel of electronic communication between themselves and parents (BECTA 2004). We are aware that this will need our attention. We might also wish to include learning resources to support home learning and the possibility of it being an interactive site.

Sometimes I can have frustrating days with the computers and laptops experiencing connection and performance problems. This can happen just when you need to access information and print it out. I often find myself trying to do several things at once because many things seem to be needed immediately. Recently, because we were having problems with our software, I went with the SENCO to another school to meet with their SENCO to learn more about IEP Writer. This was outside of my paid working hours. It seems to me that technical problems often come with ICT but mostly we solve them or find some way around them.

Conclusion

Do I enjoy the role of SENCO's assistant? Yes, as there are so many different aspects to it and I am able to put many of my previous and current skills to use. However, it might be easier to have one role to concentrate on instead of three because it can feel like I'm being pulled in many directions. It is likely that my SENCO assistant role will expand further, especially in terms of its ICT element. I have a strong sense that more SENCO-related and wider school-related ICT work could come my way if ICT plays a much greater part in learning, teaching and administration in schools. However, if I had to make a choice between my three support roles it would actually be difficult as, like most of my teaching assistant colleagues, I actually enjoy all of what I do.

References

BECTA (British Educational Communications and Technology Agency) (2004) http://www.becta.org.uk/research/research.cfm?id=2606#basic

DfES (2003) *Professional Standards for Higher Level Teaching Assistants.* London: Teacher Training Agency.

Wallace, S. (2001) *The Government's Expectations for Learning Support Assistants are Unrealistic in Comparison to the Training and Support Provided,* unpublished dissertation, Advanced Diploma in Child Education, Weymouth College, Dorset.

Chapter 7

Making sure Nadia's education is working

Katie Clarke and Pat Rangeley

Katie Clarke is the mother of Nadia and Pat Rangeley is a learning supporter working with Nadia at Savile Park Primary School, Halifax. They both talked about Nadia at a conference called 'Learning supporters and inclusion' run by the Centre for Studies on Inclusive Education in Manchester on 21 June 2002. What follows is an edited transcript of their presentation.

Katie: Nadia is a bright, happy and confident nine-year-old. She has, however, various diagnoses to put on her CV such as: she has *severe* athetoid cerebral palsy, *severe* communication difficulties and *profoundly* deaf. Nadia uses sign language and various forms of communication, including low tech and high tech symbols. She's one of my six children. There's Sean who's ten, Nadia is nine, Nicky's seven, Ray is five and I've got twins, Jake and Samara, who are both two. So as you can imagine it's a rather hectic, chaotic, but very fun household. And Nadia is very much part of this household and we work very hard at making sure she's included, and it's not an easy job. We also work very hard at making sure she's included in the community.

Two years ago we lived in Northumberland, beautiful rural Northumberland. Nadia had gone to mainstream nursery and it was, in our eyes, very successful. She still talks about the learning support assistant, Margaret, who was the main force behind it being successful. However, getting Nadia into a local primary school was much more of a struggle. The LEA felt that Nadia's education couldn't be accommodated in a mainstream setting, and we felt we couldn't accommodate living in an area with an LEA who didn't want our daughter in a mainstream school – in the same school as her brothers and sisters. So we moved. It was pretty radical at the time and our decision attracted a lot of publicity. We moved to Calderdale, which was a hundred miles away, where we knew they had a more positive inclusion policy. We moved so that we could walk to our chosen school, Sevile Park Primary, with Nadia in the wheelchair with her siblings. Surely it's something that most parents do every single day with their children?

I want to introduce you to Pat who works at Savile Park and who's one of Nadia's two learning support assistants (Kath Williams is the other). They are part of a dedicated team ensuring that Nadia's education is meeting her needs.

Pat: This is just a snippet of my day with Nadia. I could have written a book, believe you me. At Sevile Park we have seven hearing impaired children, six LSAs, one teacher of the deaf and one deaf instructor, and numerous other support staff. Nadia is one of the hearing impaired children, only Nadia has cerebral palsy as well. Nadia's day begins in the school yard. I have to fight my way through the many children coming into the school. They all want to come in and I'm trying to get out. So eventually, when I get out of the door, Nadia's waiting patiently in the yard. Once we get her into school we try, as quickly as possible, to take her either into assembly or into class. Three times a week she goes into a standing frame for assembly, which is quite difficult to get into. Kath, my learning support partner, helps with this. This is followed by the usual 'good mornings' with everyone, and 'did you have a good weekend' and so on. Once in the standing frame and secure, we scan through the home–school book which Katie brings in every day, and if there's anything we need to know it's in there. Off she goes into assembly. Every assembly has a signer.

During assembly, her cochlea implant sometimes falls out several times. (Obviously, a lot of people here today know about that particular problem.) Nadia's implant is low down on the side of her head so she can sometimes accidentally knock it off by moving her head from side to side. For some children it's above their ear. Even the collar on her coat can knock it off, and sometimes so can her hair.

After assembly is over Nadia is helped back into the electric wheelchair. Children are chit-chatting in class. They start to sign across the room as soon as Nadia comes. She's got lots of friends and some of them are excellent signers – better than me in fact.

I'll now talk about Nadia's school work. In literacy, we do need to modify the work. We might blow it up and put it onto A3, and sometimes prepare 'Clicker' for her. Clicker is a computer programme that offers children with communication impairment a grid containing words, phrases or pictures which are linked to a joystick. It can be programmed by LSAs or teachers to relate to the curriculum area being studied. Nadia loves it. I love Clicker too. It's been superb for Nadia. We've got so many different ways of approaching her work but, to me, Clicker is really good. When she starts working I can leave her and walk around the classroom and generally help some of the other children. If she wants me she either signals, or she comes and finds me.

The teacher comes over to look at Nadia's work, 'Well done Nadia, a sticker for you.' The bell goes and she stays in her electric wheelchair for playtime. Because there are six of us, one of us takes her out at playtime on a rota basis. Nadia wanders round playing games, perhaps tig, or just making conversation. A problem of summer playtime is that the children are allowed to play on an area of grass that we have and Nadia cannot access this. She has a buggy that will go on the grass with somebody pushing it, but the time it takes to change her over, she'd only be getting about five minutes.

So the bell rings and it's toilet time now. Now this is a scheduled toilet visit that we do every day. It may seem strange because we are supposed to take children when they want to go. But this is now a routine of Nadia's, and Kath and I take her to the toilet at about a quarter to eleven, so as not to miss any literacy or maths, or whatever subject she's doing. It's usually quickly done. Every adult and child in our school knows the sign for toilet. So if at any time Nadia's signing for the toilet they understand straight away.

I next go and work with two other hearing impaired children up to lunchtime and Nadia goes into maths. We have to be quick as maths has started. Kath takes her to the classroom and Nadia is excellent at maths, she's absolutely superb. It's a lot easier for Nadia to access maths because of the signing. You know, five times five and she's got it there in her hand. The answer's immediate to her.

It's usually all hands for maths, and of course Kath writes down anything that needs to be written down. Lunchtime arrives and we sometimes cover Nadia's lunchtimes as getting a lunchtime assistant for an hour a day isn't very easy. Not a lot of people want five hours' work a week in the middle of each day. The person that we've got at the moment is pregnant so she'll probably be leaving in September. Kath and I do lunchtime on a rota basis, and whoever takes Nadia for lunch will have their lunch after that. But, unfortunately, that means another child is missing out on support during that time.

So off Nadia goes with a group of helpers over to the canteen with a packed lunch. Everybody wants to sit next to Nadia. I mean, she's been at Savile Park School for three years and children are still fighting to get next to her at the dining table! Conversation is going on as Nadia's eating her dinner. At home she would eat a lot of it herself unaided, but there isn't the time in school because it's only a short time for lunch.

It's one o'clock and the bell has gone so it's back to work. Now the first twenty minutes is reading time and children look at a book with a friend. Nadia goes to the friend she wants to be with and takes them back to where she's working. We've got twins who have just started, Camilla and Antonia, and she likes them because they remind her of the twins in her family. So she goes and picks one of them and they look at a book together. At this time the teacher and I (or the teacher of the deaf) would be discussing the afternoon's work and how best we can put it to Nadia.

It's science today which is difficult, especially for me. We're doing force meters and I haven't got any idea of the sign for 'force meter'. So I have to sign a spring balance, which is the nearest I can think to a force meter. I use the word 'force meter' but I use the sign of a spring balance and this is a little difficult for Nadia. We do have an instructor for the deaf who sometimes comes in but it's not her day to come so I have to deal with the signs myself.

Clicker's now ready. It's so easy to add words to it, words I'm going to need like 'force meter'. So the teacher demonstrates the force meter, tells me how it works, and how it measures in 'Newtons'. None of the children know anything about Newtons at all. So the only way I can put it over to Nadia is to introduce Isaac Newton and how he discovered gravity.

We're lucky enough to have, in Halifax, 'Eureka' (an interactive museum for children) where there is a massive Isaac Newton ball which drops down into a bath every hour. Nadia understands the connection between 'a Newton' and Isaac Newton. But with signing you've got to put things over the best way that you can if you don't know the meaning of a word or the sign.

Mr Richards, the teacher, wants all the children to try out the force meters and asks Nadia if she'd like to have a go at trying to pull a force meter. We've had them for years and they're stiff so they don't actually work very well. We get down to the worksheet and Nadia's copying from Clicker the relevant words. When she's finished we print it off and there's a space to draw a force meter. On this occasion, she asks me to draw the hook that was attached to the force meter.

Then Nadia wants the toilet. So I rush off to the other side of the school, open all the doors so she can access the way out, straight into the disabled toilet. I have to tell you that this toilet is also for all staff. So, if there's somebody in there, we have to wait. We've got thirty five staff and we've got two toilets including the disabled toilet. I get a colleague to help me and we're quickly in the toilet. It's then straight back into class. I ask Mr Richards if we can spend a bit more time to finish the work. So, we draw a force meter and Nadia concentrates extremely hard. Mr Richards comes over, has a word with Nadia and praises her work.

It's 3.10 pm and it's time to go home. Kath and I meet in the unit room. Such is the electric wheelchair that one of us has to take her out and hold her while the other one transfers the seat onto another, manual, wheelchair.

So that's the procedure that we go through. Every day has its ups and downs for Nadia, some good some not so good. Perhaps she's had a restless night after going several times to the toilet. All these things we try to take into consideration. She works very hard and she's also very curious. She always wants to know what's happening, 'Why's Jamalba crying?' or 'Why's Mr Richards cross with Keith?'

This has been a typical school day for Nadia. I've been working with her for three years now and I'm still learning all about her. We're always trying different methods of supporting her but, of course, we're no miracle workers. We're trying our best and we're striving for a better education for Nadia. We never turn any ideas down. Last week we had someone from SCOPE and we thought she might suggest something that we hadn't tried, but she didn't and strangely that made us all feel good. It did, you know, because it made us feel nobody has all the answers but (*looking towards Katie*) you read that bit because I might get upset.

Katie: It says, 'We're all working at Nadia having a happy and fulfilling life and we all know we'll be a part of it'. So, this is how I see the role of Pat and Kath (see Figure 7.1).

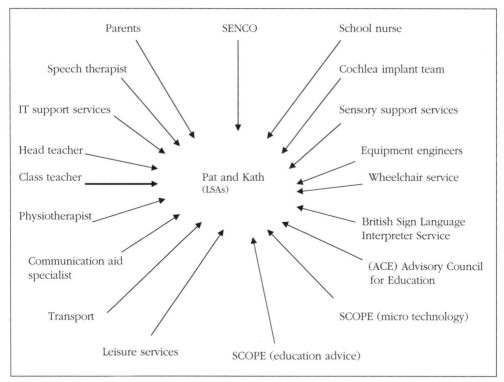

Figure 7.1 Pat and Kath co-ordinating advice and services for Nadia

There are so many people involved with a child with such complex needs. There are many people telling Pat and Kath what to do at school. Some of the people actually don't value Pat and Kath. All these services have to be co-

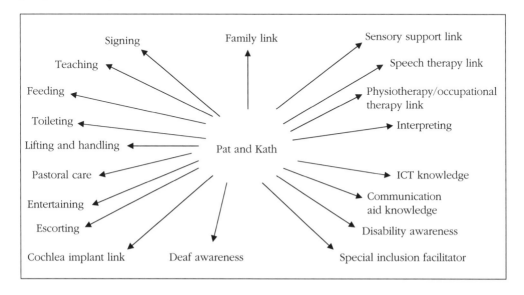

Figure 7.2 Roles performed by Pat and Kath

ordinated and Nadia's needs change daily so the links have to be there and the links of the family are absolutely vital. I'm so lucky I can go into Savile Park whenever I want. I pop in, I write in the handbook, but I'm there to help make sure that Nadia's education is working. There are two or three meetings a week that I attend, some with the learning support assistants, some with the various agencies.

There are a lot of services advising the LSAs but this is how I see Pat and Kath. I see them as powerful and actually as the main persons involved. They've got so many skills and there are more skills that I could have mentioned. They've got to do all these things to make sure that Nadia's education is working (see Figure 7.2).

That's how we're going to end our presentation and it's with thanks to Pat and Kath and also Anne, who's Nadia's teacher of the deaf. Because they are the body, they are the team; they are the key workers behind making Nadia's inclusion work in a mainstream school.

Chapter 8

Providing learning support in a mathematics lesson

Jennifer Colloby

Ofsted, the school inspectorate for England, suggests that teaching assistants provide important support for up to one-in-four primary school children (Ofsted 2003). Jennifer Colloby, a Staff tutor with the Open University, provides a closely observed study of Caroline Higham, a teaching assistant working within the context of a mathematics lesson. Her chapter highlights the complex nature of learning support.

Caroline is employed in a small rural school with just over ninety pupils and four staff including the head teacher. She has worked as a teaching assistant for several years. She has two children who were previously educated at this school. She now works full time, i.e. 35 hours a week. She would eventually like to be a qualified teacher and is studying to complete her BA degree.

Since working at the school Caroline's role has grown, both in the number of hours she is employed and in the nature of her responsibilities. She has responded willingly to these developments. She has responsibility for organising and maintaining the school's reading programme and works closely with the head teacher on this. She enjoys the associated responsibility for children's progress and attainment. She keeps records of the individual children she supports and updates these at the end of each school day and shares them with staff. Caroline's experience has given her increased status in the school. She is invited to and participates in staff meetings.

Parents do seek her out for advice but Caroline knows when to pass them on to teachers. She is compassionate and fiercely loyal to the children. She has commitment, patience and determination.

Her own work area in the school is welcoming with interesting displays on the walls. Here, she sometimes supports small groups of children or individuals. Her current timetable involves her supporting a group of Year 4 and 5 pupils (9–10-year-olds) each day for their mathematics lesson.

The mathematics lesson

Caroline makes her way to the classroom and greets the class teacher. A quick discussion between them confirms both the plan and objectives for the lesson. For numeracy the pupils are grouped according to ability and she will be supporting a group of four low-attaining pupils.

She counts out pencils and rulers, ensuring that the groups have sufficient supplies. Her preparation for the lesson involved meeting with the teacher earlier in the week (not always easy) so she was aware that the theme was 'pictograms'. From this planning session she knows which books are needed and hands them out. The pupils are in an extended assembly and arrive late for the lesson. She moves quickly, assisting the teacher in settling the children. She has thought about how she will prompt and encourage children by taking part in the mental warm-up activities. She knows she will need to explain, repeat, assist and encourage her group throughout the whole class activity and group work.

As the lesson begins, she positions herself near her group. Pupils are chanting two, five and ten times tables. This is an animated activity and she joins in. An exploration of mid-way points begins with the teacher asking, 'What number lies halfway between 20 and 30?' Caroline's group offer no answers but she shows an active interest in the lesson, which encourages them in their silent participation. The teacher moves onto the topic of pictograms and talks about conducting a survey on the colour of cars. Pupils volunteer colours such as red, blue, silver, white and gold and the class finds much amusement in the teacher's drawing of a car on the board. The teacher admits it looks like a submarine and then jokes with the class saying, 'Don't criticise and don't drive one of these particularly on a Thursday morning!' Caroline laughs and then her group does too.

After 15 minutes of whole class activity the pupils move back to their desks. Caroline goes round the class handing out worksheets. She settles them and then returns to sit with her group. She reminds them what they have to do and Amy is struggling to understand. Caroline explains this again while acknowledging that Beth has progressed to worksheet two. Caroline moves and crouches down beside her. Mistakes are found and Caroline suggests they count together. Beth chants along with Caroline. As Beth's confidence grows she returns enthusiastically to her work. Caroline quickly moves back to Amy, collecting her own chair on the way. Amy is still experiencing difficulties so Caroline moves to the board to make use of the number line as a visual aid. Caroline demonstrates and repeats the activity the teacher did with the class. She checks that Amy now understands by posing questions for her to answer and encourages her to continue.

Caroline moves back to the group. Cassie is not perturbed that Caroline finds mistakes in her work. Caroline encourages her to have another go before shuffling her own chair next to Diana, the quietest member of the group. Diana has made little progress and Caroline explains the task. Cassie asks for help and Caroline moves to her but is aware that Diana is struggling again. Cassie is now trying to work out the quantities represented by the shapes on pictograms and Caroline explains this. Caroline moves back to Diana but is still questioning Cassie on the pictogram. 'I'll come back to you,' Caroline promises Cassie as she turns her attention to Diana and her troubles with the number line. Fifteen minutes have gone by and the teacher calls for the class's attention. Caroline moves back to her chair, positioning herself well to observe the whole class activity. The teacher wants to emphasise the need for accuracy with bar charts as well as explaining the challenge of extension work from the textbook.

It's back to her group for Caroline. She moves her chair to be with Amy, ticking answers and asking for Amy's explanations. Amy enjoys talking with Caroline and there is a natural bond between them. Caroline moves her chair next to Beth who hardly seems to notice. Have Beth and Cassie worked out question three? asks Caroline, and turns her attention to Beth's work.

The teacher passes by and Cassie is eager to tell him she has finished the first work sheet. Caroline does not confirm this but neither does she express surprise to Cassie. Amy and Diana are on their feet bringing their worksheets to be marked. Diana has her arm round Caroline as she marks her sheet. It's congratulations all round. Amy and Diana have done well and are told to get out their exercise books and find page 31. Cassie is now on her feet but Caroline asks her to sit down and moves close to her. Two boys have arrived and are asking Caroline about page 31. They are Peter and Jonathon whom Caroline has supported since Year 1 in a range of subjects. Caroline quietly explains that they should speak to the teacher today, and adds she is looking forward to working with them later. Off they go and Caroline returns her attention to Cassie. Cassie can now begin to work from the textbook and Caroline kneels by Diana who is looking at a bar chart in the textbook.

The teacher asks the class to listen to two boys at the board who want to conduct a quick survey on favourite subjects. Caroline remains kneeling and tells Diana to think of her favourite subject. Caroline expresses delight that it's maths. The pupils are voting and Caroline reminds Cassie to vote. Cassie won't be voting for maths or science! Amy is not listening and Caroline reminds her to do so. Diana claims she is now 'going slow' because she doesn't want to do any more of the bar chart. The teacher is explaining to the class about 'scaling the axis' on a bar chart but Caroline is absorbed with Diana who further claims not to have 'a Friday' on her chart. 'Friday' is found and Caroline moves on to Amy to discuss her answers to questions from page 31. Amy can explain her answers well and Caroline shows she is pleased with her understanding.

The door to the classroom opens and two men enter. They see Caroline and move to her thinking she is the teacher. They explain that they wish to test the electrical equipment in the classroom. Caroline quietly directs them to the teacher. She returns her attention to Amy and finishes discussing her work. She then moves to Beth who has done very little. The teacher tells the whole class to close their books and look his way. Caroline ensures her group does so and sits down.

The teacher is explaining on the board about labelling the axis for the bar chart on favourite lessons and Caroline is watching him. A mobile phone rings! It belongs to one of the men who are checking electrical equipment and the teacher comments on this. Caroline smiles but continues to watch the board and the interruption by the phone passes almost without notice.

All pupils are now finishing off their work. The group have to think of their own title for the 'favourite lesson' bar chart and this causes difficulty for Beth. Caroline offers assistance suggesting words that could be used. Diana asks her how to spell 'favourite' and Caroline asks, 'How does it start?' Diana begins to sound it out and Amy joins in. Caroline is encouraging Diana who is responding well when Amy recognises the word is already written on the board. Caroline congratulates them both – but for different reasons.

Caroline returns her attention to Beth who is having difficulty choosing a scale for the bar chart but she wants Beth to choose it. Together they start to count to ten in twos but the teacher now tells the whole class to close their books, as it's nearly the end of the lesson. Caroline quietly continues with Beth until ten is reached and then ensures the other three have packed away. Beth is talking to Caroline about today's work and Caroline asks both her and Cassie if it was hard. Cassie replies that she knew the work would be 'more serious' in this class. Caroline senses the enjoyment and achievement of this group of pupils (including Beth), tells them well done and they go off to playtime.

Over a cup of tea in the staffroom Caroline advises the teacher of her group's progress. She reports they worked well, concentrating and trying hard to complete the task. Caroline is pleased with their use of vocabulary and will update their individual records later. Together they decide that Caroline will support this group tomorrow to complete the week's work but now it's nearly time for the literacy hour.

Conclusion

What is it that teaching assistants do when they provide learning support to children and classroom support to teachers? Caroline's practice provides insights into the complex nature of the role. It is a many-sided mix of personal and professionally acquired skills. For instance, she connects with the plan of the lesson and its stated objectives. She links with individual children and groups – explaining, questioning, prompting and reminding them of what it is they are meant to do, so keeping them focused on the planned lesson. She also links with the class as a whole, always aware and reacting to spontaneous changes to the lesson plan.

Caroline mediates between 'her' children and the demands of the teacher-led, larger classroom experience. She enables learners to engage with the learning objectives of the lesson by prompting children when they need to be involved in a whole class activity. She also mediates between learners and their sense of achievement by ensuring her children can access the tasks through her additional explanations, encouragement and support.

With regard to spontaneous requests from children, she reacts by reinforcing, redirecting and consolidating the links between knowledge and understanding. She also adjusts to unforeseen events in such a way that the classroom continues to be a productive learning environment. Finally, she supports the teacher's management of the teaching and learning within the classroom in such a way that children can model her attitude and behaviour.

This sweep of 'mediating' support skills exhibited by Caroline is part of a repertoire of skills that might be drawn upon by a teaching assistant. However, perhaps they tend to be taken for granted. This close description of practice suggests they are very important for the effective support of both children and teachers.

Reference

Ofsted (Office for Standards in Education) (2003) *The National Literacy and Numeracy Strategies and the Primary Curriculum*, HMI 1973. London: HMSO.

Section 2
Learners and learning

Roger Hancock and Janet Collins

In this section the focus shifts from learning support *per se* to a consideration of what we mean by learning and what learners do when they learn. Chapter 9 reminds us that when we concentrate on the immediate details of school learning we also need to consider the purposes of education in a broader sense. Schools, Guy Claxton argues, need to prepare learners for a life-long involvement with learning.

Chapter 10 looks at learning through the eyes of children. When asked to imagine the school that they would like, children suggested that too much learning in classrooms is arid and de-contextualised. They emphasised the importance of having opportunities to learn outside school and the need for learning to be both active and enjoyable. Chapters 11 and 12 take up the related theme of informal learning but within the context of home education. Alan Thomas has researched 100 home educating families in Britain and Australia. In his chapter he examines the nature of informal learning and suggests that teaching assistants are well placed to promote it. In Chapter 12, Claire Young writes of 'living and learning' with her three home educated sons. Claire reminds us that learners can have highly individual approaches to learning.

If children are provided with the appropriate resources, there is much that they, as self-directed learners, can learn for themselves. Chapter 13, written by Amrit Dhillon, provides an example from the streets of New Delhi where internet connections were provided in public spaces for children's use. This chapter illustrates the great promise of new technology in terms of its ability to stimulate and support the process of learning. Chapter 14 brings this discussion back to the classroom. Sue Crowley and Mike Richardson offer teaching assistants and teachers suggestions with regard to how they might work together with children to increase their ICT confidence and maximise the use of ICT in classrooms.

Chapters 15 and 16 address the theme of assessment from two different perspectives. The call for higher standards has given impetus to monitoring and assessment in schools and many teaching assistants have become involved in assessing children's learning – a task that hitherto was seen mainly as a teacher's responsibility. In Chapter 15 Janet Kay reviews assessment practice and identifies an expanding role for teaching assistants. Chapter 16, by Ian Eyres, describes a team approach to observation and assessment which is geared towards the justification of a play-based curriculum.

The last chapter in this section addresses the learning that can arise from homework. Julian Stern, in Chapter 17, considers the reasons behind certain kinds of homework and the implications that this can have for parental involvement. The chapter argues that schools need to take care when sending work home and for staff to recognise the variety of pupils' home circumstances.

Chapter 9

What is education for?

Guy Claxton

With the concerted focus on measured standards in education, it's important not to lose site of the deeper reasons why children attend school. Guy Claxton, professor in education at the University of Bristol, has written extensively on creativity and learning. In this chapter, he emphasises the role of education in preparing pupils for a changing world and offers a rationale for lifelong learning.

At root, education is what societies provide for their young people to help them get ready to make the most of the world they are going to find themselves in. We want them to be able to make a living in a way that is fulfilling, enjoyable and responsible. We want them to be able to use their leisure productively: to have fun in a way that does not harm other people or the common resources of locality or planet. We want them to be able to make successful relationships, to be good parents, to be capable of being (and disposed to be) loving and kind.

We would like them to be naturally respectful of people of different beliefs, faiths and persuasions, especially those who are less fortunate. We would like them to feel able to take part in the public life of their community and nation. We would like them to have clear values and principles, and to live by them. We want them to live, as much as they can, without fear or insecurity. We would like them to be happy.

Different people and different societies might express their aspirations for the next generation in different terms, but all education rests on some such statements of hope.

The attitudes, beliefs and capacities young people will need in order to achieve those goals depend crucially on what their world is going to be like. And the education they will need therefore depends on the accuracy with which the current generation, the designers and providers of education, anticipate what the major challenges and opportunities of the future are going to be. It is no use providing education that prepares young people, however effectively, for a world that they are not going to meet, perhaps one that no longer exists.

In stable times, where the culture is relatively homogeneous and the demands of the future relatively predictable, education can provide young people with the knowledge, skills, and ways of thinking that *we* know *they* are going to need. It is a truism that we do not live in such times: a truism because it is so obviously true.

For the vast majority of young people on the planet (and many of their parents), the world is confusing, complicated and rapidly changing – and likely to get more so over their lifetime.

Most people agree that the only thing we can say with any confidence about the year 2025 is that there is not much we can say about it with any confidence.

In this situation, education has to take a step back. Of course we want to give young people the knowledge and attitudes we value: the trouble is, most societies are now a jumble of different we's. Young people are subject to a welter of conflicting advice and images about what matters, and how to be. It's as if they were standing in the middle of a circle of street-lights, each casting their shadow in a different direction. In a world like this, the only sensible role for education is to get them ready, as much as it can, to cope well with complexity, uncertainty and ambiguity – and to handle the high level of responsibility for crafting their own version of a satisfying life that this challenge entails.

The way the world is going

It does not take an astrologer to know the way the world is going. Mobile phones, e-mail, satellite TV and video games, the internet, cheap international air travel…a host of technological innovations have changed the face of work, life and leisure in dozens of ways. Millions of people in the UK work at least part of the time from home. Many of them do daily business with people they have never met. Instead of a 'steady job', people are getting used to being employed for the life of a project: having to adapt quickly to the particular languages and worldviews of team members from diverse professional and cultural backgrounds, and then move on. Microelectronics companies come and go, chasing the best costs-to-skills ratios around the globe, leaving a legacy of deepened insecurity, middle as well as traditionally working class, in their wake. Business people look for security to their financial bonuses, pension funds and their fattening C.V., not to company loyalty.

The traditional heavy industries, and the community life which they supported, are things of the past. The gap between those consultants and 'knowledge workers' who are doing well out of globalisation, and the millions at the poor end of the service industries, packed into call centres, forced to smile on the minimum wage, is widening. As Doug Ross, Assistant Secretary for Employment and Training in the US Department of Labor, told an international conference a few years ago, 'the new poor and marginal in the societies of the developed world will be those who cannot or will not engage in lifelong learning.'

Chapter 10

Learning: 'Let us out...!'

Catherine Burke and Ian Grosvenor

This chapter arises from a *Guardian* newspaper competition asking children to describe 'The School I'd Like'. Catherine Burke, a lecturer at the University of Leeds, and Ian Grosvenor, the director of Learning and Teaching, University of Birmingham, consider what children said about their school learning. The children's responses highlight the importance of promoting learning which is active, engaging and fun.

Learning, like play, is a natural activity in childhood. There are biological and neurological impulses towards learning that children are not entirely conscious of but occur as part of growth and development. Early educators such as Pestalozzi, Montessori and Dewey believed strongly that one of the most important roles of a teacher is to create or adapt an environment which does not fetter this natural process and to know when to stand back and allow such natural activity to take place (Pestalozzi 1894; Montessori 1912). However, the routines of traditional schooling, and particularly the language of reward and punishment, indicate a belief that the child will only learn under certain imposed conditions. Children recognise this paradox and in their alternative visions remind the adult world of their natural proclivity to learn.

One commentary, describing an imagined school of the future, challenges the current assumption that children must be forced to learn.

In this school, lessons are not strictly divided by subjects. Most of the time, lessons in Maths, English, Geography or Science can be taught as one. Students learn concepts by doing – seeing, smelling, hearing, touching, and tasting as well as thinking either creatively or logically. All their senses are utilized in all sorts of manners so that learning is meaningful and practical – not something so alien that they have to be forced upon to do. When children find learning meaningful, they will naturally want to learn more and hence, they will be self-motivated and do not need to be pushed by adults to learn.

Oliver, 13, Loughborough

The school, as traditionally conceived, is only one possible site of learning. There has been a massive growth in the cultural and leisure industries in recent years which has spawned a new generation of 'interactive' learning environments visited by children with other family members outside of school time. Gardens, museums, nature reserves, galleries and ecological centres often employ education officers whose job it is to liaise with schools and to enhance the educational impact of the site. These developments have led some to consider what the experience of children and their families when visiting such sites can tell us about alternative contexts of learning.

The Eden Project in Cornwall, opened in 2001, is a garden theme park consisting of several bio domes containing representations of the world's eco zones. When school groups visit such sites, they can be observed to adapt classroom-style, task-oriented approaches which contrast with the 'natural learning behaviours' manifested by family groups visiting at weekends (Griffin and Symington 1997). Such behaviours tend to be less formally organised, more random and led by curiosity rather than design. It has been argued that school-imposed task structures inhibit the natural tendency to learn at such sites. 'Worksheets encouraged "tunnel vision", box-ticking and emphasis on literacy rather than environmental objectives' and surveys have indicated that 'most teachers and pupils felt that learning would have been more effective if there had been unstructured time for exploration, open-ended questioning and consolidation through structured discussion' (Peacock 2002: 10).

The comments of children about their ideal learning environment unite across time with the cry 'Let us out!'. For some this means having more opportunity to learn outside of school boundaries, to see, touch, smell and feel real artefacts or nature. Many children dream of escaping the confines of the walled and windowless classroom to learn in the school grounds or in special open-air classrooms designed for the purpose. Blishen (1969) found that children were:

> begging that they be allowed to *get out* of the dead air of the classroom - to be freed from that sterile and cramped learning situation in which the teacher, the text book and the examination-dominated syllabus have decided what should be learnt, and how it should be learnt, and that virtually everything should be presented as a hurried intellectual abstraction.
>
> (Blishen 1969: 55)

Once more, the tediousness of lessons, the failure of teachers to inspire and the boring methods to communicate facts are criticised. However, there is no doubt that children want to learn and they believe that changes in the organisation, design and structure of education can allow learning to happen more readily.

Learning will happen with ease when it is allowed to be fun and when children are regarded less as 'herds of identical animals', but as individuals who are made comfortable in mind, body and spirit. Part of the sense of comfort and stimulation will result from being granted some control, choice and direction in their learning. Children and young people long to be allowed more activity, experimentation and continuity in the task; once started, they want to be allowed to finish. A recent study comparing secondary school pupil experience of learning in three European countries, Denmark, France and England, found that the English children 'enjoyed school and lessons the least and were the most likely to want to leave school as soon as they could and to feel that school got in the way of their lives' (Osborn 2001: 274). The same study found that an important cross cultural 'constant' among young people was the pupils' concern that learning should be active and that lessons should have an element of 'fun' or humour.

This is what some children had to say about schools and learning:

In the pretty, lively school there are lots of different classes. There are language lessons on French and German, also there are maths and history lessons. You can go to whatever class you feel like any day. The teachers are kind and interested in the children's ideas . . . The most important thing is learning is fun.

Alix, 7, Oxford

The School I'd like . . . could slow down a little occasionally. They all speak too fast. Some of the children can sign and all of the staff do but it's all usually too fast. Normal schooling is very heavily based on hearing and reading the English language. There are too many words and too many letters. I can understand key words and simple sentences. It is really helpful if I can see a photograph, an object of reference, a symbol and signs accompanied by hearing the sound of the word. The school I'd like could do more sensory things, more hands on, more touchy/feely. Everyone has loads of senses. We can feel with different parts of our body, we can see, hear, taste, smell. How many senses does the national curriculum focus on? Sometimes I find life in the classroom boring and sometimes the pace is too fast and I switch off. Well, who wouldn't – day in, day out, literacy hour, numeracy hour, registration. How about smelling hour, tactile hour, music hour and physical activity hour. What about employing Charlie Dimmock to fill the school with wonderful water features that we could see, hear, touch, smell and feel?

Hugh, 6 (with help from his mum), Wellington

One change that we would make would be to in summer have some lessons outside. In summer in a classroom you get hot and bored. Outside we would be a lot happier and work harder. There could be special outside areas in the school grounds with tables and chairs and the teacher could book lessons there.

Alex, Jessica and Sarah, 12 and 13, Okehampton

The place must be unafraid of kids staring out of windows and must not insist on 100% attention or even 100% attendance . . . It is a terrible pressure for kids to have to pay attention and think what they are told to think. I would encourage people to dream more and enjoy the sun and the sky, the growing grass and the bare boughed trees. I would encourage kids to look beyond the classroom, out of the classroom and see themselves doing different things.

Hero Joy, home educated, 14, Kent

The best thing about the maths classroom is that when our teacher enters, hundreds of sparkling numbers tumble down from the ceiling and then disappear as they hit the floor. And all of us scurry around clutching nets in our hands, trying to catch them. If you're quick enough, you might find you've caught the golden number which gives you the answer to that day's homework.

Jade, 9, London

When we were doing the Vikings in history, we didn't see any of their weapons up close we only saw them in pictures. It would be better if we were taken to a museum to see them. We should be taken on trips as part of our topics, it would help us understand more.

Richard, 12, Glasgow

Time to learn and see a task through to its completion is very important to children, suggesting that they may often be frustrated by the school timetable and its demands. Children recognise too that school is not the only place of learning. Many interactive and imaginative learning resources are now to be found outside schools. Also, the application of electronic devices such as televisions, computers and mobile phones gives community- and home-based learning distinct advantages over the seemingly restricted regime of the school. [Editors]

References

Blishen, E. (1969) *The School That I'd Like*, London: Penguin.

Dewey, J. (1916) *Democracy and Education. An Introduction to the Philosophy of Education* (1966 edn), New York, NY: Free Press.

Griffin, J. and Symington, D. (1997) 'Moving from task-oriented to learning-oriented strategies on school excursions to museums', *Science Education*, **81**, 763–79.

Montessori, M. (1912) *The Montessori Method*, New York, NY: F.A. Stokes Company Inc.

Osborn, M. (2001) 'Constants and contexts in pupil experience of learning and schooling: comparing learners in England, France and Denmark', *Comparative Education*, **37** (3), 267–78.

Peacock, A. (2002) 'Making the environmental message more effective: working with children for ecological awareness at the Eden Project'. Paper presented at the 'Beyond Anthropocentrism' Conference at the University of Exeter, 16–17 July.

Pestalozzi, J.H. (1894) *How Gertrude Teaches Her Children*, translated by Lucy E. Holland and Frances C. Turner, London: Swan Sonnenschein.

Chapter 11

Informal learning

Alan Thomas

Alan Thomas, visiting fellow at the Institute of Education, London, has carried out research into the approaches and experiences of British and Australian parents who educate their children at home rather than send them to school. In this chapter he considers the nature of informal learning and the support for learning that can be provided within the context of home education.

As home educating parents gain in experience, they begin to realize that structured learning is not the only route to an education. A potent influence which brings about the change is that many children resist 'school-type' learning, sometimes strongly. As some parents respond by reducing more formal lessons, they see their children still seem to go on learning.

It is worth restating that formal and informal learning have different meanings at home compared with school. Formal learning at home would probably be regarded as rather informal in a school setting because it is child-centred and highly flexible. Informal learning at home is specific to home because little if anything is prescribed. Children learn through living, from everyday experiences, much as they did in infancy. This kind of learning is not feasible in school.

There can be few professional educators, or anyone else for that matter, who would expect much learning could accrue from simply living at home. There is no doubt, however, that school-age children who learn informally really do learn, which is intriguing at the very least. It challenges nearly every assumption about how children of school age should learn. For obvious reasons, very little is known about informal learning for children of school age – they are in school all day. We do not even know much about informal learning in early childhood. It is taken for granted. It is only relatively recently that research into language acquisition has demonstrated how language is learned almost entirely informally. Apart from this our knowledge of informal learning is quite scant.

A continuation from early childhood

The best support for the proposal that school-age children can go on learning as they did in infancy comes from those parents who, when their children reach school age, just go on doing what they are already doing. They have certain unstated goals obviously, to continue to develop their children's oracy, literacy, numeracy, scientific, geographical and historical understanding, general knowledge, emotional maturity, social competence and physical skills. But these goals do not have to be spelt out any more than they did when their children were younger. These parents are simply continuing their children's apprenticeship to the culture. There is no reason why learning should have to undergo a radical change at the age of 5 or so. Neither does the curriculum of the culture suddenly have to be compartmentalized into relatively autonomous components as it needs to be in school.

Children who start school have to abandon earlier approaches to learning that served them so well in infancy. But if they have the opportunity, they will go on learning in a similar vein. In fact, the idea of continuation was one of the reasons given by parents for deciding to home educate in the first place.

- When he reached school age we just continued: nothing changed.

- At the start it was just a continuation of what had gone before . . . learning will take place anyway. I'm a trained teacher.

- We felt there was nothing to lose. Why interrupt something that had been going on from before the age of 5?

- We've gone on doing exactly the same things as when she was younger. It will be better for her than for [her older brother who was taken out of school at 13], less structure, more of an evolution.

- I was doing a lot with [him]. He's really bright. He takes in any information. We always talked when we were out. I thought then, if only I could I'd keep it like this . . .

One parent who saw education as a continuation, still wanted at least to mark what would have been the first day of school. So, on the day, she and her daughter caught a bus and kept the ticket.

The lifestyle of these families attests to their reliance on informal learning, again being highly reminiscent of life in early childhood.

- Sometimes days go by without anything special happening.

- There is very little that is organized . . . We start the week doing lots of things and get to Sainsbury's by Friday.

- Sometimes I think we should do something but mostly things just happen.

- Children can learn a lot at home, not by having school at home but just by living at home – learning happens naturally.

The parent's role

Although children who learn informally have a large measure of control over what they learn, they are not going to learn much if left to their own devices, any more than they would have in early childhood. The parent is as indispensable for informal as for more formally organized teaching and learning. The child has to acquire knowledge about the culture from the parent who has to play an active role in transmitting or mediating it. How do 'informal' parents do this? Partly by cottoning on to what the child is interested in and extending it, and partly by suggesting things the child might be interested in and seeing if they are taken up.

- Basically, I supply resources, tap into my wealth of information, see opportunity where it arises, listen and observe...

- I'm with him all the time, as a guide.

- I follow them around. I try to be subtle and there when needed. Then they go on on their own. There is no entity of knowledge, just learning how to learn.

- Generally, they just did what they wanted, made things, working out money for other things and how much they would have to save. They'd watch TV, especially wildlife – that was their chief interest. Generally, I'd wait until they wanted to know something...but I wouldn't then make them read or write about it. If they wanted to know about something they'd remember it – if not, if it came from me, it was far more likely to be forgotten.

- [It's] a question of offer and respond. If you have an idea of what might be of interest you make a suggestion and see how it goes; alternatively you cotton on to something that has caught the child's attention or is otherwise of interest...

- We have antennae out all the time, sensitive to our children's needs, difficulties, interests, etc.

Conversational learning

If there is one aspect of the informal 'curriculum' which, above all others, contributes to learning, it is conversation. We have already seen how important dialogue is in more structured learning, allowing parents to strike while the iron's hot and deal with any problems immediately they arise. But informal conversation was also stressed by parents, whatever their approach. Again, this is an extension of the kind of learning that occurred in early childhood, exemplified by the work of Tizard and Hughes (1984), who demonstrated the opportunities there were for learning through everyday social interaction.

- ...lots of walks, we talk a lot.

- After morning tea they are 'banging their gums' all the time. It helps them develop ideas.

- During a visit to [a nature reserve] he asked me: How do they harvest the reeds? We talked about the water table, end of summer harvest, drying out of land, etc. He didn't have to write about it; he had the answer immediately he wanted to know. It was a real life situation, no books, just human interaction.

- I always preferred going places and talking about things and giving them my attention, than sitting down with books.

- We talk and do things without too much organizing them. It just happens...All the things you talk about...It's incredible.

- Most of their education is talking to them. That's how I do most of it. If you answer questions truthfully and talk to them as adults...Their questions are often at great depth.

- They share a lot in our talk – this is good except when you need time for yourselves.

- We talk an awful lot, from the time they get up till the time they go to bed...It's constant, non-stop.

- We discuss things beyond his years. He's interested in politics. He picks up a lot of general knowledge from me because the two of us are in the house together most of the time.

- Lots of questions come up especially at meal times. We talk about people and relationships and difficult people, interaction with older children, being spiteful, being excluded, how to cope. Also moral questions, how you should try and be with different people; otherwise anything from ethics to astrophysics.

- We do talk a lot. He's a chatting child. When he was 3 we did a lot of talking too, I remember.

- They learn more from talking than with pen and paper.

- We talk together a lot on the long car journeys. You don't realize how much you learn.

- They learn a lot through everyday conversation and also learn to talk about their feelings.

- A lot of talking happens in the car.

- I'm convinced most happens through conversation...I spend a great deal of time talking to her.

- A lot happens in talking, for example: 'Why don't we make this?' – or TV, for example: [a politician in the news] was 'stabbed in the back' – with metaphorical meaning. There is time to listen, and you can hold it till later. At home you can do a lot of talking and a lot of listening...I talk to [her] about issues way above her head – this helps to give her a more mature outlook. I also listen to her – she might argue a point and be right. I did not see this in her school days – the relationship is not 'us and them' type of thing.

- [She learns] from being next to me, asking questions, watching...What is important is me giving my time and not rushing off. We can take half an hour to walk down the street.

Children in school have reduced opportunities to converse with adults. Most classroom talk, whether with teachers or teacher assistants, is directed at the task in hand. But teaching assistants do have more opportunities to converse informally with their pupils, simply because they often work with small groups or individual children. In such situations it is the normal run of things to break from work from time to time and talk about other things, just as people at work do. An important aspect of this informal chat will be just helping children to feel comfortable with themselves in the classroom, enjoying a social relationship with an adult as well as a teacher–learner one. But what is, on the surface, simply social conversation, will almost certainly include opportunities for learning informally from someone who has a much greater knowledge of the world. Teaching assistants are also 'around' more than teachers and able to extend interaction with them in the playground, over lunch and during school events, performances and visits outside school. Learning that occurs may be incidental, just in passing, related to news events in the wider world or some issue in school. Family and social life outside school also provide topics of conversation. Talk about your own life – well, up to a point anyway! The lives of school staff are always of interest to children. There is also the opportunity to discuss children's interests and develop threads of conversation across days or weeks. But the main thing is to make the children feel comfortable about talking – topics will emerge anyway.

Informal learning need not be sequential

In keeping with the above, some parents came to realize their children learned a great deal in apparently unrelated bits and pieces.

- A lot of what happens might appear to a school teacher to be fleeting, inconsequential and muddled – but part of this is the opportunity there is to drop and pick up interests as and when you want.

- Children only learn if you are interested in the same thing. I have a prejudice against knowledge stuffing. Learning comes in a very higgledy-piggledy manner – we organize and reorganize as we go along.

- Teachers want things done sequentially. We don't learn to talk like that – not sequentially...Some things we may spend five minutes on now and then pick up two months later...I started with very little structure, but a sort of mental sense of what they should be doing. I had this big thick book. I wrote down what we did every day, for quite a while. I felt I had to prove I was good at what I was doing and I needed a record to show anyone. I found it really hard to keep a diary. We'd start on one subject and then go through a heap of things and end up 'somewhere'. They might read ten books in a day; we had tons of books. We went to the library book sales...For the school inspector I wrote down what we did in one hour: make a cake, do maths, flour, wheat, birds, flying, bird book, flight and feathers, timing the cake, heat, plan for evening, etc.

If there is one body of knowledge the learning of which requires structure and sequence, it is maths. Nearly all parents, including the more informal ones, followed a maths course. Even so, the amount of maths that could be learned incidentally and informally, certainly at the primary level, attracted comment.

- Organization is pretty open though I keep a maths course going, but more maths seems to happen outside maths.

- They do a lot of maths if [their father] is at home because it is almost a social thing around the kitchen table.

- We've used maths books, mainly to fill in the gaps with what they learn anyway, but lots of maths is with 'real things', practical rather than abstract...Recently they built a cardboard castle with some friends. It involved building turrets, working out floor space, how to cut a spiral...and no one mentioned the word 'maths'.

- A lot of maths occurs just through something cropping up...maths just crops up. The children are always more ahead than you expect them to be.

- Maths just happens, though he was taught 'carrying'.

This is not as surprising as it at first appears if you consider that most children informally pick up fundamental concepts in maths before starting school, and that a great deal of maths at the primary level is what adults use on a day-to-day basis, capable of being assimilated informally along with other common cultural knowledge. There are echoes here of the well-known study in which Brazilian children informally acquired mathematical skills through working in the local market (Carraher *et al.* 1985).

Of course, informal learning does not just 'happen' without outside guidance. Parents have to seize opportunities to extend their children's knowledge as and when they arise. But opportunities do crop up very often in day-to-day living, even in maths. In cooking alone there is estimation, fractions, volume, weight, temperature and timing, not to mention biology, chemistry, health, environmental issues, etc. Then there is shopping (including price/weight comparisons), saving and spending pocket money, etc. In the car there is distance and speed and the relationship between them. These are just by way of example. It is essential for parents to involve their children in such activities. Even multiplication tables can be learned informally, just as learning the alphabet was, chanting them in the car, in bed, in the kitchen or out walking. Finally, parents need to react to their children's observations, answer their questions, follow up some of their interests, constantly extending and building on what they already know.

Summary

Informal learning has much in common with learning in infancy. A great deal of it occurs through everyday living and social conversation, but which on closer analysis contains many opportunities for learning. To an observer it might seem somewhat chaotic but if a child educated at home can progress informally even in a subject as structured as maths, then informal learning is very powerful indeed. It is as if the children themselves impose their own sequence on what they learn. Of course, in school, teachers and teaching assistants do not spend anything like as much time with pupils as do parents at home. Nevertheless, they do have opportunities to further pupils' knowledge in the course of naturally occurring social conversations, both during lessons and at other times. This painless kind of learning generally goes unnoticed but what pupils get out of it may have a positive influence on their progress through school, both social and academic.

References

Carraher, T. N., Carraher, D. W. and Schliemann, A. D. (1985) 'Mathematics in the streets and in the schools'. *British Journal of Developmental Psychology*, **3**, 21–9.

Tizard, B. and Hughes, M. (1984) *Children Learning at Home and in School*. London: Fontana.

Chapter 12

Living and learning

Claire Young

Claire Young has been home educating her three sons and keeping a diary about this experience for some eight years. In this chapter she looks back over what she and her three children have learned together. Her piece provides important insights into the process of learning and, particularly, the importance of children's interest and motivation.

Our learning took place as we lived life to the full; we are a family who love reading and talking and being out of doors. That just about sums up how we home educated. I know families who played musical instruments for hours each day, and others who painted, sewed and trailed through charity shops. Each has produced well socialised children who are active learners. Success comes when adults actively engage with children in whatever way comes naturally to both parties.

Learning memories

Remembering incidents from when my children were younger, it amazes me that so much learning took place in and around ordinary living. Some was planned, but more often it happened as we did chores, met friends and even while having arguments. At the time it felt as if they never stopped learning, it was 24 hours a day education. Actually, I think everyone home educates, like it or not. It's just that some people also send their children to school.

In January 1993, Tony was 6 years old, Michael 4, and Paul 1. One Sunday after church we went to a country park, running, hiding and watching motorised model boats. On returning I wanted to make a phone call to my brother in Canada. We used the atlas to look for date lines and time zones and ended up discussing pie charts and colour keys. Tony asked for us to sew a Canadian flag; we discussed the relationship between the words 'Canada and Canadian' and 'Britain and British'.

In November 1994, Tony got a Lego container ship for his birthday. We read books about ships, looked up our junior encyclopedia on ports and container ships, and then visited a container ship base in Gourock. This was how a lot of learning happened, by picking up on something happening in the family, and seeing what else linked in via newspapers, library books, conversations with friends. I wanted them to see the range of options for following an interest. This would probably constitute a 'project' at school, but ours only ran as long as it sustained the child's interest, the learning being the aim, not project presentation.

Michael and Tony wanted to collect a cereal box special offer; this resulted in much counting of pocket money and they very swiftly became competent with pounds and pence. When Paul was 6, he was given 5 pounds per person for Christmas presents, and by having to work out prices in shops, swiftly came to a similar understanding. Decimals were never a problem in maths.

In December 1995, Paul, aged 3, was inclined to fall asleep if we travelled in the car after 4.00 pm – not a good idea as he then stayed up late. To keep his interest, we started counting Christmas trees in people's houses. This became the way Michael, then 6 years, learned to count past 10. By Christmas he could count to 90.

The concept of learning subjects or concepts in a particular sequence didn't seem to apply at home. There would be spurts of interest and then a lull with no apparent learning, only to have them bound forward a month or so later. I had made myself a 'mind map' of the maths concepts for primary-aged children and about every six months I'd glance at it to see if there were any yawning gaps. For instance, if we hadn't done graphs we'd do a survey of birds coming to the feeding table and draw a relevant graph.

Travelling down to Grand-da at Christmas we looked at maps to help pass time. Enjoying maps has become a feature of our family life. We have used a world map pinned on a dining room wall to talk about news items or understand history books, road maps to plan holidays, and town maps to plan cycling trips to friends. Talking about scales and keys of maps came up naturally.

By this stage Tony and Michael had a small 'desk-work' programme which I put together. This would take about an hour each day and was fitted around chores and trips to the park and long, daily sessions of reading together.

Normally children develop speech and walking without being taught. However, I don't believe it happens in the same way with writing, reading or written maths. (There are, however, home educators who have proved me absolutely wrong!) I used a variety of exercises found in books at the Teachers Resource Centre, local stationers and ideas from friends. Maths was as practical as possible, reading and writing little and often.

In June 1996, the toy library was threatened with closure. The boys asked 'Why?' This resulted in a discussion which covered councils, their functions, their funding, decision making and democracy. This conversation ran for about three days, and, as I have no particular political interest, involved asking many other people for the answers.

That year, with Tony 9, Michael 7 and Paul 5, they each had their own piece of garden and grew plants of their own choice. Gardening has always been a great source of learning opportunities, for example organic versus chemical, different types of soil, root formations, and the need for light and nutrients.

There was a General Election May 1997, and the boys, taking note of this, decided to run their own soft toy elections. The Tyrannosaurus Rex Party won, on the promise that they would set up burger bars for the carnivores and investigate DNA storage to prevent extinction. I always enjoy sharing interesting things I've been reading with them so the week before had read them a brief article on DNA and cloning.

A week did not go by without us doing something together in the kitchen. Cooking is a rich area of learning; making a cake, we would discuss what made it rise. When melting chocolate, we would discuss reversible reactions. Recipes require reading, measuring gets learnt naturally, and discussions about nutrition would arise from why it wasn't a great idea to make toffee shortbread every week.

As they got older I found we did about two or three six-week sessions of 'homework', as we termed it, per year and for the rest just read copiously, covering every subject under the sun, in fiction or non-fiction. Book work included a variety of maths and English work and I'd add in science, geography or history, depending on the child's interests or lack of. One child was physically a little lazy, so he had exercise on his list.

I set a weekly quota from textbooks and work books and put up the social diary for the week so they could decide when to work. If we got to Thursday and they wanted to play out but had done no homework, as agreed, the answer was 'after work'. I have always told the boys 'School is optional, education is not.' Having said that, home education can only be done by mutual consent, which I think is one of its strengths. We have talked together using Edward de Bono's 'six hat thinking' and Tony Buzan's 'mind maps' to get the children to take responsibility for their learning.

In November 1999 Paul, aged 7, continued to collect bones and interesting rocks, and noticed on a walk the clear layers of different rock in a freshly eroded river bank. He still has an abiding interest in the out of doors – fishing, Scouting, hawking lessons, reading adult-level books on survival and fishing.

Ways of learning

Answering questions as they came up was one way they learned.

As a 6-year-old Paul asked, 'What does "hotel" mean?' I replied, 'You know what it means.' 'Yes,' he said, 'but what does it really mean?' 'Do you mean where does it come from?' I asked. (Noise of possible agreement from him.) I said, 'Find me a dictionary.' (I was probably cooking dinner at the time.) Paul fetches me the big dictionary which he knows shows word origins, not just spelling, so I take it I have correctly guessed what his question meant. We look up 'hotel', read it out and he goes off with no further comment.

Aged 7, Paul came in holding a cardboard toilet roll with a mini rolling pin as the plunger and a plasticine 'cannon ball'. 'Look how far it can fire,' he said. I look. He says, 'Hmm not very far, but if I aim it higher.' He tries again with more success.

When 9 and cuddling up in bed in the early morning, Paul says, 'If we had a glass almost full of water, just air at the top. If we closed it and turned it over where would the air go?' After puzzling that through, he then moved on to ask 'What would happen if you had a metal box of air and you closed it and squashed it?' This led onto a discussion of how a pressure cooker works – there being a well known family story of when a pressure cooker blew beetroot all over the kitchen!

I have had to adapt to their ways of learning, otherwise it would have been just a waste of time. It took me till one child was four to realise he was scared of new things. I actually love new things and was making his life difficult by emphasising 'new' as we started anything, even swimming lessons. He needed to know he would be in the same pool and wearing the same costume and not that he had a *new* teacher and was in a *new* class. When I realised this tactic also worked academically I would approach a new step in learning saying it was a slightly different way of doing something that he already knew. So division was introduced as multiplication done backwards.

Our family has several of the learning types Howard Gardener has identified, and it's been a challenge to learn how to present the same thing differently. Tony learned to read easily with phonics. Michael wanted to be able to read at 5, but disliked being taught. I eventually gave up when he was 6, as it was causing such fights. A year later, I discovered he could read even complicated words like 'through'. Paul proved to be different again, much more a physical learner. So he has 'run' letter shapes out in the garden, laid rope out in their shapes and then written them on the patio in chalk. While learning to read he had to get up and run around the house between each few lines because his legs went 'funny'. He always came back to work, but found concentrating such hard work he needed to blow of steam. He finally learned to read at the age of 9, and by 10 was well up to his reading age, now happily immersing himself in books for hours.

I often felt the tension between letting a child discover for himself and actively teaching. On one occasion, Michael, of his own accord, made a set of traffic lights. I made several comments on how to improve the design, and he ended up crying because I had confused him with too many ideas. If I believed in self-discovery, why did I still want to butt-in?

What did not come naturally with any of our boys was writing. I found getting the boys to write was like pulling teeth and early on decided I was going to use our time to learn, not fight over pages of writing. Most 'creative writing' was done orally. I would type out stories they told, or just listen to their endless imaginative accounts. Michael would, of his own accord, draw a detailed picture and then come and tell me about it. Tony and Paul would make complicated clay models of an island, or a mine, and then tell me the story behind it.

I never worked out whether it was better to present a new concept practically or via a book at first. It was easier to read a book about estuaries when we had followed a river to the sea, but we discussed racism in reading books like *Kim* by Rudyard Kipling. In a way we might not have done otherwise in our mainly white town.

We have often joined with other home educators for group events, numbers varying from eight to 28 children. These have included felt-making with a friend, a talk on Romans at a museum, a series of art lessons and a technology workshop. Paul loved rock and bone collecting, so a geology trip should have been his favourite. However the man who took us was newly graduated, enthusiastic to share with us his new-found knowledge and understanding, and that was over Paul's head. Children who were older, 14 years old, learnt a lot.

The drama workshops were taken by a home educating mother, who'd been a professional actor. She was brilliant in her ability to set a theme and then work in all the ideas the children came up with. With her interactive approach she totally hooked the children.

We found group learning benefited only a few in the group and seldom equalled one-to-one conversation, because the child tends to get talked at rather than with. However, the children remember the group events as happy times and so as socialising times they were useful.

The love of learning

I was pro-home not anti-school. I never wanted to teach, but I did want them to be hooked on learning. I home educated because I did not believe young children needed teachers. I think they need loving and enthusiastic companions in learning, and a normal environment. We eventually had to make a decision as to when, and if, to use the school system. I wanted them at home at least long enough for them to see learning as enabling and interesting, not 'boring' as I often hear children describe it around here.

Many home educators, in the USA and here in the UK, have continued right the way through to school-leaving age, not sitting exams, and found the children are actively welcomed into colleges and employment. Home education has been reported as producing mature, active learners who will give of their best.

We have chosen to put the boys into the last year of primary school, for a settling-in year, and then on to secondary in order to sit exams. I've been delighted, and relieved, to find our minimalist approach to written and formal work has, so far, resulted in two of the boys doing very well in all subjects. They found the first year in school a steep learning curve in terms of speed and quantity of writing expected, but did not struggle in any other way. With one son, I told the teacher, after the first month, he was very aware of how little he wrote compared with others. The teacher's reply was she'd rather have one paragraph of his writing than a page of the others because the quality of ideas and word use was so much better.

My third son, the one who takes book learning and writing like medicine, has struggled with his first year at school and has a long way to go before he realises his ability. He is bright, but I sense that school is never going to suit his interests and style of learning. He continues to have an enquiring mind with subjects he values; they just aren't in the school curriculum!

Watching children develop, mind, body and spirit, is a source of wonder for me. To be involved as an enabler and encourager, perhaps like a sports coach, has been hard work sometimes, but it's been great fun and so rewarding.

Chapter 13

Net gains for 'slum' children

Amrit Dhillon

There is time-honoured debate in education about how children should learn in school. On the one hand, it is said they learn best through a detailed curriculum that is planned and 'delivered' to them. On the other, there is a belief in their abilities to learn much from their own endeavours assisted by teachers, teaching assistants and parents. Amrit Dhillon, a writer, provides an example of what children can learn for themselves when they are provided with the means to do so.

Go to a slum district of Delhi, put a computer with an internet connection into a public wall and leave it on. Wait and watch through a remote video camera rigged up on a nearby tree. Children who cannot read or write, with no English but blazing with curiosity, come along and start fiddling with the weird contraption that has surfaced out of nowhere.

Eight minutes later, children who do not know what a computer is are navigating the web. By evening more than 70 are surfing the net. Days later they are playing games, creating folders, cutting and pasting, creating short cuts.

A fluke? That is what Dr Sugata Mitra, who conducted the experiment three years ago, thought, too. So he repeated it. Even in remote wildernesses, where the only mouse that desperately deprived children knew was the furry kind, Mitra kept seeing the same extraordinary results: children learning basic computer literacy on their own, with no instruction.

They invented their own vocabulary to define terms, so the cursor is 'sui' (Hindi for needle) and the hourglass is the 'damru' after the hourglass-shaped drum that the Hindu god Shiva plays.

When Mitra, who heads the Centre for Research in Cognitive Systems at one of the world's largest computer-training institutions, the National Institute for Information Technology (Niit), added sound, the children discovered what MP3 was and began playing their favourite Hindi film songs. 'They didn't know what any of this was called,' Mitra says. 'But they would say, "if you take this little box, and you drag this file into this box, it plays music." They gain a functional literacy very fast.'

At Daksllinpuri, another slum district of the Indian capital, seven-year-old Rajendra cranes his neck to see the screen. 'I'm learning English by using it,' he says proudly. 'I know words like save, delete, folder. With him is ten-year-old Akansha, clutching a baby sister on her hip. Asked what the internet is, she replies: 'It's where we can do everything, even if we don't know anything?'

The computer kiosks are designed to exclude adults (they are set low in the wall, with a keyboard angled so that taller people find it awkward to access), and are engineered specially to endure India's searing heat, dust storms and monsoons. They are also designed to have a high fault tolerance; if some software is damaged, for example, the computer notices and restores it. There is also software to prevent Windows from hanging so that children do not have to know how to reboot.

The key insight from this hole-in-the-wall experiment is that if India's poorest children can become computer literate by learning on their own, or in groups, they do not need formal computer education.

The implications for India's primary education system are staggering. Starved of resources, schools lack books, paper, chalk, everything. Some have computers, but not enough for the 700 million Indians under 18. As the world lunges farther into the information age, the most socially fragmented society on Earth faces the emergence of yet another social divide – between the information haves and have-nots.

But if children need no formal training to use computers, it means that precious time and money can be freed up for teaching them what they cannot learn on their own. In the process, India might just succeed in bridging the knowledge gap that will otherwise condemn millions to exclusion from the modern world for ever. James Wolfensohn, the president of the World Bank, is taken by the experiment because it suggests a bold new way of tackling rural education. That is why the bank is giving $1.6 million (£966,000) to a joint venture – the Hole in the Wall Company – for setting up the project in 108 locations in India.

'If we can put in 100,000 kiosks, I reckon that we could get 500 million children computer literate in five years, at a cost of $2 billion. If you educated the same children using traditional methods it would cost twice as much,' says Mitra.

But the application of Mitra's findings is potentially much wider. What Niit and Mitra are now exploring is how far a computer in an urban or rural slum district can go in delivering a classical primary school curriculum to children who will never go to school.

This is an important question, and explains the World Bank's excitement. In India and the rest of the developing world, the economics of the classical bricks-and-mortar model do not work. There is not enough money to build and equip all the schools that are needed.

So maybe on-line education is the solution. 'I am not saying that if we put computers in all slums, children can become literate on their own,' Mitra says.

'I am saying that in situations where we cannot intervene frequently, you can multiply the effectiveness of ten teachers by 100 if you give children access to the internet.'

Chapter 14

Information and communication technology

Sue Crowley and Mike Richardson

In this chapter Sue Crowley and Mike Richardson, lecturers at Liverpool Hope University, review the role of ICT in school learning and highlight ways in which teaching assistants and teachers can further develop their ICT knowledge, skills and confidence – not least by supporting each other and learning alongside children.

Introduction

Information and Communication Technology (ICT) can be an extra, versatile tool for learning, which sits alongside books, pens, glue and other vital items in the primary and secondary teacher's toolbox. In the past, children were introduced, sometimes reluctantly, to many such tools from slates to slide rules, and Heppell points out in the Foreword to Loveless and Ellis (2001) that they have even had innovations such as the ballpoint pen and mobile phones confiscated. However, it is now time to embrace new technologies and use them to change and improve pedagogy. The desire of the teacher should not be to set a standard that all children must achieve, but rather to enable children to realise that ICT offers practical and fun ways to achieve more. The assistant in the classroom needs to be prepared to reinforce this ethos and support the use of ICT if it is to become firmly established as a learning resource in school. We believe our children need to know about the use of ICT in everyday life around them and its potential for the future, but more importantly they deserve opportunities to begin to realise the full potential of ICT as a tool to support and present their developing learning and creativity.

One ultimate goal of the use of ICT in education is that the pupils are able to use the technology independently and appropriately. Moseley *et al.* (1999) found that successful teachers of ICT gave children choices rather than directing them. Teachers who were not confident users of ICT would employ another adult to help and direct the children with ICT and hence not use ICT in any way to change pedagogy. The teaching assistant can prepare specific resources and activities. In addition, the assistant will help the children learn how to use ICT for learning. Pupil empowerment is more desirable than receiving instruction or completing work from an adult's point of view. Naturally, children need to acquire certain skills, which need teaching. However, once basic skills have been learned, ICT offers a medium that is ripe for experimentation. Children show fewer inhibitions than adults and are more willing to try different icons and menus without fear of damaging the computer. They may not experiment if an over-zealous adult tells them what to do, or presses the keys for them.

Confidence and skills

Monteith (2002) suggests that teachers who are skilful in ICT are most likely to develop skilful pupils. It is important that the teacher and the assistant both feel confident that they can support their children with ICT skills and have sufficient knowledge to be able to plan appropriate ICT activities into the curriculum for all children. This chapter does not include guides to software but we hope that both the teacher and assistant are aware of areas for their own personal development. Remember that nobody needs to know everything about the appropriate software to be effective. It is important to stay open-minded as your learning continues, so that you will be able to support pupils' ICT work appropriately.

The teacher and the assistant should work in partnership to develop ICT capability for themselves and their pupils. If both adults have little experience, then it might be best to take different aspects of ICT to develop personally, then pool and share their knowledge and ideas. If the assistant is new to ICT, and the teacher has some knowledge, then they could spend some concentrated time, i.e. an in-service morning or afternoon, going through the core skills in relation to the ICT planned for the term/year. It is better to spend time learning, and teaching each other, away from the busy school day. Ideally, teachers will give the assistant time and opportunities to get to know all the ICT peripherals so that he or she will be able to do what is required with ICT. For example, the children will benefit from the assistant's ability to use a digital camera immediately when a situation arises. Too often, we miss the opportunity of catching children's smiles of satisfaction when they have recognised a significant achievement.

The general principle we are trying to promote here is that teachers and assistants should try, as much as possible, to pre-empt potential causes of frustration. You can promote a positive attitude to the subject by refusing to allow the computer or any ICT equipment to become a 'nuisance in the corner'. When all the adults in the room are prepared to cope with the difficulties and know when to refer difficulties to a technician, the more they will view the computer as a valuable learning and teaching tool. We need to be positive about ICT no matter how we feel! When unsure, we must seek help from a sympathetic technician, friend, colleague or relative and explain that we want to learn how to do things for ourselves (not just be shown). The secret of becoming a confident user of ICT is to use it a little and often at first and be prepared to ask for advice. We practise what we preach; we have been using computers for personal use and in our teaching for nearly 20 years, but we will still come into each other's rooms and say 'How can you do this?' or 'Is there another way to...?'

As a confident user of ICT, a teaching assistant can be invaluable to a school, as one assistant from Castlefield Infant School, Rastrick (DfES 2003a) stated:

> I advise, I teach ICT in small groups, I keep my own records, run parents and pupils sessions and a lunchtime ICT club, and by fair means or foul have encouraged the other staff to use e-mail. I used the children's enthusiasm for e-mail to influence the teachers.
>
> (www.teachernet.gov.uk, accessed June 2003)

The head teacher from Mission Primary School (DfES 2003b) has also praised his teaching assistant on her knowledge of the use of ICT:

> Julie exemplifies the progressive development of the TAs. In addition to her classroom support duties she has also become expert in training pupils in the use of ICT. Julie has a powerful influence in ICT. In partnership with the designated teacher, she has reviewed the QCA requirements for ICT. She has then selected the most appropriate software to deliver the curriculum. I have tried to promote the idea that each TA develops a specialist expertise such as literacy, numeracy or special needs, and that these skills are then practised across the curriculum. In this way the TAs develop two focuses to their work: one will be class-based but the other is related to the whole school curriculum. Like Julie with ICT, each TA then becomes an important additional resource in a specialist area. The response of the TAs has been overwhelmingly positive.
>
> (www.teachernet.gov.uk, accessed June 2003)

Many primary and secondary schools in the north-west of England are now employing assistants with particular ICT expertise to work in the classroom.

Making opportunities, planning and assessing

Whether it is a whole-staff or departmental approach, the ICT co-ordinator's or the class teacher's plan, the curriculum at all levels should include ICT for the whole year. In this way, ICT opportunities can be broad, balanced and progressive. Planning should start with the big picture: a table of topics in all taught subjects in the year with identified opportunities where ICT can support the subject. Obvious examples might be:

- a Key Stage 2 mathematical topic on 2-D shapes, involving work with a programmable toy
- a Foundation Stage topic on the seasons, using an art programme to show what a tree looks like at different times of the year, e.g. a picture could be pre-made by the teacher or assistant of the trunk and branches, and the children complete the picture.

Once all the obvious ICT is in place for the year, an audit needs to be made of the types of ICT used to ensure a balance. Auditing is a simple process of gathering information about ICT. As teachers are very busy, any lightening of administrative duties that help to inform their teaching is generally welcomed. Hence, the teaching assistant may find that he or she becomes involved in the auditing process. There needs to be some of each aspect of ICT across the curriculum, i.e. communication, information retrieval, information handling in the form of data collection and graphs, presentation, modelling, monitoring and control. If one type of ICT is lacking from the first scrutiny of the year plan, then teachers should seek opportunities to extend the range where it would be appropriate. At times, it may be relevant to plan a discrete ICT project in order that aspects such as control or modelling are taught as part of a specific ICT lesson. In addition to ensuring the ICT curriculum is taught, an audit will look at the resources needed to deliver the lessons. For example, some equipment may need servicing or need the batteries changed. Although the ICT co-ordinator, head of department or technician is the person who has primary responsibility for ensuring these resources are in place and working, he or she will rely heavily on other members of staff at the school to inform them when these maintenance or preparation tasks are required as well as help with suggestions on how to improve provision. A teaching assistant working closely with children using ICT will make a valuable addition to the team.

Using individual or small groups of computers

Individual or small groups of computers are often found in both primary and secondary school situations. The primary classroom might have a single stand-alone computer, or one linked to the Internet. In both primary and secondary schools, there is often one or more dedicated ICT suite. Teachers use these facilities in different ways to suit the curriculum and the situation in the school.

Teaching the skills

Inevitably, computer skills such as inserting and moving images need to be taught to most children at some time in order to carry out planned projects. For example, in making a poster/leaflet to advertise local amenities, in a geography project, the assistant and teacher will have to do the following preparatory work. First, they will need to discuss a list of skills required. These skills will include:

- the ability to use font sizes and colours appropriately
- the use of text editing features such as centring, underlining and **bold**
- the insertion, resizing and moving of images
- the use of digital camera
- the use of word art
- the use of three columns to make a fold-over leaflet.

Prior assessment of the children's knowledge and ability will need to be carried out and a plan of action drawn up as to who needs to be taught what. You should not need to teach the entire class all the skills. If the children are in small groups of similar ability, then the teacher or assistant can teach each small group the skill required for the project; this would move them forward from where they are in their computer knowledge. These small ICT ability groups may not fit in snugly with numeracy and literacy groups in a primary school situation. We suggest that at primary level the assistant can take them out of the subject lesson for 10–15 minutes and teach computer skills related to the planned subject ICT activity. It is quite feasible in many schools, as long as it fits in with the subject expectations. Once the project is underway, the, children will learn from each other any particular skill they really want.

When children are learning from one another, some may see this as an opportunity for feeling superior or even carrying out minor bullying. We can prevent such bullying by establishing a good ethos in the school that leads to a clear etiquette for computer use. Peer tutoring principles can help. The key features are the selection of children as tutors, training in mentoring skills and clear expectations given of what was involved. Such a system needs to be a whole-school strategy.

Using the computer as a tool

Once the teacher or assistant has taught the skills of a project, then the children can use the classroom computer/s on a rota system for small groups or as individuals to produce and present their work. Ideally, no other adult should be required for this project; however, ideal situations and computers don't always mix! The children should know that if they have an important query either the teacher or the assistant is available. Therefore, only one of these adults should be working with concentration with a group of children while the other is available to ensure the computer project can progress, allowing the children to work independently. The children need to know who is on 'computer duty'; you could follow the example of a colleague of mine who used to put on an apron with a large cat on the front when she didn't want to be disturbed! A wall display containing 'prompts' is very useful for older children at Key Stages 2 and 3, especially if situated near the computer area. Such a display aids independence.

Some computer activities may require planned intervention in order to encourage thought and reflection. For example, when producing computer graphs from data collected from an investigation, there needs to be the prompt 'What does your graph tell you about your findings?' or, when using a modelling program that includes decisions, 'Why did you take that path?' This need not occur often but it is a good opportunity for speaking and listening skills to develop alongside reflective thought. However, the teacher and assistant need to discuss whatever is going on that day and decide on the teaching strategy and who will do what, whether it is teaching, planned intervention or waiting for invitations to help. This kind of approach works well in situations where there is less time pressure on the curriculum. For example, in Sweden where the compulsory element to the curriculum is approximately half that of our own, teaching assistants are able to provide support to children as they engage in independent learning activities.

Conclusion

Teaching assistants will need to work alongside teachers in preparing for the use of ICT in lessons by:

- ensuring they understand how to use equipment
- making resources and assisting with their use
- supervising computer use and assisting children with their developing ICT skills.

Although some people claim to be techno-phobic, with a little perseverance these technical skills are well within their reach. After all, much of the equipment or in some cases software is designed for use by children. Most problems come because things are done out of sequence, due to assumptions made by the user. The best advice is to spend some time with unfamiliar equipment or software so that you are aware of the pitfalls and dangers. All the best users of technical equipment can tell the tale of the time when they came unstuck because they didn't prepare themselves. If you don't like doing it on your own, then find others who will be prepared to join you in a practice session. Finally, children love having people who are prepared to learn with them and good teachers and teaching assistants have been doing it for years.

Websites

www.ncaction.org.uk – the DfES website.
www.standards.dfes.gov.uk/schemes3 – a site for guidance on the QCA schemes of work.
www.teachernet.gov.uk

References

DfES (2003a) '"Castlefield Infant School": a case study in support for the curriculum', at www.teachernet.gov.uk/management/teachingassistants/Management/casestudies/, accessed June 2003.
DfES (2003b) '"Mission Primary School": a case study in support for the curriculum, at www.teachernet.gov.uk./management/teachingassistants/Management/casestudies/, accessed June 2003.

Loveless, A. and Ellis, V. (2001) *ICT, Pedagogy and the Curriculum*, London: Routledge Falmer, pp. xv-xix.

Monteith, M. (ed.) (2002) *Teaching Primary Literacy with ICT*, Buckingham: Open University Press, pp. 1-29.

Moseley, D., Higgins, S. and Bramald, R. (1999) *Ways Forward with ICT: Effective Pedagogy Using ICT for Literacy and Numeracy in Primary Schools*, Newcastle upon Tyne: University of Newcastle upon Tyne.

Chapter 15

Assessment

Janet Kay

With an increased attention on measured standards, assessment and recording have become very important school activities and many teaching assistants have been drawn into these teaching-related tasks. Janet Kay, lecturer at the University of Derby, reviews some of the skills involved in assessment and suggests ways in which teaching assistants might collaborate with teachers.

Introduction

Teaching assistants have a significant role to play in the monitoring and assessment of groups of children and individual children whom they are involved in supporting. Assessment is a more major part of the activities in primary classrooms, more so since the introduction of the National Curriculum and the Early Learning Goals formalized the curriculum for young children. The role of assessment in monitoring the performance of individual children, whole schools and the broader education system has been well established over the last few years.

But what is assessment for? O'Hara (2000: 102) states that assessment is to ensure that teachers know:

- what children know
- what they can do
- where they need to go next.

Assessment provides the basis on which the next round of planning for teaching and learning can take place. If assessment is ongoing and accurate, teachers can plan teaching and learning from a baseline of knowledge as to where the children have already progressed.

Assessment is not a single process, nor does it all take place formally or at preset stages in the school year. Formal assessment has a role to play, but is only one part of the wide range of assessment processes which take place throughout each school year. Children are formally assessed at the end of each Key Stage through Standard Assessment Tasks (SATs), which measure children's progress against a nationally determined range of criteria across particular parts of the curriculum. SATs results give the teacher feedback on the child's progress and abilities. They also give the school feedback on the whole class achievement, which can be compared with previous classes at the end of each Key Stage, and compared with other schools' results within the LEA, and nationwide. Each school will have set targets for achievement and the SATs results will be judged against these targets. [...]

But SATs are only a small part of the assessment process in schools. Although they have a high profile because they are nationally determined and the results are published, they rarely tell teachers and schools much they do not already know about the children in their care. While SATs can be typified as 'summative' assessment – assessment that takes place at the end of a phase of the curriculum – schools are also involved in ongoing, formal and informal 'formative' assessment. This type of assessment is the day-to-day monitoring and judging of children's work, which informs teachers of the ongoing progress of individuals and the whole class.

All assessment is vitally important in the teaching and learning process because:

- It gives feedback to teachers on the effectiveness of learning and teaching strategies.
- It helps teachers become aware of areas that the whole class needs to work on more or in a different way.
- It helps teachers to recognise specific problems or areas of lack of progress a particular child may have.
- It helps teachers to assess the rate of progress the class and individual children are making.
- It is the basis of feedback to children as a group or individuals and provides material for giving praise and acknowledging progress.
- It provides information which can be shared with parents.
- It can help teachers and heads to become aware of deficits in resources, both human and physical.
- It helps teachers judge their own performance and planning and make adjustments as required.

All assessment is based on the process of judging children's progress and achievements against known criteria. When SATs are taken, this is a more formal process based on clearly stated criteria. However, during the more informal processes of assessment, the criteria are not necessarily so clearly stated and the assessment is not usually achieved through tests. [...]

Types of assessment

A number of different types of assessment are used with young children. It is important to note that the choice of type of assessment is not random. We choose the type depending on what we want to assess and for what purpose. The type of assessment used must match the outcomes required if it is to be effective. This does not mean that there are no choices to be made. Very often there will be different ways in which a particular assessment can be made. Choices may depend on the resources available and the forms of assessment that are most familiar and seem most effective to those involved. In some circumstances, it is helpful to draw information for assessment purposes from more than one source, to strengthen the judgements that may then take place.

Choices of assessment must also be geared to the needs of young children and the possible impact of different assessment methods on their confidence and progress. There have been some criticisms of formal testing of 7-year-olds because of the possible negative impact of this type of assessment on some young children's self-esteem and confidence. The type of assessment used must therefore both fit the purpose of the assessment process and meet the needs of the children involved. While some types of assessment are so 'feather light' the children are more or less unaware of them, others are more obvious and therefore have more impact.

Summative assessment

As discussed above, summative assessments take place at the end of a specific phase of learning. Summative assessment, such as the SATs described above, sum up what the child has achieved at a specific time or stage of learning. [...] Summative assessment usually also takes place at the end of each school year, providing a basis for teachers to feedback to parents on their children's progress within the school year. This end-of-year assessment can also be used to inform the teacher of the next class up, in terms of his or her planning. It can be used to determine if special educational needs (SEN) are evident in respect of individual children, and what sort of support is required to assist the child to make progress. Not all summative assessment is based on a formal process. End-of-year assessment is often based on both informal and formal formative assessments that have taken place over a period of time.

Summative assessment is important in checking each child's progress against expected levels of attainment (criteria), but has less use in helping teachers plan their teaching and learning or give regular feedback to children and their parents, because it only takes place periodically.

Formative assessment

Formative assessment is more ongoing, whether it is based on formal methods or informal methods. It is the constant feedback teachers use to decide what sort of teaching and learning, support and encouragement their pupils need, either as individuals or as part of the whole class. This feedback comes from a wide range of informal sources:

- daily examination of children's work
- feedback from reading records
- the answers children give to questions
- the questions children ask
- the mistakes children are making and the problems children are encountering with specific activities
- comments and concerns of parents
- comments and concerns of the children.

More formal sources include assessment that is planned beforehand such as:

- tests, e.g. spelling tests, maths tests
- criteria-based assessment (assessing children during tasks against pre-set lists of criteria)
- homework.

Formative assessment comes from a wide range of sources of information which are collated and seen as a whole by the class teacher. This type of assessment draws on the skills of all staff and volunteers in the classroom and the wider school, on the views and observations of parents and children, and on the expertise of specialist staff from outside the school. Formative assessment can help to diagnose particular difficulties children may have, as well as provide an ongoing record of the children's progress.

For example, Kerry, 6, had problems with her handwriting to the point where she actively avoided writing tasks and sometimes refused to write. In discussion with her parents, it became clear that they were concerned about aspects of Kerry's physical co-ordination as well as her performance at school. Kerry's parents arranged paediatric assessment for Kerry through the local children's hospital. The physiotherapist found that Kerry had poor strength and stability in her shoulders and upper body, which made writing a difficult task for her. In consultation with the teacher and the Special Educational Needs Co-ordinator (SENCO) and the direct involvement of two support workers, Kerry was supported with a programme of physiotherapy at home and at school in order to help her gain strength and stability in her upper body, and ultimately to help her make progress with her handwriting. She also received extra help in class and was encouraged to use the computer to develop literacy skills so that her writing delays had less general impact on her literacy development.

Approaches to assessment

There are a number of different measures against which a child's work can be judged, and it is important to know which is being used and why. They are:

- national criteria such as the National Curriculum level descriptors, which set general attainment standards against which work can be measured
- the average of the class, which may not reflect the above, but which can give information about the level of development in relation to the rest of the group
- the child's own progress rates in terms of his or her individual development.

[…]

Judging a child's progress against his or her previous achievements is a sound basis for giving praise and encouragement and helping unconfident children to recognise that they have progressed. Children with SEN have this process formalized through their Individual Education Plans (IEPs) which set targets for the child to progress towards, their targets reviewed on a regular basis. This helps the child, parents, teachers and support workers to recognize and praise areas where progress is being made, and review support in areas where progress is less evident.

Effective assessment is usually based on a range of different approaches to provide the assessors with a full picture of the child's abilities. One type of assessment may simply not give enough information or may not provide all we need to know about the child's ability to learn and progress to date. For example, when Dan was 6 his delays in learning to read and write seemed to dominate the view of his learning progress held by his parents, school and, sadly, himself. With the support of other types of assessment, however, Dan's oral skills became a much stronger focus for assessment giving a broader and more encouraging picture of his progress and ability to learn. Dan's self-confidence and self-esteem benefited directly from this wider view of his abilities and this more positive view of self was reflected in his learning.

Using different approaches also means that different individuals involved in the child's learning can contribute to the assessment process. Different assessment methods may be effective with different children depending on a number of factors:

- gender
- culture and language
- particular skills and strengths
- response to different assessment methods.

Assessing to determine children's strengths as well as their areas for further development in an important basis for positive and encouraging feedback to both parents and children.

[…]

Feedback

Giving feedback is a crucial element in the assessment process. It is not much use to children to be assessed if the outcomes of that assessment cannot be or are not translated into information that will support and encourage the child's learning in the future.

Feedback comes in many forms, formal and informal, written and verbal, instant and delayed. Some feedback is associated with summative assessment, for example, annual reports and discussions at end-of-year parents' evenings, and SATs results. Some is associated with formative assessment, and can include feedback on written work or oral work, groupwork and individual work, projects and play. It can include written comments and verbal comments, grades and marks out of a total, for example spelling test results. Feedback appears as comments in a child's reading record, ticks and comments on written numeracy work, praise for the whole class or a particular group, a child being asked to show work to the class or even to the whole school. Feedback can come in the form of stickers ('Star of the Week'), certificates ('Super Speller') or comments to parents at home time.

Whatever the form feedback takes it should always be based on the following principles:

- Feedback should be positive as well as negative.
- It should be considered and pertinent to the particular achievement.
- It should link that achievement to the child's overall progress where possible.
- It should suggest areas for further development where appropriate.
- It should not be critical, overly negative or condemning.
- It should involve the child's views and opinions which should be actively sought.
- It should be shared with others where appropriate.
- It should never damage a child's self-esteem or confidence.
- Praise should be genuine and based on progress.

Feedback is often given at a high level in primary schools, based on the principle of supporting self-esteem and good levels of self-confidence. Children need to know they are doing well and progress is being made. They will benefit from being in an environment where praise and encouragement are the norm. However, there are a few pitfalls, which need to be considered alongside this positive approach. Children will not necessarily benefit from the 'that's nice, just pop it over there' syndrome, which can be found in some establishments. If children learn that standard praise comments will be issued for every piece of work they do, this may not promote high standards. Work needs to be properly examined and discussed, and the child's view on its quality sought, in order to give genuine and valuable feedback. Feedback has more meaning when it is focused on a few pieces of work or aspects of progress rather than being general. Over-use of praise can devalue it in the children's eyes, so although praise is very important, children should feel it is based on real progress or achievement. For example, Damien, 7, was so used to 'smiley faces' on his work, to encourage his slow progress, that he drew them on his work himself before completing it. Any value they had as a form of positive feedback had faded by this stage, and new methods of giving Damien praise had to be sought. Giving feedback that is carefully considered, immediate and based on a considered assessment of the child's work, however, can be a vital part of the learning process and central to the child's overall development.

[...]

The teaching assistant's role

The role of the teaching assistant in assessment will vary considerably depending on the specific work you are each involved in. All assessment activities will be agreed with the teacher and possibly other members of the school staff or other professionals involved with a particular child. The teaching assistant's role is to:

- Make assessments as agreed with the teacher and record these as planned.
- Report back to the teacher on the progress of individual children and groups of children as required.
- Identify learning points which will inform future planning, e.g. areas of a subject that the child or children needs to do more work on.
- Identify successes, achievements and breakthroughs and share these with the teacher.
- Give feedback to the child as required.
- Report back to any other professionals or parents as agreed.

Much of the assessment you do will contribute to the teacher's formative and summative reports. Some, however, will be the definitive record, particularly where you work directly with one child. The formative assessment you are involved in should contribute to the teacher's planning process and the teaching and learning which takes place in the classroom.

The role of the teaching assistant also includes ensuring records are fair and open, and that they avoid subjective and possibly damaging comments about the child. It is very easy to develop a particular view of a child, which may then affect all our dealings with that child, especially if the child has difficult or demanding behaviour patterns. These fixed views or stereotypes can prevent us from seeing the child's progress and achievements clearly, as we tend to observe only the aspects of the child's behaviour that support our fixed view. Stereotyping children can limit the effective support they are given, it can reinforce negative self-esteem and poor self-confidence in the child, and it can mean the opportunity to build on areas of strength goes unnoticed.

Finally, it is important to remember that your role is not just as a human recording instrument, passing information on to the teacher. You bring your own skill and expertise, knowledge and understanding, to the process, enriching the assessment with your own evaluation and interpretation of what is observed or recorded. This is a very valuable aspect of the teaching assistant's role in assessment and recording and one that should be developed to the full. The sorts of knowledge and understanding which can be usefully brought to bear when evaluating assessment information are:

- how young children learn best
- child development and developmental delays
- your specific knowledge of individual children's learning needs
- your knowledge of the child or children's ongoing progress and achievements
- your knowledge and understanding of how best to support children sensitively and effectively
- your knowledge and understanding of effective verbal and written communication.

Conclusions

Teaching assistants have a major role to play in the assessment processes taking place in primary classrooms. Teachers need assessment information for planning and for tracking pupils' progress, yet often the logistics of assessing large classes are highly challenging. Teaching assistants have increasingly supported the assessment process in partnership with the teacher and other staff. Developing confidence in your ability to use assessment processes effectively and to understand the types and purposes of assessment is a key role for teaching assistants. Giving feedback to children and recording and evaluating assessment information are all tasks that are becoming more a part of that role. As teaching assistants continue to gain prominence in classrooms, this role seems likely to continue to expand, requiring the further development of the range of skills and abilities discussed above.

Further reading

O'Hara, M. (2000) *Teaching 3–8*. London: Continuum.

Chapter 16

Fighting the fuzzies

Ian Eyres

How might play be justified in schools? This chapter describes a collaborative approach to observation which supports the use of a play-based curriculum. Ian Eyres, a lecturer in education at The Open University, considers the nature of observation in an educational setting, and highlights the way in which nursery-based staff take steps to ensure objectivity and rigour.

Located in central Cambridge, Brunswick Nursery school offers half-day places to 80 children. The diverse intake usually includes several with English as an additional language and a relatively high proportion with special educational needs. The staff comprises the headteacher, two teachers, (one part-time – 50%), two nursery nurses and four learning support assistants attached to individual children.

Curriculum and play

The curriculum is planned according to the Qualifications and Curriculum Authority's Early Learning Goals (QCA 2000: 26–116) and gives children opportunities to develop in the six identified 'areas of learning'.

Play is central to the curriculum as the staff have always believed that 'well planned play is a key way in which children learn' (QCA 2000: 7). On one afternoon, for example, children were to be seen engaged in playing with wet and dry sand, sharing picture books with an adult, making models from recycled materials, hammering nails into a section of tree trunk, looking at and drawing logs, using a computer programme to sort geometrical shapes and engaging in make-believe play in the 'house'. All these experiences had been carefully planned to provide opportunities for 'playing, talking, observing, planning, questioning, experimenting, testing, repeating, reflecting and responding to adults' (QCA 2000: 6) as ways of deepening their understanding within the six areas of learning.

Children are not directed, but are free to follow their interests and become absorbed in activity and enquiry. Staff therefore need to be skilled in seizing opportunities to both assess and foster development towards particular Early Learning Goals on the basis of what the children actually do.

Key to the success of any early years setting, then, are the adults' understanding of how children learn and develop and of the curriculum and, based on these understandings, their ability to observe, respond and plan appropriately. This approach has been judged to 'meet the needs of the children and successfully promote their intellectual, physical and personal development' in the context of 'a rich and balanced curriculum' (Ofsted 1998).

The rest of this chapter is based on discussions with three staff members: Colette Williams (nursery nurse), Jane Holt (teacher) and Nicola Davies, learning support assistant (LSA) and special educational needs coordinator (SENCO). For an LSA to be a SENCO is unusual. It should, however, be noted that Nicola undertook substantial training for the SENCO role and was already a qualified (secondary maths) teacher. Her appointment offers additional evidence of the non-hierarchical nature of the school. Since the original draft of this chapter was written the picture has been further complicated by Nicola's appointment to a part-time teaching post in addition to her LSA post.

Observation at Brunswick

> By observation I managed to develop proper respect for what they're doing. Concentrating on one child does show you a much greater depth of understanding and powers of 'reasoning things out' than I would have credited young children with.
>
> (Jane Holt)

At Brunswick, all adults are actively involved in the observation process, most directly by watching carefully and noting details of what children do and say on Post-it notes. This may be done alongside a child or by writing up observations immediately afterwards. The information collected is sorted weekly by Jane, Nicola and the headteacher (Marian Funnell) who look for evidence of learning in each of the six areas. Gaps and uncertainties in this record influence future observations and support.

Observations provide particularly valuable information to inform the support given to children with special educational needs, both for the statementing process and as the basis for termly targets. The detail of the assessment means that very precise targets can be devised and progress towards them closely monitored and supported. Social development, a crucial factor in inclusion, is particularly closely monitored. Even for apparently sociable children, systematic observation (noting the number and nature of contacts with peers) can be revealing. They may be talking to other children without getting a response or simply talking to themselves. What looks like interaction may be parallel play, where two children play independently alongside each other.

Children of all kinds can suffer if they are 'labelled'. Continuous detailed observation helps shape the curriculum for individuals and the nursery by eliminating inappropriate expectations and overgeneralizations.

Although the curriculum is planned to provide for particular learning outcomes, sometimes surprising evidence emerges. One child, for example, faced with a set of objects which included a toy crocodile, spent some time using the crocodile's jaws to measure the other objects, and then arranged them according to their size. Another child used coloured blocks to make an elaborate symmetrical pattern. Without constant observation these aspects of the children's mathematical knowledge could have been overlooked, and opportunities to challenge and develop their understanding lost.

Children's achievements are assessed in a natural context and staff have access to evidence gathered in different contexts by a number of observers. One child was able to join in the counting of children before the distribution of mid-session fruit but had difficulties in counting the number of bean bags thrown into a hoop. Although on the face of it these are 'the same task', in the former example the child has the support of a well-rehearsed routine and of the arrangement of the children (sitting in a circle – a single curved line). This knowledge helped staff find ways of supporting more difficult forms of counting, for example by encouraging the child to arrange the bean bags in a single line. Continuous observation also enables staff to cope with the 'three steps forward and two steps back' nature of learning. It is also the basis for the planning of 'next steps' both for individuals and for the nursery as a whole.

At the end of their first week at the nursery, staff pool all their observations and construct a preliminary sketch of each child and formal reviews are conducted regularly throughout the year. In staff meetings towards the end of the first term, there is discussion of how well each child has settled, and of their strengths and needs in all areas. Similar meetings are held in the spring term shortly before Jane and Marian meet parents individually to discuss each child's progress and development.

Facts or fuzzies?

> …even though all observers are likely to be less than objective, objectivity can be aimed for.
>
> (Hurst and Joseph 1998)

While absolute objectivity is practically impossible, staff work towards it through an agreed approach to what is recorded, and through the way in which knowledge is shared.

Nicola introduced colleagues to the notion of 'fuzzies', imprecise comments which describe an interpretation of an event rather than what the observer has actually seen. For example, the note, 'Tom enjoyed this activity' is an interpretation, not hard evidence. Noting that 'Tom smiled', or that he 'remained at the activity for more than five minutes' provides facts which can be evaluated alongside other observations. Newcomers sometimes need to unlearn the skill of interpreting underlying emotions and motives, in order to develop the practice of reporting dispassionately on what they see. Enjoyment cannot be seen – a smile can. Some events are more easily reported, for example if they are quantifiable: how long did an activity take? How much of a puzzle was completed? ('50%' may convey more information than '5 pieces'). Noting children's talk (always the exact words) provides much evidence about their language and wider learning. A concentration on what can be observed also helps to separate the observer's (inevitable) bias from what is noted down.

The way assessment data is shared among the whole staff also supports objectivity. Often, the evidence accumulated on a particular child is mutually confirmatory, illustrating different facets of consistent behaviour. Fragments of dialogue noted in the context of home-corner play, painting and doing puzzles may all support the conclusion that a child is developing the ability to interact purposefully with peers, for example. Where discrepancies are identified they need to be investigated and sometimes existing evidence will have to be challenged. This process may begin in a staff meeting or in informal conversations. If different observers report a different dominant hand for a particular child, for example, everybody would be alert to the need to observe the child drawing, painting, building and so on; a flood of observations usually follows. In this example it may be that the child has not yet developed a preference for using a particular hand, or that one hand is preferred but not used exclusively. Further discussion would then focus on what intervention, if any, might support the development of appropriate motor skills.

Sometimes the nature of the area of learning calls for multiple assessments, as the 'counting' example demonstrated. Counting with correspondence cannot be 'ticked off' after a single sighting. It must be seen in a variety of contexts. Sometimes this means setting up a situation which repeats or re-presents what has been observed already, though never in a way which leaves a child feeling they have been tested.

Of course, sometimes multiple perspectives simply fit together like the pieces of a jigsaw. For example, someone might note that a particular child 'hasn't gone to the collage table today'. Others might add 'That's because he was very busy at the computer', 'But he took a model home last Friday' and so on. Not visiting the collage table then becomes part of a larger picture which shows the child's varied interests and perhaps a tendency to concentrate on one thing at a time. On the other hand, successive observations may show that he never visits the collage table. By working together, the team builds a picture of each child's learning.

Making individual assessments in context and basing conclusions on the totality of children's nursery experience means that this is an 'authentic assessment' approach (Pollard 1997: 287) offering higher validity than one based on less frequent observations or specially devised activities.

Challenges

> We're always aware that we can improve.
>
> (Jane Holt)

Observation is something you have to keep doing all the time or the child's record can quickly develop gaps. However, it is important to strike the proper balance between the desire to record and the need to fulfil other roles.

> It can be difficult making time to get all the observations in, especially during a very physical or messy activity – you can be covered in clay or paint and in any event you want to be interacting with the children as well. Sometimes you can hold something in your head while you finish working with a child and then make notes afterwards. It can be difficult to know when to start writing something down; should you wait and see how the activity develops and then see if you can remember it to write it down later? If you do that, you have to hope nobody comes in with wet knickers in between!
>
> (Jane Holt)

'Saving an observation for later' is all the harder when recording something that a child has said, as it has to be memorized exactly. Sometimes the choice has to be made between collecting something for the record and using the observation as a starting point for supporting further learning.

Some children are very adept at drawing attention to what they are doing, while others simply don't want to interact with an adult, preferring to end an activity and move off. Staff know to make the time to observe the children who might otherwise be overlooked. It's obviously easier to make notes on the children who do verbalize their thoughts or who volunteer things at story time. The temptation to record many sayings of children who say 'the most fascinating things' has to be resisted. You must also remember to make observations of *how* children play as well as what they say, and that can be more difficult to record.

Staff also guard against following their own areas of interest exclusively, and against being influenced by preconceptions which might arise from discussions about a child; they must not fall into the trap of simply looking for evidence to prove a theory. Each practitioner records more about the children she knows best, but as every child's record has contributions from several adults this is no cause for concern. Although the team is aware of many pitfalls in the process, there are established strategies to deal with most of them, and an awareness that practice can always be improved.

Working with parents

> She hasn't brought much home – is she doing anything?
>
> (Brunswick parent)

Parents hold Brunswick in high esteem and they overwhelmingly want to work with the staff to support their children's learning. They often express surprise at how well nursery staff know the children. Observation data plays an important part in opening and developing the dialogue between home and school; through sharing observations, and through seeing how carefully they are made, parents appreciate the value of what the nursery has been doing.

Any parent's understanding of a child's behaviour may differ from the nursery's. Expressing different interpretations as 'conflicting' is not a good starting point for a dialogue, while sharing impressions and interpretations can provoke unhelpful responses. Fortunately, a record of things the child has actually done offers a basis for more dispassionate discussion. A practitioner might say, 'Your child really seems to finish the puzzles.' Whether the parent replies, 'Yes, he plays with them a lot at home', or 'Does he really? I haven't seen him do that', a dialogue has begun. Parents who begin by thinking that they disagree with the nursery's view of their child usually come to see that apparently conflicting information is, in fact, complementary. Areas where parents do not recognize the picture painted of their child are explored in much the same way as contradictory observation evidence.

Parents find it easy to make sense of evidence of things that are practical and observable that they can easily relate to their own knowledge of their child. They may say s/he 'doesn't do that at home', or that the things which haven't been observed in the nursery are the things s/he spends hours doing at home. The nursery meets different needs for different individuals. An only child may look forward to the nursery session as a time for socializing, a child from a larger family might seek out quieter activities and opportunities for sustained concentration. Parents help staff build up a full picture of a child's interests and accomplishments and the dialogue can help parents understand how their children are learning. Of course, information flows two ways and a discussion may begin with some concern of the parent.

Working together

> Everyone's opinion is valued. That works against the setting up of a hierarchy and supports the ethos of working together; supporting each other.
>
> (Jane Holt)
>
> You can't run a nursery if you don't all get on; we are a team.
>
> (Colette Williams)

One important feature of the observation process is the way in which it reflects the ethos of the nursery. Just as every child is valued, so is the contribution of every member of staff, whatever their job title. All are actively involved, on the one hand in observing and recording children's learning in context, and on the other in interpreting observations and identifying 'next steps'. All are equally involved in talking and listening with children, supporting them physically and supporting and extending their learning; children rarely make a distinction between different kinds of adult they meet in the nursery. The observation strategy emphasizes the fact that everybody's views are valued equally. There is no sense of hierarchy during the nursery day, even though some staff may have special roles in respect of the analysis and presentation of observation data.

The pooling of information emphasizes the necessity of team working: colleagues take ideas from each other and give each other advice. There is no place for criticism, and differences of view are reconciled in a professional way. This cooperative *modus operandi* offers a good model to children, who also enjoy working together.

Observations can contribute more directly to the school's ethos too. Noting what children are doing gives them an explicit signal that their work is valued. Observing and recording what children *can* do has the potential to raise their self esteem and this can be especially valuable in respect of children exhibiting anti-social behaviour. Additionally, if a child with special educational needs has behaviour problems then the behaviour of other children around him or her would be noted too.

At Brunswick children never feel under pressure to demonstrate particular areas of learning. They may be encouraged to follow a certain activity, but never directed: a new skill is noted when a child is ready to use it. Because of this, play (by definition a self-motivated activity) can remain the principal medium through which the curriculum is taught.

All this emphasizes the view that the most important role of the nursery is in fostering the development of individual children. Close observation leads to a greater respect for a child.

> You understand, particularly with children who have special educational needs, the efforts they are actually making when there is no adult there to help them; you see how hard things are for them and how they cope by really struggling. The level of effort is something you need to remind yourself of time and time again.
>
> (Nicola Davies)

Final words

> Observations really do make you aware of what you're doing and what you're expecting the children to do.
>
> (Colette Williams)

> One of the things I enjoy very much. You always learn something about a child, you always learn something about the other people in the nursery.
>
> (Nicola Davies)

Everyone at Brunswick agrees about the value of observations and about the sense of satisfaction they give. Observation offers a way of ensuring that every child is considered as a whole person.

Observation enables a play-based curriculum to be implemented rigorously and in a way which fully supports the demands of the Foundation Stage. The assessment strategy supports inclusion by ensuring that all children receive the attention and support they are entitled to. As a bonus, every day staff learn more about the children, more about successful planning and teaching strategies and more about making and interpreting observations.

The strategy has grown out of the underlying values of an established staff who have respect for each other and for children and for children's rights to receive a broad and balanced education which is stimulating and enjoyable. All at Brunswick are convinced that play is at the heart of early years education and that their assessment strategy is the key to making a play-based curriculum effective for all.

References

Hurst, V. and Joseph, J. (1998) *Supporting Early Learning: the way forward.* Buckingham: Open University Press.

Ofsted (1998), *Inspection Report: Brunswick Nursery School.* London: Ofsted.

Pollard, A. (1997) *Reflective Teaching in the Primary School: a handbook for the classroom.* London: Cassell Education.

QCA (Qualifications and Curriculum Authority) (2000) *Curriculum Guidance for the Foundation Stage.* London: QCA.

Chapter 17

Homework

Julian Stern

Julian Stern, head of the Centre for Educational Studies, University of Hull, has a particular interest in ways of involving parents in schools. Here he considers the potential impact of children's homework on home life, and suggests ways of making it meaningful in order to promote closer home–school understanding.

[…]

A teacher friend of mine was burgled. When the police came around, they were tremendously sympathetic, as the burglar had not only stolen the video and jewellery, but had wrecked the house too, throwing things all over the place. The burglar had in fact been very tidy: it was teaching that had left no time for housework. […] Suppose that teacher decided to get a grip of the housework, and when there was no time to do the ironing at home, it was brought into the staffroom, and during staff meetings, the teacher stood at the back, doing the ironing. What would you, as a colleague, do? Whenever I have asked this question, incidentally, the respondents have said that they would ask the teacher if they would do their ironing as well. Nevertheless, most people recognize that school is not the best place for ironing. Housework is best done in the house and it disrupts the school to bring housework in and complete it there. Likewise, much of schoolwork is best done in school, and it disrupts the home to complete schoolwork there. Let us consider three kinds of homework that schools can set, each having different implications for the involvement of parents.

First we could use homework to 'expand' the 15,000 hours of schooling currently suffered by children, making parents into cheap and unqualified school teachers, working in the worst possible conditions. This is perhaps based on the 'vanity' model of governments and schools, suggesting that no learning happens outside school without schools *making* it happen. The most common 'expansion' homework task is 'finishing off' – the most common homework task of all, and the one that most disadvantages slower workers who generally need most help from teachers. Other expansion tasks might be to complete lists of questions or general 'research' tasks (such as 'find out about the Second World War'). It is no wonder that expansion homework is rarely liked and is likely to have little impact on learning (as in Stern 1998). Involving parents means using parents as prison guards ('you're not going out until you finish your homework') or as pupils themselves ('I'll look it up for you'). Parents may welcome this, as homework can be a genuinely helpful means of control: a bargaining tool in the battle of the generations. And parents may really enjoy looking things up in encyclopaedias, or completing maths questions – even if this means they will also get upset by low marks for their work. However, these ways of involving parents are not generally the best ways of exploiting what parents are good at, and can distance parents further from the whole schooling process. Expansion homework is also one of the main reasons why parental support for their children's homework is so reduced as children move to secondary school – with 57 per cent of primary pupils getting regular help from parents, and only 17 per cent of secondary pupils getting regular help from parents (MacBeath and Turner 1990).

A *second* way of looking at homework would be to use it in such a way that the 15,000 hours of schooling could be applied to the rest of the child's world. 'Application' homework is based on the idea that school subjects need to be relevant, or that school learning consists of a set of 'apprenticeships' in the world:

- Food technology should help with food preparation in the home, and is about being an apprentice in catering.
- History should help pupils understand causes and implications of current local and national situations and the community's place in history, and is about being an apprentice historian.
- Science should help pupils understand how the physical world works and how to test this, and is about being an apprentice scientist.
- PE is about physical and sporting understanding and control, and is about being an apprentice sportsman or sportswoman.

These and similar ideas, more popular in secondary than primary schools, are often popular with members of subject-based professions and with governments concerned with the usefulness or value to the economy of schooling. When it comes to application homework, parents are more likely to be enablers than helpers. For example, parents might allow a child to shop for and make one meal a week, or investigate the home in order to find evidence of the age and original use of the building, or grow plants on a window sill. Similarly, pupils studying musical styles might analyse the music used in a range of adverts on the television, pupils studying French could choose a song they like and write some French lyrics for it, or pupils studying moral systems in different religions (such as the ten commandments and the five precepts) could see how many moral rules are broken in particular soap operas. Parents are invited, not assumed, to be enablers. For example, letters sent home from a primary school (quoted in DfES 2003 as examples of good practice) said:

Today we have been learning about floating and sinking. You can help your child continue the experiments by putting some objects made of different materials in the bath to see which float and which sink. See if your child can guess what will happen!

And:

Today we made some fruit salad. We used…You could ask your child to look at and name any fruit you have at home. Also, children could look at the fruit in the market and supermarket, and practise saying the names as often as possible.

The *third* way of looking at homework is based on the imbalance in time mentioned at the start of this book. There are 15,000 hours of schooling up to the age of sixteen, which leaves 125,000 hours spent by pupils with their families and friends, or on their own, outside school. Homework could be used to ensure that these 125,000 hours of childhood be made use of in school. The homework tasks capture the child's world for the schoolwork. 'Capture' homework sees school as largely derivative of non-school life, especially home life. It recognizes that schooling and subjects are primarily about humanity and the world, rather than being about subjects for their own sakes. Parents and other adults can be 'interviewed' by their children about their views or experiences of life, rather than their knowledge of subjects:

- How could the area best be developed (for geography)?
- What was school like when they were young (for history)?
- What sports do they enjoy watching or participating in most or least (for PE)?
- What do they think is the most important moral principle (for RE)?
- How do they choose a candidate, or choose whether or not to vote, when it comes to elections (for citizenship)?
- What were their favourite stories when they were young (for English and other languages spoken by parents)?
- What five pieces of music would they take to a desert island and why (for music)?

Parents and other adults can be sketched for art, measured to provide a set of data for work in statistics, asked to rank a set of statements about or pictures of types or styles of clothing (for technology), and so on. To involve parents with capture homework, means to capture the worlds of parents, including the languages of parents, and use them in school. Then, when parents visit classrooms or look at pupils' work, they will recognize a little bit of themselves, and will recognize aspects of the lives of other parents. There will be something familiar (as well as something unfamiliar) in the classroom, and school will be that much more inclusive. It is a puzzle that parents who are themselves teachers, and who are incessantly 'educational' with their children ('Ooh, look at that interesting cast-iron Victorian lamppost!' accompanying a walk to the park), still often feel stressed by the need to support homework. 'Homework is hell', a teacher-parent once wrote to me, and causes 'endless friction between concerned and caring parents and their teenage children'. If homework includes plenty of capture homework, grabbing hold of the world beyond the school, then parents can be involved more painlessly and imaginatively.

Whatever kind of homework is set, teachers should be aware of the variety of pupils' home circumstances:

- All pupils, and especially pupils who themselves have family responsibilities, may welcome breakfast, lunchtime or after-school homework clubs. This means that they are less stressed by multiple responsibilities around the home, and the family is less pressured.
- Pupils who split their time between two homes, for example of separated parents, may welcome a full week to complete homework tasks. This means they will be able to make use of people or facilities – such as computers or books – in either home.
- Pupils whose parents are less likely to be in a position to help with homework, for whatever reason, will welcome tasks being set that say 'ask an adult' or 'talk to a grown-up, such as a parent or someone who works in the school'. Providing opportunities for pupils to ask other adults around the school – support staff of all kinds – has the advantage of bringing the whole school together to support learning. I remember a quiz set by a history teacher, where the pupils had to ask adults in the school what famous women they could name from history. This created a real 'buzz' around the school, as all through break and lunchtimes teachers and administrators and premises staff and supervisors were being quizzed by very competitive pupils.
- When there is homework about families or homes themselves, make sure that you do not make things difficult for the pupil by asking for information they may not want to share with you or other pupils, or may not know. Avoid questions such as 'draw your family tree' (who is who on the tree, and whom shall I call 'father'?), or 'count the number of rooms in your house' (which house, or if a local authority care home, how much of the house?). A simple alternative would be 'think about a family/house you know well – either your own family/house or the family/house of a friend or someone else you know', followed by the task. This allows pupils to put a little distance between themselves and their responses.
- Sleep is a good idea. Children and adults alike, these days, apparently get too little sleep. Homework should not mean that children get even less sleep. It is important to say to pupils and parents how long homework should take, overall, and to see this as a maximum rather than a minimum amount of time. Even though a teaching contract does indeed look like this, few adults welcome a work contract that says 'be at work for a certain number of hours, but the work may take much longer', and few children would like a lesson that started 'this lesson may take an hour, or it may last for several hours'. Yet this is a common attitude to homework, which therefore seems endless and more stressful – and more likely to be completed at the expense of much-needed sleep. I

recommend asking pupils to write at the end of each piece of homework how many minutes it took to complete. They then have an incentive to complete the task in good time, and to underestimate, if anything, how long the task took – as they do not want to appear too slow.

If there are to be breakfast, lunchtime or after-school homework clubs (popular in UK schools at least since the 1930s, as in Great Britain Board of Education 1936), then these will need financing and staffing – providing further opportunities for involving parents in school, either as fund-raisers or paid or unpaid helpers in the clubs. If there are effective family learning activities, then these will help parents become more confident in their dealings with their children and with the school, as well as supporting parents' own further learning (as described in Stern 2003).

[...]

References

Department for Education and Skills (DfES) (2003) 'Parental Involvement'; www.standards.dfes.gov.uk/parentalinvolvement.

Great Britain Board of Education (1936) *Homework (Educational Pamphlets, No. 110)*, London: HMSO.

MacBeath, J. and Turner, M. (1990) Learning out of school: Report of Research Study carried out at Jordanhill College, Glasgow: Jordanhill College.

Stern, L. J. (1998) *The OoSHA Review: Out of School Hours Activities in Lambeth: Report for Lambeth LEA, Spring 1998*, Isleworth: Brunel University.

Stern, L. J. (2003) *Progression from Family Learning*, LSC-funded research report for Hull CityLearning, April.

Section 3
Learning relationships

Roger Hancock and Janet Collins

This section is concerned with the relationships within which learning for children is often embedded. In Chapter 18, Priscilla Alderson argues that we should respect the opinions of children more than we do and involve them in our decision-making, not least so that we can learn from them. The theme of learning collaborations between adults and children is continued by Henry Maitles and Ross Deuchar in Chapter 19. They argue that teachers and teaching assistants should approach education for citizenship with enthusiasm and that it should not be unduly adult-led and controlled. Children, they suggest, need to be fully involved as participants. Chapter 20, by Janet Collins, recommends that some children may need focused support in order to fully participate as learners. Children who are habitually quiet in school, she suggests, may find it easier to express their feelings and ideas to teaching assistants and peers within the context of small group activities.

Eating disorders often make the headlines. However, although many children have individual preferences for food, even idiosyncrasies, most do not develop serious difficulties. Nevertheless, it is important that teachers, teaching assistants and lunchtime supervisors have insights into the causes of potential difficulties and a sense of when a difficulty becomes a potential disorder. Chapter 21, by the Royal College of Psychiatrists, provides advice.

The next two chapters consider the needs of two distinct groups of children who may be at risk of not being included sufficiently in school learning. In Chapter 22, Gwynedd Lloyd and Gillean McCluskey provide information and challenge some commonly held stereotypes with regard to the children of Gypsies and Travellers. Chapter 23 similarly provides important background understandings for the often overlooked experiences and needs of children in public care. Tony Eaude and Jude Egan also offer practical advice for teachers and teaching assistants.

Bullying is extremely upsetting for children who experience its effects and potentially very disruptive to their learning and their lives. We therefore felt it appropriate to include three chapters on bullying in this Reader. Chapter 24 reports on the views of children. It is written by Christine Oliver and Mano Candappa and arises from a study involving nearly 1,200 primary and secondary pupils. The following chapter, by Helen Taylor, summarises research she conducted as part of a Masters degree into the issue of gender differences and bullying. She concludes that anti-bullying strategies need to be more focused on girls' experiences of being bullied. Lastly, Pete Johnson examines the reason why many bullied boys feel they must hide their unhappy experiences.

The two final chapters in this section look at the relationship between children's learning and their behaviour. In Chapter 27, Stephen Lunn writes of his involvement, as a learning support assistant (LSA), with a pupil who finds it difficult to accept school norms and to engage easily with school learning. This chapter illustrates the way in which LSAs, often a front-line resource for inclusion, can sometimes find themselves in deep waters. Chapter 28 reviews support practice with regard to learning and behaviour. Janet Kay highlights the potential contribution of teaching assistants to a 'positive' learning environment both in terms of supporting the teacher and also within their own remit, working with groups and individuals.

Chapter 18

Institutional rites and rights

Priscilla Alderson

Priscilla Alderson, professor of childhood studies at the Institute of Education, London, gave her inaugural lecture on 4 June 2003. This chapter draws together three extracts from that lecture. The first considers the 'institution of childhood' and the way adults define and organise this for children. The second extract considers how schools, places where adults have all the power, might feel through the eyes of children. In the third extract, the conclusion to the lecture, it is argued that even the youngest children can be helped to make informed, responsible decisions, and that children need to be more involved in planning and organising the institutions that exist for their benefit.

Institutions – childhood

Childhood itself is an institution with its established laws and formal customs. It is often thought of as a biological and inevitable stage of life. It is, however a social stage, lasting until around 7 to 12 years in some societies, or up to the mid-20s for some young adults in modern western societies. About 150 years ago in Britain, after a short infancy (infant meaning 'without speech') working-class children were very much treated as adults – and most adults were treated rather as children. They had few rights or possessions, heavy workloads, little leisure, the anxieties and hardships of poverty. As far as we can tell, many had strong ties of affection and loyalty. Childhood has since gradually been subdivided into babies, toddlers, pre-schoolers and so on, including adolescents – they were first officially classified in 1904 (Hall 1904).

Children are real living people. But childhood is a set of ideas about what children are and ought to be like, and how they should behave and relate to adults. These ideas change very much over time. Near our London school, mosaics on the library walls recorded how Chaucer's pilgrims set out from that street over 600 years ago, with their highly educated young squire. Around 2,000 years ago, some local families lived in the newly imported Roman style. Today, pearly princes and princesses undertake regal duties in the area. Incidentally, the images record waves of immigration, from Italy, France and the Caribbean, each wave bringing new ideas about childhood and education.

Children are so confined today, that it is often assumed that they cannot, and should not, take an active part in their communities. Less than a century ago, their lives were far more closely woven in 'adult' society, and still are today in the poorer majority world. Children aged 4 or 5 years would go alone on errands across a busy city, use public transport, shop and barter, or ramble in the countryside (Ward 1994). Today, millions of young children ably help their parents, by working in homes, farms and streets. In war-torn, AIDS-torn Africa, children head households (Muscroft 1999: 74), as 12-year-old Sophia Ingibire Tuyisenge's story tells. She is caring for her two sisters and despite many problems is 'coping just fine' (McFerran 2003: 66). In Britain today, thousands of children aged from 3 years upwards help to care for a sick or disabled relative (Aldridge and Becker 2002). The point here is not whether this should happen, but that it does happen, and shows young children's strengths and competencies. Perhaps children are happier today, with more toys, books, games, clothes, comfortable homes, food, education and care services planned for them. We cannot know. Certainly they are lonelier, with so many fewer children per family and per street, and are far more confined. Fashions in childcare swing from harsh to indulgent, from fairly loose to tight control (Hardyment 1984). Today, alongside indulgence, children are often controlled more rigidly than ever before.

Just as women's views are largely missing from history, children's views are almost wholly absent. Instead we have adults' records, discussions and images of childhood (Hendrick 1997). What was it like for a 5-year-old to sit still hour after hour on cramped benches? How did those older boys and girls feel, who were beaten for being 'thick' and 'idle' but who could do fairly skilled work that would bring in money their family desperately needed? And what did older sisters in large families think about being 'taught' to do tasks they had been doing at home for years?

Local doors have closed, while virtual and global ones have opened throughout the past century for western childhood, more than ever before. Today, children may not know their next-door neighbours, partly because of current stranger-danger fears, but they may know lots about rain forests or space travel, and have perhaps been to Florida or Pakistan. In Derby in 1902, Margaret, aged 5 years, took a pushchair across the city to collect her sister Elizabeth, aged 3 years, who had been in hospital for weeks. The matron was annoyed that their mother had not come, but assumed that the girls were old enough to go home on their own. Cities were dangerous places then, with plenty of horses and other traffic, muddy cobbled roads and no zebra crossings or traffic lights. Myths have grown up that children cannot and should not do these things. Researchers ask to whom does childhood belong, when parents and teachers assume they must organise and oversee almost every moment of children's lives (Shamgar-Handelman 1994).

Adulthood is assumed to mean being strong and informed, reliable and wise, and childhood means being vulnerable and ignorant, unreliable and foolish.

Schools are planned on this assumption and constantly reinforce it. A curriculum is 'delivered' to children, as letters are posted into letterboxes, until children turn into adults. These institutionalised 'laws and customs' seem too obvious and natural to be worth noting, but are they true?

[...]

How would adults react to being treated as many school students are?

We could review a typical secondary school day. Nowhere safe to leave your coat and belongings, which must be carried everywhere. Regular crowded mass treks from one part of the campus to another. Queuing to wait, sometimes in the rain, until a teacher arrives to unlock doors. Up to a quarter of your time taken up with silent queuing and marching (Griffith 1998). Much reduced break times. Petty rules about uniform, jewellery and hints of individual expression, that in turn stop freedom of speech: 'We cannot have a school council because all they want to talk about is uniform and they cannot do that,' some teachers reported (Alderson 2000a, 2000c). Britain and Malta are the only European countries to have uniforms (Hannam 1999), which indicates that they are not essential.

Would you care to arrive home and hear your partner say, 'Your boss has just phoned to tell me you broke that agreement I signed with her. You were late back from lunch and she says I must stop you watching television for a week.' You might reply, 'But I was helping a friend whose mobile was stolen.' 'Tough,' your partner will say, 'I don't want any more lame excuses. Now get on with that work you have to give in tomorrow.' And so you labour on through a 6- or 7-day week that far exceeds the European limits for adults' working hours. With breakfast clubs and after school clubs, even young children may spend 50 hours a week at school. Most children would prefer not to attend the clubs, if they had the choice (Smith 2000; Smith and Barker 2002). Many children are not happy about the growing alliances between home and school, and mothers being turned into teachers, and they would prefer there to be a clear gap (Alldred *et al.* 2002). By the way, you are not paid a penny, your pocket money may be stopped too sometimes, and your work, however skilful, complicated, hard, interesting, beautiful or original, does not count as 'work', but as mere practising or learning for your benefit (Morrow 1994). You cannot have the satisfaction of feeling that you are helping or benefiting others; adults insist that they help you.

Teachers can act as claimant, witness, judge and jury if students are accused of misdemeanours. Despite this complicated overlapping of roles that the justice system exists to separate, children may be punished and even excluded without routine means of appeal or fair arbitration (UNCRC 2003). Home-School Agreements are the reverse of a legal contract, which is an informed and unpressured agreement freely negotiated between equal partners. The Agreements appear to assume that any alleged misdemeanour will be entirely the child's fault, and not possibly be linked to mistakes or other problems in the school. Parents who support their child can be criminalised, fined and even sent to prison.

Mothers of 4-year-olds have told me about class teachers advising them to 'ground' their children to punish alleged inattention and misbehaviour. During small discussion groups about rights in schools (Alderson and Arnold 1999), some children mentioned their fear that when teachers call their parents into school to complain to them, 'my mum will beat me up'; 'my dad whacks me'. So although the 1993 Education Act banned physical punishment in state schools, this has been exported, in some cases, to the home, rather than abolished. Children are the only members of British society who can, by law, be hit, as if somehow they do not mind as much as adults would, or as if 'a smack is the only language they can understand'. Yet research shows that young children can feel deeply hurt and rejected (Willow and Hyder 1998). The dire state of the toilets in many schools is another sign of disrespect for bodies that adults' institutions would not tolerate. A colleague who read a draft of this paper commented,

> My daughter aged 9 has to sign a book whenever she goes to the toilet at school and then sign back in. The teachers want to find out who is vandalising the toilets. She won't go to the toilet in case she gets blamed and because they are unpleasant. She won't drink so she is dehydrated but longing to go to the loo. How can she learn?

Instead of making all the children suffer when a few offend, another approach is to involve everyone in planning and carrying out positive solutions. This often requires some funding, and effective school councils see budgets and have some share in deciding how certain funds are spent.

Despite all the discouragements in schools, most young people do work very hard and creatively. They enjoy at least some of their schoolwork, and they rate time at school to be with their friends very highly, especially as there are so few free public spaces where they are encouraged to meet outside school. As they become older and more competent, however, their enjoyment and interest fall (MacBeath and Mortimore 2001: 85; Alderson 2000c; Pollard *et al.* 1997). Yet we treat all school students as if most of them, instead of only a relatively tiny minority, were potential truants, by making schooling compulsory and enforced with heavy sanctions.

[…]

Conclusion

At the end of his novel *Vanity Fair*, Thackeray says to his readers, 'Come, children, let us shut up the box and the puppets, for our play is played out' (1847: 733). This lecture concerns trying to close away old ideas of children as puppets, to make space for children as persons. I began by asking:

- What can adults do that children cannot do?
- At what age can children start to do activities that are often seen as 'adult' ones?
- What is the difference between children and adults?

If you thought before hearing this lecture that there were clear and large differences between adulthood and childhood, I hope that now you believe there are considerable overlaps, and that many of the differences result from how we (mis)perceive and treat children rather than from children's actual capacities. Perhaps you will also agree that a rigid double standard, of respect and rights for adults, and compulsion and control for children, is neither principled nor productive. How can we possibly encourage children to be responsible agents, as many school brochures claim, by treating them as helpless dependants hemmed in by many rigid rules, often listed in the brochures? We might as well expect frogs to turn magically into princes, and drudges into princesses (Griffith 1998).

This is an 'inaugural' lecture, a rite that implies that a new, youngish professor inaugurates or institutes a programme of work for the next 20 to 30 years. I do not have that long time ahead of me, and so instead I will propose a programme that I hope the Institute will inaugurate – plan and develop – over the next century. As we have seen, dominant thinking in the Institute over the past century has sometimes mistaken the nature of childhood and education. Instead, in the twenty-first century, we could take more heed of Marion Richardson's faith in 'sincere free' relationships, and in those nineteenth-century working people's respect for education where the learners would 'go first and the master would follow' (Godwin 1797). These ideals are practised to some extent in some Italian early years centres, Rajasthan night schools, Colombian schools (Hart 2003), and in some schools in Britain and around the world (Apple and Beane 1999).

Surely universities are places for exploring new and alternative ideas carefully, instead of dismissing them. The philosopher Mary Midgley (1996) compares thinking with plumbing. Beliefs and pipes tend to be invisible and ignored until something goes obviously wrong, such as leaks or blockages. Then the importance of hidden pipes, or hidden assumptions, becomes clear, and the most practical thing to do is to sort out the (mental) plumbing. Instead of simply suggesting new techniques or practices to improve schools, at the level of patching leaks, it is time to look more deeply at what is going wrong and why. Unlike 1902, 2003 is a time when British adults assume that their rights, choices and responsibilities should be respected. Childhood has been left behind in a historical limbo and this has skewed relationships and double standards between the institutions of childhood and adulthood. It is as if a great dam has grown higher over the past century to exclude children and young people and direct them into separate channels away from mainstream society. Adults claim that this is to protect and cherish children, but the system can very much harm children, young people and adults while tending mainly to serve adults' economic and political interests.

Suppose we took seriously the hope that there are better ways for children and adults to work together in schools, such as in the words of the Danish law that schools must 'build on intellectual freedom, equality and democracy' (Davies and Kirkpatrick 2000: 22). A logical step is that school attendance would become voluntary instead of compulsory. The vast majority of children and young people would attend school voluntarily for three reasons they value very highly besides learning: to gain necessary training and qualifications for the next stages of education and employment; to enjoy time with their friends; and to have opportunities and resources especially for the arts and sports (Alderson and Arnold 1999). Most children start school eager and able to learn. Black children, particularly, do very well at first and then fall behind (Gillborn and Youdell 2000). With the fall in interest in secondary schools already noted, this suggests that many problems may arise in schools rather than at home. The benefits of voluntary attendance would include respect for students as the informed 'consumers' or, far better, co-creators in their education, supported by their parents and carers, besides a creative, positive, welcoming school ethos. So much time, frustrated energy, and wasted resources could be re-channelled into working with the majority instead of trying to work against a resistant minority. That would release many teachers from administration and management back into teaching, with better teacher-student ratios, resulting in more personal and rewarding relationships. There would be more time to help the small minority who are unhappy, resistant or absent, and to work with them towards solutions, whether the difficulty is with reading or maths, bullying from children or adults, parents who keep them at home too much, or other problems (see, for example, Katz 2002).

There could be a programme of research and teaching to address the advantages and problems associated with voluntary school attendance, and to support the necessary new policies and practices. In the programme children, young people and adults would share the responsibility to:

- rethink the meaning and relevance of childhood and children's competencies and rights
- work to plan better curricula, real learning and teaching, and improved teacher training
- map new approaches to education itself and to schooling that can accommodate a new mutual respect and voluntary (willing) partnerships between learners and teachers
- plan how to prevent and resolve problems
- devise new effective systems of intrinsic rewards, credits, and paced flexible learning for core and optional subjects
- wrestle with the challenges of trying to combine liberty, equality and solidarity in schools
- recognise children as contributors and resources, instead of assuming that respecting their rights means increasing their expensive dependence
- seek to change society's treatment of and attitudes towards children and young people – the views of parents, 'experts', journalists, politicians and all others who influence public opinions and policies.

Children can see though the current hypocrisy of repressive schools and token school councils. 'We get played like fools,' they say (Morrow 2002). An 8-year-old girl succinctly summarised how rights are trivialised and distanced, in vain attempts to conceal how children's rights are disrespected in schools: 'It's so boring when they keep telling you that making the world a better place means picking up litter and not killing whales' (Alderson and Arnold 1999; Alderson 1999). The aim of changing the blocked plumbing of compulsion, and rigid though ineffectual control, into new channels of shared willing human agency would be that, whatever future forms schools take, all children and young people and adults will be able to flourish in civilised, respectful and caring communities. In the words of the UNCRC, respecting the inherent worth and dignity and the inalienable rights of all members of the human family promotes social progress and better standards of life in larger freedoms, and lays foundations for justice and peace in the world.

References

Alderson, P. (1999) 'Human rights and democracy in schools: Do they mean more than "picking up litter and not killing whales"?' *International Journal of Children's Rights*, **7**, 185–205.

—(2000a) 'Practising democracy in inner city schools', in: A. Osler (ed.), *Democracy in Schools: Diversity, identity, equality*. Stoke on Trent: Trentham Books.

—(2000b) *Young Children's Rights*. London: Jessica Kingsley/Save the Children.

—(2000c) 'Citizenship in theory or practice: being or becoming citizens with rights', in: R. Gardner, D. Lawton and P. Walsh (eds), *Citizenship and Education*. London: Continuum.

Alderson, P. and Arnold, S. (1999) 'Civil Rights in Schools'. *ESRC Children 5–16 Programme Briefing no. 1*. Swindon: ESRC.

Aldridge, J. and Becker, S. (2002) 'Children who care', in: B. Franklin (ed), *The New Handbook of Children's Rights: Comparative policy and practice*. London: Routledge.

Alldred, P., David, M. and Edwards, E. (2002) 'Minding the gap: children and young people negotiating relations between home and school', in: R. Edwards (ed.), *Children, Home and School: Regulation, autonomy or connection?* London: Falmer/Routledge.

Apple, M. and Beane, J. (1999) *Democratic Schools*. Buckingham: Open University Press.

Davies, L. and Kirkpatrick, G. (2000) *The EURIDEM Project: A review of pupils' democracy in Europe*. London: Children's Rights Alliance for England.

Gillborn, D. and Youdell, D. (2000) *Rationing Education*. Buckingham: Open University Press.

Godwin, W. (1797/1976) *An Enquiry Concerning Political Justice and its Influence on General Virtue and Happiness*. Harmondsworth: Penguin. Quoted in Ward, C. (1991) *Influences*. Bideford: Green Books.

Griffith, R. (1998) *Educational Citizenship and Independent Learning*. London: Jessica Kingsley.

Hall, G.S. (1904) *Adolescence.* New York: Appleton.

Hannam, D. (1999) 'Biodiversity or monoculture – the need for alternatives and diversity in the school system'. Summerhill Conference: The Free Child. Summerhill School.

Hardyment, C. (1984) *Dream Babies: Child care from Locke to Spock.* Oxford: Oxford University Press.

Hart, R. (1997) *Children's Participation: The Theory and Practice of Involving Young Children in Community Development and Environmental Care.* London: Earthscan/UNESCO.

—(2003) 'Children and youth on the cultural front line: the radical challenge of authentic participation in different settings'. Paper presented at ESRC Seminar Series: Challenging social inclusion: perspectives for and from young people, 2nd Seminar on Participation, Strathclyde University, Glasgow, 8–10 April.

Hendrick, H. (1997) 'Constructions and reconstructions of British childhood: An interpretive survey 1800 to the present', in: A. James and A. Prout (eds), *Constructing and Reconstructing Childhood.* London: Falmer.

Katz, A. (ed.) (2002) *Parenting Under Pressure: Prison.* London: Young Voice.

MacBeath, J. and Mortimore, P. (eds) (2001) *Improving School Effectiveness.* Buckingham: Open University Press.

McFerran, A. (2003) 'A life in the day'. *Sunday Times Magazine,* 6 April.

Midgley, M. (1996) *Utopias, Dolphins and Computers: Problems of philosophical plumbing.* London: Routledge.

Morrow, G. (1994) 'Responsible Children? Aspects of children's work and employment outside school in contemporary UK', in: B. Mayall (ed), *Children's Childhoods: Observed and experienced.* London: Falmer.

—(2002) '"We get played like fools": Young people's accounts of community and institutional participation', in: H. Ryan and J. Bull (eds), *Changing Families, Changing Communities.* London: Health Development Agency.

Muscroft, S. (ed), (1999) *Children's Rights: Equal rights? Diversity, difference and the issue of discrimination.* London: Save The Children.

Pollard, A., Thiessen, D. and Filer, A. (eds) (1997) *Children and their Curriculum: The perspectives of primary and elementary school children.* London: Falmer.

Richardson, M. (1938) quoted in R. Aldrich (2002). *The Institute of Education 1902–2002: a centenary history.* London: Institute of Education.

Shamgar-Handelman, L. (1994) 'To whom does childhood belong?', in: J. Qvortrup, M. Bardy, G. Sgritta and H. Wintersberger (eds), *Childhood Matters: Social theory. practice and politics.* Aldershot: Avebury.

Smith, F. (2000) *Child-Centred After School and Holiday Childcare.* Swindon: ESRC Research Briefing from the Children 5–16 Programme.

Smith, F. and Barker, J. (2002) 'School's out. Out of school clubs at the boundary of home and school', in: R. Edwards (ed), *Children, Home and School: Regulation, autonomy or connection?* London: Falmer/Routledge.

Thackeray, W. (1847/1967) *Vanity Fair.* London: Pan Books.

UNCRC (United Nations Committee on the Rights of the Child) (1995, 2003)

'Consideration of Reports Submitted by States Parties Under Article 44 of the Convention, Concluding Observations: United Kingdom of Great Britain and Northern Ireland'. Geneva: United Nations.

Ward, C. (1994) 'Opportunities for childhood in late twentieth century Britain', in: B. Mayall (ed), *Children's Childhoods: Observed and experienced.* London: Falmer.

Willow, C. and Hyder, T. (1998) *It Hurts You Inside: Children talk about smacking.* London: National Children's Bureau/Save the Children.

Chapter 19

'It's not fair – anyway, we've got rights!'

Henry Maitles and Ross Deuchar

Education for citizenship is now a national priority, and the creation of an open, trusting and participative school ethos is essential. In this chapter, Henry Maitles and Ross Deuchar, both from the University of Strathclyde, provide practical illustrations of the way in which primary school pupils can become engaged in discussing controversial social and political issues as a means of enhancing their understanding of, and potential participation in, a democratic society.

There is increasing recognition that the general ethos within a school can have a profound impact on the teaching of citizenship education, and the full understanding of the principles underpinning democracy. Schools should ensure that their daily practices do not conflict with or undermine their perceived aims for democratisation. The exposure of pupils to the controversial issues of society is a vital step towards encouraging pupils to develop empathy with the interests, beliefs and viewpoints of others; to value a respect for truth and evidence in forming or holding opinions; and to participate in decision-making, and value freedom and fairness as a basis for judging decisions. Such exposure is therefore vital for enabling pupils to fully understand what it means to live in a democratic society and behave with respect.

For classroom assistants and teachers, the creation of a positive classroom and school ethos is key. All research evidence (although limited at the moment) suggests that classroom assistants who understand the need for democracy and consultation can give the necessary impetus in the class to develop a better ethos; moreover, having additional adults in the room gives some teachers the confidence to effect that positive classroom ethos. Dobie (1998) argues that the way in which a school is run transmits messages to pupils about the nature of society, and cites pupil councils as having a huge role to play in the process of encouraging pupils to have a sense of ownership in the life of the school community.

There is no set way to form a pupil council. Most schools in Scotland now have them but they have been set up in different ways, usually due to a mixture of the school's individual circumstances and the thinking of the senior management. Most councils are elected and representative, either of classes or of year groups. They should be used to discuss issues of interest to the pupils; most common topics are toilets, school meals and issues such as bullying. Some councils, however, have budgets and clear input into some quite major school issues. It is to be hoped that classroom assistants will become increasingly involved in school councils, providing, as they do, an important adult non-teacher perspective. This may be especially significant where classroom assistants are parents and/or members of the local community. We would welcome further research and the identification of positive examples here. Our investigation into best practice throws up a number of areas, best explained by the following example.

A pupil council in action

A large Scottish primary school in an area of socio-economic deprivation with a predominantly ethnically white pupil body has had a school council in place for almost eight years. The school has routine weekly meetings in which representatives from Primary 1 to Primary 7 (5 to 12 years) get together with their headteacher to discuss the various points on their agenda, which is informed by class suggestion boxes and council representatives' own ideas. At one series of meetings, observed by one of the authors, items included the possibility of raising money for the local hospice, the development of a school newspaper, introduction of new features in the school dinner hall such as flavoured milk and fruit, and the ongoing difficulty of fighting on the football pitch between Primary 5 and Primary 7 boys. For each issue on the agenda, the headteacher acts as facilitator, encouraging pupils to think about and reflect upon the feasibility of the ideas or how to solve any difficulties. Where appropriate, she also makes suggestions or provides relevant information. The pupils take the lead in the discussion, and are able to speak up at any time. Decisions are made jointly and, where necessary, by means of a vote. At the end of their meeting, pupils decide to consult with classmates about the type of fundraising activities they would like to do for raising money for the local hospice, to name the school newspaper 'The Newsflash', to present ideas to the dinner ladies about new types of fruit that could be introduced and to suggest to Primary 5 and Primary 7 boys that they might share the school football pitch at lunchtime through the use of mixed-aged teams.

Council members are reminded by the headteacher to report back on these decisions to classmates immediately following the meeting, and that members will announce the pupil council decisions at assembly on Friday. Teachers in the school, although sceptical in the beginning, now embrace the aims of the Pupil Council and see the benefits. They encourage pupils to report back from meetings immediately on their return to the classroom. Indeed, there may be a particular role for classroom assistants in supporting the reporting-back stage.

Pupils are elected to the Council by democratic means: pupils in each class write down two people (a boy and a girl) who should be elected, and the most popular choice is elected. Children who are on the Council feel that it provides a forum to have an opinion listened to, and that they see change happening as a result. They feel proud when they are elected to the Council. Non-Council members also seem happy about the process; they know that they can come back and re-discuss ideas, if they are not happy with initial decisions. Many changes have come about as a result of the Pupil Council, apart from those outlined above, such as new equipment in the gym hall, different cakes in the dining hall, a 'Golden Bench' for children who are bullied, and a 'buddying' system for Primary 7 pupils to assist new Primary 1 children.

Even where there are functioning and well organised pupil councils, there should be space in the classroom to discuss socially or politically sensitive issues, whether that be bullying, local issues, drugs, animal welfare or international events, such as wars, conflict or terrorism. There is evidence suggesting that although youngsters are turned off formal party and government politics, they are very interested in single issue campaigning politics (Roker *et al.* 1999). Again, a case study showing good practice follows.

Democracy in the classroom

In this large non-denominational primary school located within a prosperous section of a West of Scotland town, Primary 7 pupils are encouraged to bring in news stories that are of interest to them as part of their weekly 'international news day' session. The discussions provide a forum for pupils to express aspects of their political interest, and demonstrate their strong engagement in world affairs, often at a very mature level. The main philosophical view underpinning the class teacher's approach appears to be the need for openness and creating an ethos of encouragement for pupils to express their opinions, often in relation to quite controversial issues. Among many of the issues for which she has noted particular pupil interest in recent years, she highlights teenage pregnancy, the use and misuse of drugs, animal rights and the debate about the teaching of religion in schools as being the most common. She noted a strong interest developing among pupils about issues surrounding terrorism and the Iraq War in the spring of 2003.

The media appear to play a large part in stimulating these particular pupils' interest and curiosity about the Iraq War, and the use of interactive sessions on international news issues provides a useful setting for them to share their curiosity, interest and personal opinions and also for the teacher to address some particular misunderstandings. Although she clearly encourages pupils to express their opinions and sees the importance of demonstrating the value of these opinions to children, this teacher also takes up the stance as advocated by Ashton and Watson (1998) of 'critical affirmation' in allowing pupils to develop their arguments. The relationship, trust and respect between the pupils and the teacher becomes central in such an approach. Although proven to be highly successful, this teacher feels that this approach is not as common among other teachers as it should be. Through her own experience, she has observed the reluctance of some teachers to value pupils' opinions because of their fear of 'losing control' of classroom discipline. Her own view here is that teachers who have the confidence and courage to allow pupil participation and to value its worth can, in fact, minimise indiscipline because children will be less frustrated at school.

During their discussions about the Iraq War (Maitles and Deuchar 2004), these pupils displayed a rich knowledge of topical and contemporary issues at international levels, as well as an awareness of the nature of democracy through their views about the future of Iraq and how it could and should be decided. Their concern for humanitarian issues related to the war reflected their growing understanding of the nature of diversity, social conflict and a concern for the common good. In addition, they were highly reflective about the underlying causes of the war, illustrating their ability to engage in a critical approach to the evidence presented via the mass media. The pupils displayed a strong concern for human dignity, equality and the need to resolve conflict diplomatically, and are increasingly able to recognise forms of manipulation that may be used by political leaders in their attempts to justify the need for war. They appear to have a growing understanding of human cultures, political structures, human rights and the underlying sources of conflict between communities.

They also appear to be developing a capacity to imagine alternative realities and futures for the people of Iraq through their discussions, and their ability to empathise with other communities and create reasoned argument in favour of democracy and against war is clearly providing the foundations for active citizenship, permeated by a sense of social and moral responsibility (Advisory Group on Citizenship 1998; LTS 2002). It is clear that there has to be a supportive atmosphere and a positive ethos for this to work effectively; classroom assistants (and, in particular in these kinds of issues, those from ethnic minority backgrounds) can be vital here.

It is evident that the particular class teacher involved here firmly believes that these children's interests in single-issue, environmental and third world issues is not untypical of the wider primary-aged pupil population. However, it is also clear that she feels that her intense valuing of pupil opinions is not so typical among teaching colleagues in the wider profession. The evidence of her positive results with pupils helps to confirm the view that, where there can be developed a respectful, trusting relationship between the teaching and support staff and the pupils, and the teacher encourages the pupils to develop their opinions, even the most controversial issues can be sensitively discussed in classrooms. The type of social empathy and tolerance that may emerge from such discussion combined with the ability to engage critically in the consideration of conflict resolution strategies may also assist pupils in dealing with more local controversial issues and incidents as they occur within their own lives in the school, playground and at home.

Conclusion

We are still in the infancy of education for citizenship, although many of the ideas and practices described above flow from long established practice in schools. While there is evidence of much good practice and we describe some major examples, it is also true that education for citizenship can be boringly, routinely introduced so as to appease audit forms and inspectors. This is a shame as its enthusiastic introduction can lead to better relationships, better behaviour, less bullying and better learning as the pupils feel some ownership of their work patterns. Hart (1997) outlines eight stages of participation from teacher-led, manipulated and controlled to pupil-initiated and shared. He shows the importance for democracy and learning if education workers (and particularly senior managers) encourage less of the former and more of the latter. Our evidence endorses that.

References

Advisory Group on Citizenship (1998) *Education for Citizenship and the Teaching of Democracy in Schools.* London : DFEE.

Ashton, E. and Watson, B. (1998) 'Values education: a fresh look at procedural neutrality'. *Educational Studies,* **24** (2), 183–93.

Dobie, T. (1998) 'Pupil councils in primary and secondary schools', in: D. Christie, H. Maitles and J. Halliday (eds) *Values Education for Democracy and Citizenship.* Glasgow: Gordon Cook Foundation/University of Strathclyde, 72–5.

Hart, R. (1997) *Children's Participation: the Theory and Practice of Involving Young Citizens in Community Development and Environmental Care.* London: Earthscan Publications.

LTS (Learning and Teaching Scotland) (2002) *Education for Citizenship in Scotland: a Paper for Discussion and Development.* Available at: http://www.ltscotland.org.uk/citizenship/files/ecsp.pdf.

Maitles, H. and Deuchar, R. (2004) 'Why are they bombing innocent Iraqis? Encouraging the expression of political literacy among primary pupils as a vehicle for promoting education for active citizenship'. *Improving Schools,* **7** (1), 97–105.

Roker, D., Player, K., and Coleman, J. (1999) 'Young people's voluntary and campaigning activities as sources of political education'. *Oxford Review of Education,* **25** (1–2), 185–97.

Chapter 20

Hearing the silence

Janet Collins

Quiet children are easily overlooked in today's busy classrooms. Janet Collins, a lecturer in primary education at The Open University, offers teachers and teaching assistants insights into the needs of children who say very little. Teaching assistants, given their work with individuals and small groups, seem particularly well placed to support children who are quiet in school.

It is by talking to children, and listening to what they have to say, that teachers and teaching assistants assess and support children's learning. For pupils to be successful and make the most of the learning opportunities offered it is important that they become active participants in the discourse of the classroom. Children who are unable or unwilling to talk freely to adults in school are at an acute disadvantage when compared with their more vocal peers.

My research (Collins 1994, 1996) highlighted the fact that quiet children are often very anxious about talking with, or in front of, others, especially during whole class discussions. They can become extremely embarrassed when adults try to persuade them to talk against their will. This anxiety prevents quiet pupils from taking an active role in their learning. It can also make them feel inadequate, especially in comparison with their more confident peers.

For example, Mandy recalls how uncomfortable she feels when she is 'picked on' to answer a question in class when she does not have her hand up: 'I feel horrible. I don't like it. Because I don't know the answer...I just sit there. Sometimes I gave him an answer...but sometimes not'. In situations like this, quiet pupils can appease the teacher by offering an answer, or they can satisfy their own need to be silent by refusing to speak. Mandy's obvious discomfort at being asked to speak suggests that neither response is easy or likely to enhance her self-esteem.

When quiet children do not join in class discussions it is extremely difficult for teachers and teaching assistants to assess the extent and depth of their understanding or to support further learning. This problem is compounded by the fact that quiet children find it very difficult to ask for help from adults even when they are experiencing serious difficulties. As the following example shows, a lack of contact with a teacher or another adult can have a detrimental effect on a pupil's learning and may lead to the development of a negative self-image.

Mandy decided to do extra homework in order to progress quickly through the school's individualised maths scheme. As the teacher was unaware of this decision he was not in a position to encourage this commitment to learning. Moreover, he was unaware that while Mandy was clearly well-motivated, she had not understood the work to be done. Working without guidance from the teacher both at home and at school, Mandy's mistakes were not identified for some time. Consequently, when her work was eventually marked she found that she had pages of corrections to do. For Mandy this was a blow to her perceptions of herself as an able mathematician. In order to avoid repeating this experience she simply stopped doing homework, thus potentially limiting her opportunities for improvement. This incident is not quoted here as an illustration of bad teaching, but rather to demonstrate how a lack of communication between pupils and adults in the classroom can disrupt learning.

When working with quiet pupils it is important to recognise that compliance does not necessarily equate with a commitment to learning. Observations suggest that quiet children might be 'playing truant in mind whilst present in body' (Young 1984: 12). Although they complete the bare minimum of work they appear to have little interest or investment in the outcome. 'They conform, and even play the system, but many do not allow the knowledge presented to them to make any deep impact upon their view of reality' (Barnes 1979: 17).

Justina's behaviour in a French lesson is an obvious example of this. Throughout the lesson, including during oral work, Justina worked hard, writing in her exercise book. Judging from the comments in this book the teacher was highly delighted with her progress. Page after page, she was complimented for the neat presentation of her written work.

However, since Justina did not speak a single word of French it would appear that she had missed the central point of the lesson. Her one interaction with the teacher was conducted in English and focused on the presentation of her work. The teacher seemed oblivious to her lack of participation in the oral part of the lesson. When I asked Justina to read what she had written she said, 'I don't speak French because it confuses me'. Justina's compliance with her teacher's expectations for her written work was matched by an equally stubborn refusal to share the language with anyone. What, I wondered, did Justina expect to learn during the French lesson? Clearly, this educational experience had not made an impression on her view of the world.

Habitually quiet behaviour can thus be detrimental to learning. In addition, such behaviour can mask acute or long-term emotional needs. However, as illustrated below, while it is relatively easy to identify the emotional and behavioural difficulties of loud, potentially aggressive pupils, the special educational needs of quiet withdrawn pupils can be easily overlooked.

Paul and Heather attended the same inner city primary school with a high proportion of pupils with special educational needs. Paul's violent, aggressive and often offensive behaviour drew attention to his emotional and behavioural needs, with the result that a variety of adults devoted a huge amount of time offering support. In sharp contrast, Heather's silent compliance meant that no one in the school was aware that she had suffered abuse at the hands of her father and step-father. Heather's story is an extreme case; clearly, quiet behaviour does not, of itself, indicate either physical or sexual abuse. However, her experience serves as a useful signifier for the quiet, withdrawn pupils who can so easily be overlooked.

Whatever the cause, habitually quiet, withdrawn behaviour should be regarded as potentially detrimental to learning. Such behaviour:

- prevents children from learning to express themselves (learning to talk)
- prevents children from asking questions and making the learning their own (learning through talk)
- prevents children from an active exploration of the subject being learned
- prevents teachers and teaching assistants from finding out what children know and thus monitoring and supporting learning
- reinforces stereotypes. Girls, especially those with moderate learning difficulties, are more likely to exhibit quiet passive behaviour in the classroom than other groups of children
- renders children invisible and can reinforce poor self-images
- can be linked with social isolation and can make pupils vulnerable to bullying
- can, in a minority of cases, mask serious emotional trauma such as bereavement, abuse, family separation.

A desire to empower quiet pupils to be active participants in classroom talk led me to carry out the four-year research project which forms the basis of this chapter (Collins 1994, 1996). This research aimed to understand the possible causes of quiet, withdrawn behaviour and to devise and implement teaching and support strategies which empowered quiet pupils to become active participants in the social and academic discourse of the classroom.

Based on this research, which involved detailed analysis of classroom observations in primary and secondary schools, I concluded that empowering quiet, withdrawn pupils essentially involves:

- emphasising the value of talk and making it the medium for learning rather than the precursor to the 'real' work of writing
- rejecting whole-class, teacher-directed talk in favour of small-group, child-centred talk
- identifying the rules of discussion and making them explicit to the pupils
- increasing feelings of security by establishing friendship groups or 'talk partners' and using them as the basis for all initial discussions
- providing activities which encouraged collaboration
- allowing pupils opportunities to consider what they wanted to say before calling on them to speak in front of large groups

- working with the pupils to devise ways of assessing talk and providing opportunities for pupils to reflect on what makes for effective talk.

In short, empowering quiet children involves recognising the importance of talk for learning and adopting collaborative small-group learning strategies. Teaching assistants and learning support staff are often well placed to 'hear the silence' and can often play a crucial role in identifying and supporting children who may be reluctant to talk in school.

References

Barnes, D. (1979) *From Communication to Curriculum.* Harmondsworth: Penguin.

Collins, J. (1994) 'The Silent Minority: Developing Talk in the Primary Classroom', unpublished PhD thesis, Sheffield University.

Collins, J. (1996) *The Quiet Child.* London: Cassell.

Young, D. (1984) *Knowing How and Knowing That.* London: Birkbeck College.

Chapter 21

Understanding eating disorders

Royal College of Psychiatrists

Most children enjoy eating and move through childhood and adolescence with very few difficulties. However, a few develop eating disorders which can give rise to considerable concern at home and in school. This chapter has been written for parents and schools by the Royal College of Psychiatrists. It reviews the signs, effects and causes of eating disorders and highlights when it may be necessary to seek professional help.

What are eating disorders?

Worries about weight, shape and eating are common, especially among teenage girls. Being very overweight or obese can cause a lot of problems, particularly with health. Quite often, someone who is overweight can lose weight simply by eating more healthily. It sounds easy, but they may need help to find a way of doing this.

A lot of young people, many of whom are not overweight in the first place, want to be thinner. They often try to lose weight by dieting or skipping meals. For some, worries about weight become an obsession. This can turn into a serious eating disorder. This article is about the most common eating disorders – anorexia nervosa and bulimia nervosa.

- Someone with anorexia nervosa worries all the time about being fat (even if they are skinny) and eats very little. They lose a lot of weight and, if they are female, their periods stop.
- Someone with bulimia nervosa also worries a lot about weight. They alternate between eating next to nothing and then having binges when they gorge themselves. They vomit or take laxatives to control their weight.

Both of these eating disorders are more common in girls, but do occur in boys.

What are the signs of anorexia or bulimia

- weight loss or unusual weight changes
- in girls, periods being irregular or stopping
- missing meals, eating very little and avoiding 'fattening' foods
- avoiding eating in public, secret eating
- large amounts of food disappearing from the cupboards
- believing they are fat when underweight
- exercising excessively
- becoming preoccupied with food, cooking for other people
- going to the bathroom or toilet immediately after meals
- using laxatives and vomiting to control weight.

It may be difficult for parents or teachers to tell the difference between ordinary teenage dieting and a more serious problem. If you are concerned about your child's weight and how they are eating, consult your family doctor.

What effects can eating disorders have?

- tiredness and difficulty with normal activities
- damage to health, including stunting of growth and damage to bones and internal organs
- in girls, loss of periods and risk of infertility
- anxiety, depression, obsessive behaviour or perfectionism
- poor concentration, missing school, college or work
- lack of confidence, withdrawal from friends
- dependency or over-involvement with parents, instead of developing independence.

It is important to remember that, if allowed to continue unchecked, both anorexia and bulimia can be life-threatening conditions. Over time, they are harder to treat and the effects become more serious.

What causes eating disorders?

Eating disorders are caused by a number of different things:

- Worry or stress may lead to comfort eating. This may cause worries about getting fat.
- Dieting and missing meals lead to craving for food, loss of control and over-eating.
- Anorexia or bulimia can develop as a complication of more extreme dieting, perhaps triggered by an upsetting event, such as family breakdown, death or separation in the family, bullying at school or abuse.

- More ordinary events, such as the loss of a friend, a teasing remark or school exams, may also be the trigger in a vulnerable person.
- Sometimes, anorexia and bulimia may be a way of trying to feel in control if life feels stressful.

Some people are more at risk than others. Risk factors include being female, being previously overweight and lacking self-esteem. Sensitive or anxious individuals who are having difficulty becoming independent are also more at risk. The families of young people with eating disorders often find change or conflict particularly difficult and may be unusually close or over-protective.

If you think a young person may be developing an eating disorder, don't be afraid to ask them if they are worried about themselves. Some young people will not want you to interfere.

These simple suggestions are useful to help young people to maintain a healthy weight and avoid eating disorders:

- eat regular meals – breakfast, lunch and dinner
- try to eat a 'balanced' diet – one that contains all the types of food your body needs
- include carbohydrate foods such as bread, rice, pasta or cereals with every meal
- do not miss meals – long gaps encourage overeating
- avoid sugary or high-fat snacks (try eating a banana instead of a bar of chocolate)
- take regular exercise
- try not to be influenced by other people skipping meals or commenting on weight.

When professional help is needed

When eating problems make family meals stressful, it is important to seek professional advice. Your general practitioner will be able to advise you about what specialist help is available locally and will be able to arrange a referral. Working with the family is an important part of treatment.

If the eating disorder causes physical ill health it is essential to get medical help quickly. If the young person receives help from a specialist early on, admission to hospital is unlikely. If untreated, there is a risk of infertility, thin bones (osteoporosis), stunted growth and even death.

Sources of further information

The Eating Disorders Association provides information and advice. Youth Helpline 0845 634 7650; Adult Helpline 0845 634 1414; www.edauk.com.

The YoungMinds Parent Information Service provides information and advice on child mental health issues. 102–108 Clerkenwell Road, London EClM 5SA. Telephone 0800 018 2138; www.youngminds.org.uk.

The Royal College of Psychiatrists' *Mental Health and Growing Up* series contains 36 factsheets on a range of common mental health problems. They can be downloaded from www.rcpsych.ac.uk.

Chapter 22

Gypsies and Travellers

Gwynedd Lloyd and Gillean McCluskey

In this chapter Gwynedd Lloyd, lecturer, and Gillean McCluskey, research associate, both from Edinburgh University, provide background information to the groups of Travellers currently living in Britain today, and consider what people think and say about them. They suggest that Traveller children are at risk of name calling and bullying at school as there is a widespread lack of understanding about their lifestyle and culture.

In this chapter we will look at some of the things that people often say or think about Gypsies and Travellers in this country. We will talk about some of the experiences that Gypsy and Traveller children have in school to promote an understanding about how their educational opportunities could be improved.

There are several different groups of Travellers living in Britain at the moment, and sometimes they call themselves different names, which can be confusing for settled people trying to understand. Gypsy Travellers in England and Wales are sometimes called Romanies or 'Romany chals'. In Scotland sometimes they are called Gypsy Travellers, Tinkers or 'Nawkens' or 'Nachins'. Irish Gypsy Travellers are also sometimes called Tinkers. Some of these words, like Gypsy or Tinker, may be used with pride by Travellers but can also be used by settled people as terms of abuse.

All these groups have been in this country for generations. They are partly descended from some people who probably left India beginning hundreds of years ago and travelled through Asia and Europe. As they went they interacted with, and sometimes settled for work or married, the people who lived in the countries they passed through. The language known as Romani can be traced back along this route. Many of these travellers settled and formed communities in these countries. In Europe they are now usually referred to as Roma, although in France they are known as Tsiganes and in Germany Sinti. The Roma communities in Europe were persecuted in many places over the centuries, culminating with their near destruction in the Holocaust, where probably around a million or more Gypsies were subjected to medical research and killed in the concentration camps.

In Britain groups of Romanies arrived over several centuries, meeting and mixing with groups of other Travellers on the roads. Although it is very difficult to get accurate figures some estimates suggest that there are around 25,000 to 30,000 Gypsies and Travellers in Britain today. The language of Gypsy Travellers in the different parts of the UK includes Romani words as well as words that reflect the cultures of the part of the country they have travelled in. For example Scottish 'cant' includes Gaelic words.

Other Gypsy groups in Britain include European Roma, many from Eastern Europe where after the second world war they were often subject to forced settlement and where children were disproportionately educated in special schools. In recent years there has been a big increase in prejudice and violence in some Eastern European countries towards Roma.

There is also a group known as New Travellers, formerly often called New Age Travellers, who include people who have, for different reasons, rejected aspects of settled life and culture in contemporary Britain and have formed themselves into alternative communities.

Many people in Britain have strong, often negative, views about Gypsies and Travellers, sometimes based on direct experience with a few Travellers but often on folk tales, popular stories, myths or stereotypes about Gypsies. In the section of the chapter that follows we explore some views that are often expressed both by ordinary people and by professionals.

Gypsies in Britain aren't real Gypsies?

Recent thinking in the field of race relations makes it clear that 'race' is a political rather than a biological term and that indeed it is racist to imply predictable personal qualities on the basis of some assumed biological basis. We all have ethnicity which means that we belong to communities with shared values and cultures. For most settled people this means that they may derive their habits of life and values from a diverse range of sources. Gypsy Travellers are still small groups with shared ethnicity, with clear historical status and traditions that they wish to protect, and recognition of this does not depend on discredited notions of racial purity. They, like everyone else, will also have different views and practices according to other factors such as age, gender and personal preference. Shared ethnicity does not mean that everyone is the same but that they agree on some important aspects of lifestyle and values.

Gypsies live in caravans?

Some British Gypsy Travellers live in caravans and still travel. However, there has been a big reduction in the places where they can camp, so some find it difficult to travel. Some live in caravans all year round on permanent sites run by local authorities. Others live sometimes in houses and travel seasonally. Some live permanently in houses but still feel strongly part of the Traveller culture and community. Some live in houses on housing estates where they hide their Traveller identity out of fear of hostility from their neighbours.

Gypsies steal?

Many people over the centuries grew up with stories of Gypsies stealing babies. There is still a widespread belief that Gypsies steal. This is very offensive to most Gypsies and Travellers, who abide by the law. Many British Traveller families belong to recent Christian church movements and have clear moral views. Gypsy and Traveller communities are characterised by a strong commitment to the extended family and families often maintain much greater control over their adolescent children than in the settled community. Of course there may be a minority within Traveller communities who commit crimes as there are within settled communities, but we do not label all settled communities as criminal.

Gypsies don't want their children to be educated?

Traveller communities often have rich oral histories. Scottish Travellers, for example, have a long history of music and storytelling. Most Traveller families today recognise the importance of literacy and numeracy; many wish their children to receive a full education in primary schools. However, many Travellers attend primary school but drop out during secondary school years. Some parents are unhappy about the curriculum, which they see as irrelevant to their lifestyle, and have anxieties about their children's safety in school. 'Many Traveller parents express anxieties about their children's moral, emotional and physical welfare in what they perceive to be a strange and hostile environment' (Derrington and Kendall 2004: 4). Some local education authorities now provide some education out of school, for example on Traveller sites. However, education support for Travellers is very patchy and Traveller Support teachers sometimes feel overstretched and rather isolated (Derrington and Kendall 2004).

Gypsy children cause trouble in school?

Research into the disciplinary exclusion of Gypsy Travellers from school found that often the exclusion occurred as a result of fighting or violence which stemmed from harassment and bullying of Travellers in school (Lloyd and Stead 2001). Racist name-calling and bullying is still clearly very common, permeating Travellers' experience at school. Traveller families often say that schools fail to understand their lifestyle and culture. Ofsted (1999) in England argued that Gypsy Travellers were the group most at risk in the education system. Some schools are resistant to admitting Gypsies and Travellers.

So there is no evidence that Gypsies and Travellers are any more or less disruptive in school than other pupils. There is evidence that they are less likely to attend and that they may experience more difficulties in their relationships with staff and pupils.

Conclusion

Many Gypsies and Travellers in the UK experience major difficulties leading the kind of life they wish. They are more likely to suffer health problems and to die younger than the rest of the population. They are subject to regular prejudice and racial harassment. They find it difficult to access appropriate places to live. Many Travellers wish that their children could receive an education appropriate to their lives as part of Traveller communities and free from bullying. This is a challenge to our education system. You might like to think about how the system could be adapted to better respond to this.

References

Derrington, D. and Kendall, S. (2004) *Gypsy Traveller Students in Secondary Schools: Culture, identity and achievement.* Stoke: Trentham.

DfES (2003) *Aiming High: Raising the Achievements of Gypsy Traveller Pupils.* London: Department for Education and Skills.

Lloyd, G. and Stead, J. (2001) '"The Boys and Girls Not Calling Me Names and the Teachers to Believe Me": Name Calling and the Experiences of Travellers in School'. *Children and Society,* **15** (5), 361–74.

Ofsted (1999) *Raising the Attainment of Minority Ethnic Pupils.* London: Ofsted.

Further reading

SEED/STEP (2003) *Inclusive Educational Approaches for Gypsies and Travellers.* Edinburgh: Learning and Teaching Scotland.

Kendrick, D. and Clark, C. (2002) *Moving On The Gypsies and Travellers of Britain.* Hatfield: University of Hertfordshire Press.

Chapter 23

Looked-after children

Tony Eaude and Jude Egan

Tony Eaude, a headteacher in Oxfordshire, and Jude Egan, a school social worker in Hertfordshire, believe that the needs of looked-after children can easily be overlooked by schools. This chapter reviews issues related to children in public care and provides practical advice for teaching assistants and teachers.

When unexpected and unexplained money arrives in a school's budget, it is tempting to keep quiet. But when the school received an allocation with two children's names attached, it seemed worth investigating. Both were 'looked-after' children, a fact that no one in the school had previously known. Not only did no one know that the LEA provided some resources for such children, but the term 'looked-after' children meant little to any of the staff.

In this article, we try, as an ex-head teacher and a social worker in Child and Adolescent Mental Health, to help busy heads, teachers and teaching assistants consider how to support this particularly vulnerable group of children. Although policies vary between areas, we are trying to set out general principles on how best to work with an often-forgotten group of children. What we say does not relate only to primary schools. But the relationships built in primary schools, and the resilience this brings, may for many of these children make an important difference to how well they succeed in later life.

Who are 'looked-after children'?

The language used is confusing and is constantly changing. Under the 1989 Children Act, local authorities are required to look after children whose parents are unable to do so. These children may '*be accommodated*' or have been '*placed on a care order*' (or an interim care order). Sometimes they are called 'children in public care', sometimes 'looked-after children'. The terms are interchangeable. We have chosen 'looked-after' children because it sounds less institutional.

If a child is *accommodated*, the Social Services Department is providing some-where for the child to live. This is usually a voluntary arrangement made with the parent/s, usually as a short-term arrangement. Occasionally it is longer term, or on the basis of respite care, to give parents a regular break, usually relating to children with a physical or learning disability. There is no change in legal status. Those parents who have parental responsibility for their child retain it.

About 62% of looked-after children are subject to a *care order* (DfEE 2000: Section 3.2). This means that a court has placed the child in the care of the designated Local Authority, under Section 31 of the Children Act. Usually, a care order follows an interim care order, often in place while the care proceedings are being heard in court, prior to a final decision. Once a care order is in place, parental responsibility is shared between the parents and the local authority. The Social Services Department may limit the parental responsibility of a parent or anyone else with parental responsibility, if they are satisfied that it is *'necessary to do so in order to safeguard or promote the child's welfare'* (Children Act 1989). Birth mothers always hold parental responsibility. Birth fathers have parental responsibility automatically only if they are married to the child's mother at any time after the child's conception. A court can confer parental responsibility on any adult including the birth father following an application by such an adult to the court. The area of legal responsibility is a minefield on which schools should take legal advice if they are not sure.

Refugees who have no means of family support are another group often in public care, whether accommodated or on a care order. They may have experienced severe disruption, at least, and horrific trauma at worst.

Where may looked-after children be living?

About 65% of looked-after children live with foster carers on either a long- or short-term basis. Alternatively a child may be living in a local Children's Home (about 12%) or with family relatives (DfEE 2000: Section 3.1). It is possible that the location of the placement and the school is kept confidential from the parents. Occasionally a child may be still on a care order but living back at home, usually when the home circumstances have changed significantly and Social Services are considering revoking the care order. One final possibility is that a child may be living in a pre-adoption placement, with parents who are hoping to adopt the child or seriously considering this. If you find all this somewhat mind boggling just imagine how it might feel for the child.

How likely is it that my school will include looked-after children?

There are over 55,000 children in public care in England – a figure that continues to rise. Around 21% of these are under 5 (DfEE 200: Section 3.1). Most of the rest are, or are supposed to be, in mainstream primary or secondary schools. Urban areas tend to have more looked-after children, and, if your school is near a children's home, your school will probably be responsible for educating looked-after children. Most refugees live in urban areas, most especially in London. The likelihood is high enough that all teachers and teaching assistants should at least be aware of what the term means, and know where to find out more when a looked-after child does join their class.

What are looked-after children likely to have experienced?

Of course, it is dangerous to generalise too much, but confusion, disruption and deprivation are common themes running through many of these children's lives. Many will have witnessed, or experienced, violence or abuse. As a result they are often both socially and emotionally disadvantaged and tend to have health, developmental, behavioural, and educational difficulties. This is increasingly so for children in care as the threshold for admission into the care system has risen in recent years and is not surprising when one considers their early experiences of abuse and/or rejection, and the multiple placements and changes in a short time they may have had to deal with. 'There are present in most of these children's lives an overwhelming preponderance of risk factors. By the time they reach adolescence, unless there are strong countervailing protective factors or processes, the odds against them are simply too high' (Jackson and Martin 1998: 571).

Of looked-after children 75% have mental health needs, some complex and severe (Richardson and Joughin 2000: v). The Social Exclusion Unit reports that 'the permanent exclusion rate among children in public care is 10 times higher than the average and as many as 30% of children in care are out of mainstream education, whether through exclusion or truancy' (cited in Richardson and Joughin 2000: 45).

While each child's circumstances will inevitably be different, a number of common themes emerge. Very often, especially if they have had a difficult time at another school, looked-after children may:

• feel insecure and uncertain in their relationships
• think that they are less likely to succeed than other children
• believe that other people, both children and adults, think of them as naughty, rather than seeing their good points.

Looked-after children are more likely to have emotional and behavioural difficulties, such as:

• knowing they are different from other children
• having feelings of anger, hurt, injustice and confusion, often not knowing why they have these feelings
• be the victim, or perpetrator, of bullying.

Most of these children find it very difficult to form secure loving relationships with adults and will try our patience in every possible way. They are very often both troubled and troublesome.

How can teachers help?

When a looked-after child enters their class, teachers and teaching assistants often are, or feel, ill-prepared to meet their needs. The child may also find it hard to cope with the experience of another move to a new school. A supportive welcome, and period of induction, is especially important, maybe by seeing that a mentor, or a buddy, helps the new child with the routines and rules of the school.

Much of what really helps is common sense and good teaching such as:

- being as calm and as consistent as possible
- giving praise and positive reinforcement
- listening with care and attention to the child's concerns
- not referring to their difference in front of the other children but letting them know privately that you are aware of some of the things that might be hard for them.

But there are definitely some extra things that the school should be aware of.

Personal issues may need to be handled very sensitively. Some 'fairly normal' things may not only be not normal. They may be very far from the experience of looked-after children. These include:

- how we talk about home and families
- being very careful if doing any work on families, such as family trees
- answering questions, or doing work, about themselves and their past.

It may help, in due course, to encourage children to attend out-of-school activities, where they learn social skills, make new friends and enjoy success.

Attendance may be a difficult issue. There may be reasons why attendance is patchy, but teachers and others need to ensure that school attendance is as regular as possible. A pattern of missing school can be very difficult to break, and is likely to make success at school more difficult.

Poor educational achievement is a consistent finding from all studies of young people in or leaving care. It is important to remember to have high, but realistic, educational expectations. One of the most important factors in encouraging the resilience of looked-after children is early success in literacy (Bald *et al.* 1995), along with the self-esteem and independence that comes with such success. Previous difficulties, or a lack of consistent support out of school, may make achieving this a particular challenge. Remember that looked-after children may not have the access to books, quiet space or adult attention that help children to achieve success.

Perhaps the most important thing is to work closely with all the important adults in the child's life. This may enable you to understand more about the child's world and what they are experiencing outside school.

We are bound to make mistakes at times, but sensitivity and attention to detail is important both for the child and for the child's parents and carers. For instance, think carefully about whom to invite to school events and remember who should receive reports and letters home. Not only does this show respect for the child, it helps to sustain, or create, supportive relationships which may be fragile or non-existent.

Who is responsible for ensuring children in public care are properly looked after?

The Local Authority as a whole, not just Social Services, is required to exercise their parental responsibility. Education departments have a duty, set out in the Children Act, to safeguard and promote the child's welfare, particularly in monitoring and managing educational progress. So social workers, teachers, teaching assistants and other professionals need to work together, along with other significant adults in the child's life, to make sure they are well looked-after.

Each local education authority should have a policy on supporting looked-after children. The level of support available varies from area to area. Some LEAs have Advisory Teachers for Children in Public Care. The Guidance on the Education of Children and Young People in Public Care, issued by the DfEE and the Department of Health in May 2000, set out that each maintained school should have a designated teacher for Children in Public Care (DfEE 2000: Section 5).

The Social Services Department should inform the headteacher of the school if a child who joins the school is looked after, or if a child at the school is taken into public care. But, as the story above shows, this does not always happen. It would be good practice for the head to tell the class teacher and the Special Needs Co-ordinator, unless there is a very good reason otherwise. While the child will not necessarily be on the special needs register, this may often be appropriate, and it may be useful to inform other professionals, such as the Educational Psychologist or Education Social Worker/Welfare Officer. Other professionals in school may need to know, such as support teachers and LSAs. Everyone concerned must be aware of the need for confidentiality and the sensitivity of certain information.

How can we ensure that everyone knows, and reviews, how best to help the child?

Every looked-after child should have a Care Plan and a social worker whose responsibility it is to see that it is carried out. The Care Plan should be drawn up within 72 hours of the child entering public care, at a care planning meeting. The first statutory review must be held one month later, and then another after three months. Thereafter there should be a review meeting at least every six months. The Care Plan will be reviewed at these meetings. All these meeting are chaired by the social worker's line manager or by an independent reviewing officer of the Social Services Department.

The social worker should always be at this meeting. For all school-age children the headteacher or teacher should definitely be invited. The SENCO, Education Social Worker/Welfare Officer or Educational Psychologist can also be included if this is relevant to the child's needs. Others invited may include the child (depending on age and appropriateness), the foster carers and their link worker from the Family Placement Team or the child's key worker from their children's home. Health professionals may include a representative from the Child and Family clinic, a health visitor or a school nurse. Parents and/or grandparents may or may not be invited depending on circumstances.

At these meetings you will get the opportunity to hear about issues and/or events impacting on the emotional life, and therefore behaviour, of the child. These may include contact issues, changes in placement, sad news of parents or siblings (including no news at all), changes of social worker, and significant anniversaries. Attending this meeting will give the teacher and/or teaching assistants a chance to get to know the multitude of people in the child's life.

In addition to the Care Plan, each looked-after child must now have a Personal Education Plan, drawn up within 20 days, similar to the Individual Education Plan, familiar for children with special educational needs. This should be reviewed after 28 days, after 3 months and after 6 months. Many of these reviews can coincide with the Care Plan. Regular careful monitoring can help to ensure that issues are not allowed to drift. Those concerned should consider involving the child as much as possible in these reviews and plans, depending on the child's age.

As with all children, careful, factual records should be kept. Because of the complexity of these children's lives, these records are likely to be even more detailed than for other children. Schools should pass the records on promptly to the child's next school when the child leaves and if possible be available to discuss the child's needs.

A final thought

If you do have a looked-after child in your class or school, remember what a retired teacher said to the mother of a 'hyperactive' child: 'the children who need love the most will always ask for it in the most unloving ways' (Barkley 1995).

References and further reading

Bald, J., Bean, J. and Weagan, F. (1995) *A Book of My Own*. London: Who Cares Trust.

Barkley, R. A. (1995) *Attention Deficit Hyperactivity Disorder*, New York: Guilford Press, cited on cover of *Helping Hyperactive Children and Their Carers*, by Herbert, M. (undated). Kenn, Devon: Impact Publications.

Department for Education and Employment (DfEE) (2000) *Guidance on the Education of Children and Young People in Public Care* (text available on www.dfee.gov.uk).

Jackson, S. (1994) 'Educating children in residential and foster care: an overview', *Oxford Review of Education*, **20** (3).

Jackson, S. and Martin, P. (1998) 'Surviving the care system: education and resilience', *Journal of Adolescence*, **21**.

Richardson, J. and Joughin, C. (2000) *The Mental Health Needs of Looked After Children*. London: Gaskell.

Chapter 24

Tackling bullying

Christine Oliver and Mano Candappa

Children can help us towards a better understanding of the causes and the consequences of bullying. Christine Oliver and Mano Candappa from the Thomas Coram Research Unit, London, report on some of the findings of a study that asked children about their experiences of bullying and school responses to it.

Our research study involved twelve schools, six primary and six secondary, and we focused on the views and experiences of pupils from Years 5 and 8, respectively.

What is bullying?

In focus groups and in the questionnaire survey, pupils provided clear and comprehensive definitions of bullying. Their understanding of bullying was that it could include verbal and physical abuse, theft, threatening behaviour, and coercion. Bullying was also understood as behaviour intended to cause distress or harm. Pupils identified a broad spectrum of behaviours of varying severity that could be encompassed within a definition of bullying and the negative impact bullying could have on pupils' sense of well-being and personal safety. Their descriptions of bullying represented a narrative of vulnerability, inequality and abuse within a complex web of power relations between pupils. Vulnerability to bullying was described as the result of personal and individual characteristics, such as physical size or appearance, or the result of more structured inequalities (such as racism, sexism or homophobia). Typically, definitions of bullying included some or all of the following elements:

> Bullying is when someone picks on someone else because they are different – their race, height, weight, or looks. It's about prejudice and discrimination and when someone gets hurt physically or mentally, or when someone is not respected.
>
> (Girl, Year 8)

Bullying is when people force others, usually smaller people, to do what they want.

(Boy, Year 5)

Bullying is intentionally causing physical or mental damage to others, like attacking them or no reason frequently, teasing them frequently, or even sexually, such as rape.

(Girl, Year 8)

How big a problem is bullying?

- Just over half of both primary (51%) and secondary school pupils (54%) thought that bullying was 'a big problem' or 'quite a problem' in their school.
- Just over half (51 %) of Year 5 pupils reported that they had been bullied during the term, compared with just over a quarter (28%) of Year 8 pupils. Considerable variation was reported in the level of bullying between schools.
- Girls were almost as likely as boys to have been bullied in both age groups. In Year 8, a higher proportion of Black and Asian pupils (33%) reported that they had been bullied this term, compared with pupils of other ethnic groups (30%) or white pupils (26%).

What are the most common forms of bullying?

Name-calling was reported as the most prevalent form of bullying for pupils in Years 5 and 8. Bullying involving physical aggression was less common, but nevertheless was reported by a substantial proportion of pupils in both age groups. Behaviour resulting in social isolation (such as gossip, and the spreading of rumours) was also common for pupils in both years, but particularly for pupils in Year 5.

A minority of pupils reported sexist, racist and anti-gay abuse, although racist and sexist name-calling was more prevalent among primary than secondary school pupils: a fifth of pupils in Year 5 reported that they had been called racist names, compared with 6% of pupils in Year 8. 11% of pupils reported that they had been called anti-gay names. However, these forms of bullying were more prevalent in some schools than others.

Contrary to some research on gender and bullying, boys and girls in this study reported similar levels of physical bullying, name-calling, and social ostracism, although some forms of physical bullying were higher for boys in Year 8. Girls also reported a higher level of sexualised bullying than boys: 5% of pupils in Year 8 (mostly girls) reported that they had experienced unwanted sexual touching.

Although the numbers are small, it would appear that bullying by electronic communication is emerging as a new form of bullying: 4% of pupils in Year 8 reported that they had received nasty text messages and 2% had received nasty e-mail messages.

Responding to bullying

How good is your school at dealing with bullying?

According to pupils' memories and perceptions, the findings indicated that participating schools were more likely to approach bullying by introducing one-off initiatives, such as discussing the topic during assembly or lesson time, than by more targeted and on-going approaches, such as appointing anti-bullying counsellors or teachers designated with specific anti-bullying responsibilities.

In the questionnaire survey, a majority of pupils (over 60%) expressed positive views about their school's attempts to deal with bullying. However, secondary school pupils were less likely to give their school a glowing report: over a third of primary school pupils (36%) thought that their school was 'very good' at dealing with bullying, compared with just over 1 in 10 of secondary school students (12%).

Key elements in pupils' assessment of their school's effectiveness concerned the willingness of teachers to listen, to express empathy, and to act appropriately on the suggestions of pupils.

> The children suggest ways the playground could be made better and teachers and the Head, listen. They take notice. They change things.
>
> > (Girl, Year 5)

> At this school it is OK. We talk about it at assembly and at the school council.
>
> > (Boy, Year 8)

Conversely, schools that had a poor reputation appeared to be less likely to listen to pupils, and to take their complaints seriously or to take firm action:

> I don't think the school handles it very well. They say leave it for now, but if it happens again, come back. But when we do that and they say they are working on it, it never gets solved.
>
> > (Boy, Year 8)

Setting a good example

With regard to the extent to which teachers might limit bullying behaviour by modelling pro-social behaviour, the majority of pupils of both age groups thought that teachers set a good example for how pupils should behave. However, pupils' views varied widely between schools. For example, in one primary school, 86% of pupils reported that teachers 'always' set a good example, compared with only 48% of pupils in a second primary school.

What are the most effective responses to bullying?

In exploring pupils' own responses in dealing with bullying, the findings indicated that the three most helpful factors in preventing, or helping pupils to deal with, bullying were friendships, avoidance strategies, and learning to 'stand up for yourself'. This section of the report discusses the costs and benefits of 'standing up for yourself', telling friends, telling teachers, telling parents and telling agencies outside the school.

Standing up for yourself

Being assertive

For pupils in Year 5, more confidence was expressed in the potential of 'talking back' and other, more assertive forms of direct verbal communication with the bully, than pupils in Year 8. Approximately a quarter of pupils in Year 5 thought that communicating verbally in an assertive way with the bully would 'always' or 'usually' work. Less than 10% of pupils in Year 8 shared this view.

Hitting back

Older pupils were more likely to believe that physical retaliation had a better chance of success: 23% of secondary school pupils and 15% of primary school pupils thought that 'hitting back' would 'always' or 'usually' work to stop bullying. Indeed, almost a third (31%) of pupils in Year 8 thought that learning a martial art might help to reduce the risk of bullying, although this was identified as a more long term strategy. However, in relation to gender, girls were less likely to support physical retaliation as an appropriate strategy. Black and Asian pupils expressed a higher degree of confidence in the positive potential of each of the strategies identified than white pupils, or pupils of other ethnic groups.

> You could learn self-defence, or Karate, but that might take some time
>
> (Boy, Year 8)

> My mum says two wrongs don't make a right, but they bullied me so much my Mum said 'just fight back'.
>
> (Boy, Year 8)

> It might not work, because the person doing the hitting back might get into trouble.
>
> (Girl, Year 5)

Ignoring the bully

A higher proportion of pupils in Year 5 were optimistic about the potential effectiveness of ignoring the bully: 38% thought that such a strategy would 'always' or 'usually' work, compared with only 14% of pupils in Year 8. A number of potential risks and benefits were associated with this strategy:

> They bully you to get you annoyed. So if you show you're not annoyed, it will stop.
>
> (Girl, Year 5)

> It might not work because if you ignore them, the bully might do something worse.
>
> (Boy, Year 5)

Telling friends

A large majority of pupils in Years 5 (68%) and 8 (71%) reported that they would find it easy to talk to a friend if they were being bullied, although younger pupils were more likely to talk to their mothers. This suggests that anti-bullying initiatives that take friendship networks into account are likely to be of considerable value to pupils.

Having a group of friends was identified as an important protective factor in preventing, and helping pupils to cope with, bullying. Unlike teachers and other adults, friends were in a position to witness bullying in and outside school, and to provide support when needed.

> It's more comfortable talking to them. They're with you when you get picked on, so they know about it.
>
> (Boy, Year 8)

> They might go up to them and say 'why are you picking on X?' Because a friend is a friend. You want them to stick up for you, and they get involved.
>
> (Girl Year 8)

However, the main risk of involving a friend was that they might also start to be bullied.

> Sometimes, if they know you're picked on, it might happen to them too.
>
> (Boy, Year 5)

Telling teachers

Just over half (51 %) of pupils in Year 5, but less than a third (31%) of pupils in Year 8, reported that they would find it easy to speak to a teacher about bullying. Telling teachers was associated with a wide range of risks, particularly in relation to possible breaches of confidentiality, failure to act on reported incidents of bullying, and an inability to protect pupils from retaliatory behaviour on the part of perpetrators.

> Verbal bullying isn't taken seriously by teachers. If you have some bruises, they might take some notice.
>
> (Girl, Year 8)

> If you tell your tutor, they have to tell someone else, and then they tell someone else. It's like Chinese whispers.
>
> (Boy, Year 8)

> You get called a grass and a dobber, and you get beaten up.
>
> (Boy, Year 5)

On the other hand, some pupils reported that telling teachers could help to stop the bullying or that, armed with relevant information, teachers might be less likely to punish a pupil should they decide to take matters into their own hands.

If you hit someone, and the teacher knows you've been bullied, they take that into consideration. If you don't tell, they might think you've hit someone for no reason.

(Boy, Year 8)

Are some teachers better at dealing with bullying than others?

Most pupils could identify a teacher that they would be most likely to speak to if they were being bullied. Such teachers were reported by pupils to be demonstrably better at listening to pupils, more prepared to take pupils seriously, ready to take appropriate action (but not without the consent of the victim), and to be 'firm but fair'.

> She (the teacher) is strict. People say strict teachers are bad but really, strict teachers are better at sorting it out.
>
> (Boy, Year 8)

> Our teacher is good...she bothers to find out what really happened. She takes you seriously. She sorts it out with the Head, or she will tell the parents.
>
> (Girl, Year 8)

Telling parents

Parents were identified as offering a potentially valuable source of help, advice and moral support. In particular, pupils reported that parents who listened to them and took their experiences seriously, helped them to cope with bullying. However, pupils also reported that telling parents could make matters worse (for example, by taking inappropriate or unilateral action, or by disagreeing about the best course of action).

> Mums, dads, mates, can give advice.
>
> (Boy, Year 5)

> I know that if I tell my parents, they'll believe me. There would be no question. And I know that if I wanted them to come to the school, they would.
>
> (Boy, Year 8)

The risk of not being believed by a parent was identified as potentially very hurtful. Some were also concerned that, by talking about bullying, they might start a family argument. Other pupils also said that they would not tell a parent if they were being bullied, because they would not want to worry them or put them under pressure.

> I wouldn't tell my mum. She'd skin them.
>
> (Girl, Year 5)

> Your mum and dad might disagree about what to do, and then start arguing, and then they say it's your fault. Telling your parents is a serious step. They might take action you don't want.
>
> (Boy, Year 8)

Seeking outside help

Pupils were asked if they would seek outside help to deal with bullying, such as talking to the police or a confidential telephone helpline. Pupils were also asked if there were any other sources of help they had found useful.

ChildLine

Pupils were divided about whether they would contact a telephone helpline, such as ChildLine. Younger pupils (39%) were considerably more likely to consider such an option than pupils in Year 8 (14%). Some pupils expressed the view that ChildLine might not know about the local context, and might therefore not be in a position to give constructive advice.

The police

Only a small minority of pupils would consider talking to the police about bullying, although younger pupils (33%) were more likely than older pupils (11%) to consider such action. Nevertheless, in a small number of cases, pupils reported that they had been encouraged by their teachers to contact the police for help. A number of risks and benefits were associated with contacting the police:

> You might have to go to court.
>
> (Girl, Year 8)

> I'd tell PC Smith. She would probably talk to them, and talk to their parents.
>
> (Girl, Year 8)

Telling a counsellor

In focus group discussions, a minority of pupils suggested that external counselling organisations might assist pupils to deal with bullying. In one focus group, pupils identified Child and Mental Health Services (CAMHS) as a proven and effective source of help, while others mentioned counsellors and advice agencies targeted at children and young people. In another focus group, pupils reported that they were aware that the NSPCC might be able to help with bullying. However, others expressed surprise at this suggestion, as they thought that the NSPCC only dealt with adults who were cruel to children.

> A cousin of mine was being bullied and had a black eye and things They told the NSPCC and it worked. I don't know what they did.
>
> (Boy, Year 5)

Confidential sources of support were also valued for enabling pupils to control the pace of disclosure. Equally important, no risks were associated with this course of action. Further, in the context of pupils' concerns about breaches of confidentiality on the part of teachers and parents, the wider availability of confidential sources of help and advice may prove a valuable anti-bullying strategy.

> If you talk to a counsellor, it's someone you don't know. They don't know your life story and they don't tell no one nothing, unless you're going to harm yourself or someone else. So it's completely confidential. They realise how you're feeling and it's a lot easier than talking to a parent or a teacher.
>
> (Girl, Year 8)

Conclusions

The findings of this research project indicated that, when thinking about how to respond to bullying, children and young people engage in a complex process of risk assessment. Pupils identified a number of different ways of tackling bullying and explored the anticipated advantages and disadvantages of each option. No tidy solutions or easy remedies were identified. Consequently, pupils' discussions about 'what works' in tackling bullying might more accurately be re-framed as 'what might work'.

Although it is common for adults to encourage pupils to report bullying, pupils of both age groups expressed a preference for 'sorting it out' and 'standing up for themselves'. Alternative strategies necessarily involve pupils in the dilemmas and consequences associated with 'telling'. It appears that, even if pupils decide to 'tell' an adult, they are very aware of the gap between how teachers and parents should respond to bullying, and how they actually respond. A pupil in Year 5 had this insight to offer on 'telling' and its aftermath:

> If the dinner ladies don't help you, tell your teacher. If the teacher doesn't help you, tell your mum. Then your mum will tell the headmistress. Then the headmistress will go and tell the parents of the bully. And the parents of the bully (pause)...well, some of the parents don't care and just say 'don't do it again'.
>
> (Boy, Year 5)

In listening to children and young people talk about bullying, it is clear that they receive a number of mixed messages from adults (teachers and parents). These mixed messages might be summarised as follows:

- Adults (teachers and parents) claimed that bullying is a serious or 'bad' thing, but pupils' experience is that bullying is often dismissed as 'child's play'.
- Pupils are encouraged to report incidents of bullying, but when they do, pupils frequently felt that they are not listened to or believed.
- Schools encouraged pupils to report bullying but are also perceived by pupils as unable to protect pupils from retaliatory action, particularly after school hours.
- Teaching involves working and forming relationships with pupils, yet often teachers were perceived as taking complaints made by parents more seriously than complaints made by pupils.

- Adults (teachers and parents) claimed that they could be trusted, but telling an adult about bullying was perceived as involving a risk that they would break promises of confidentiality.
- Adults often told pupils not to fight back, but pupils (particularly in Year 8) found that fighting back works sometimes.

These findings suggest that anti-bullying policies might be expected to have limited effect if they fail to take into account the realities of the child's social world. For this reason, it would seem appropriate for schools to consider more 'bottom up' (rather than 'top down') responses to bullying, that attempt to involve pupils in decision-making at an individual and school-wide level.

It is also clear that encouraging a child 'to tell' requires an adult willingness to listen. Often, pupils expressed a wish simply to speak to an adult in confidence, in order to unburden themselves, get advice and support, and to consider their options. Importantly, there were hardly any disadvantages and some considerable benefits associated with such a course of action, particularly in relation to pupils' emotional well-being.

Nevertheless, the findings indicate that anti-bullying policies provide a useful starting point for tackling bullying. Indeed, some pupils highlighted different approaches that were described as working at least some of the time (e.g. school councils, peer group initiatives, discussing bullying regularly during assemblies, and during class time). Pupils also recommended that anti-bullying initiatives should be sustained over the long term.

Chapter 25

Bullying and gender

Helen Taylor

It is important to be aware of the gendered dimension of bullying but it seems that bullying amongst boys has attracted most attention from schools and researchers. In this chapter, Helen Taylor, a researcher based at Cardiff University, reports on her study into the effect of gender on primary school bullying, particularly the difficulties that schools appear to have in identifying bullying amongst girls.

Introduction and context

Despite being a well-documented and recognised problem, bullying remains one of the major behavioural and disciplinary issues facing UK schools today. The media has reported extensively on the issue of school bullying and international academic research has been conducted into the issue since the 1970s. Charitable and voluntary organisations have put in place numerous campaigns to help combat the problem and provide support for victims of bullying. Even though some schools have developed effective interventions to reduce bullying over the last decade, it was not until September 1999 that schools had a legal responsibility to formulate and implement anti-bullying policies.

Definition of school bullying

Bullying can be defined as 'a subcategory of aggressive behaviour; but a particularly vicious kind of aggressive behaviour since it is directed, often repeatedly, towards a particular victim who is unable to defend himself or herself effectively' (Smith *et al.* 1999:1). School bullying is generally regarded as either taking the form of direct (physical) bullying or indirect (psychological) bullying. However, a more comprehensive classification of bullying has been devised by Bjorkqvist *et al.* (Bjorkqvist *et al.* 1992; Bjorkqvist *et al.* 1992; Lagerspetz *et al.* 1988). They classify types of bullying into three forms – physical aggression (i.e. hits, kicks, pushes), direct verbal aggression (i.e. insults, name-calling) and indirect aggression (i.e. social exclusion, nasty notes).

Emergence of research interest into school bullying

School bullying has emerged as a well-documented and researched issue. During the 1970s, Dan Olweus' (1973) book *Aggression in the Schools: Bullies and Whipping Boys* began a wave of research into school bullying. Olweus has conducted extensive research into the topic, particularly within Scandinavian countries. In Britain however, school bullying remained a low-key issue until the late 1980s. Britain's largest study into the issue was conducted in 1990. Sheffield University conducted research involving 7000 pupils and 24 schools. Disturbingly, the research revealed that in Britain ten per cent of primary schoolchildren and four per cent of secondary schoolchildren are bullied once a week.

Gender differences within school bullying

The effect of gender within school bullying has been highlighted as an important factor by previous research. There is a general consensus in the literature as to how gender differences are manifest (Lagerspetz *et al.* 1988; Bjorkqvist *et al.* 1992; Whitney and Smith 1993; Ahmed and Smith 1994; Siann *et al.* 1994; Boulton 1996; Torrance 1997). With relation to the extent of bullying, boys tend to experience bullying more than girls do. Boys are more likely to experience direct forms of bullying such as physical aggression or intimidation, whereas girls are more likely to experience indirect forms of bullying such as social exclusion and verbal forms of bullying such as teasing and taunting. Boys are more likely to admit to bullying others. Boys are more likely to report being bullied by one or several boys and girls are more likely to report being bullied by one or several girls or by both girls and boys. It is very rare for boys to report being bullied by one or several girls. Boys are more likely to report being bullied in locations away from the school.

Teachers' perceptions and experiences of school bullying

There is no reference to teachers' perceptions and experiences of gender differences within the literature. In fact, there is scant research on teachers' perceptions and experiences of school bullying generally. Furthermore, the research that has been conducted has generally involved small samples and revealed statistically insignificant findings.

Aims and objectives

The key aim of the study summarised in this paper was to examine the prevalence of bullying in primary schools since schools have been responsible for formulating anti-bullying policies, with particular regard to gender. The specific objectives were: to identify the incidence of gender differences amongst a sample of primary school children; to understand how primary school teachers perceive and experience gender differences; and to examine whether incidence of gender differences corresponded with teachers' perceptions and experiences. More broadly, the research also examined whether recognition and understanding of gender differences is important for developing effective anti-bullying strategies in primary schools.

Methods

The study adopted a case study approach in which a single primary school was researched. The case school was a mixed sex primary school. The school was made up of infant and middle school pupils from Year 1 to 6. Teaching staff consisted of the headmaster, deputy headmistress and nine teachers. A structured questionnaire was administered to 75 primary school children in Years 5 and 6 to establish levels of bullying and the incidence of gender differences (see Table 25.1). The questionnaire consisted of two parts. The first part of the questionnaire was designed to establish the extent to which girls and boys were bullied and whether this took the form of direct physical, direct verbal or indirect bullying. The second part of the questionnaire was designed to establish the extent to which girls and boys were bullying others and whether this took the form of direct physical, direct verbal and indirect bullying.

Table 25.1: Sample of children by year group and by gender

	Year 5	Year 6	Total
Boys	15	25	40
Girls	14	21	35
Total	29	46	75

Semi-structured questionnaires were administered to establish teachers' perceptions and experiences of gender differences in bullying. Eight teachers completed the questionnaire and two of these participated in additional semi-structured interviews. The questionnaire probed, via the use of both open and closed questions, teachers' perceptions and experiences of the effect of gender on bullying behaviour in their school. The semi-structured nature of the questionnaire meant that some answers were elaborated by examples and incidents they had experienced. The two follow-up interviews provided an opportunity to discuss the issues highlighted by the questionnaire with more depth and provided the study with rich data.

Table 25.2: Number of pupils being bullied by type of bullying and by gender

	Boys	Girls
Direct physical	36	19
Direct verbal	44	25
Indirect	23	12

Results

The key finding from the children's questionnaire indicated that boys were more involved in direct physical, direct verbal and indirect forms of bullying as both victims and bullies, than their female peers. The other two tables represent the number of boys and girls involved as either victim or bully in each of the three different types of bullying behaviour 'more than once during the week'. As can be seen in Table 25.2 the number of boys experiencing all kinds of bullying is almost double that experienced by girls. Even more interesting is that the number of girls involved in bullying others is extremely low compared with the boys, in all kinds of bullying (see Table 25.3).

Table 25.3: Number of pupils bullying others by type of bullying and by gender

	Boys	Girls
Direct physical	23	1
Direct verbal	27	8
Indirect	12	3

The key finding from the teachers' questionnaire and follow-up interviews indicated that the teachers' perceptions and experiences reflected the well-documented gender differences found by earlier research, but did *not* correspond with the actual incidence of gender differences in their own school as reported by the pupils.

This discrepancy can be substantiated with reference to the following key questionnaire results:

- Four teachers thought that bullying was more typical of boys than girls and four teachers that bullying was not more typical of boys.
- All eight teachers said that boys were involved in direct physical forms of bullying as both bully and victim. Four teachers said that girls were involved in indirect forms of bullying (namely social exclusion) as both bully and victim. Six teachers said that girls were involved in verbal bullying as both bully and victim, whereas only three teachers said this of boys.
- The same four teachers, who said that bullying was not more typical of girls, were the same four teachers who said that girls were involved in indirect forms of bullying.
- Six teachers perceived boys and girls to be equally likely to admit to being bullied and two teachers perceived girls to be more likely to admit to being bullied.
- Five teachers perceived boys and girls to be equally likely to admit to bullying others and one teacher thought this true of boys and one teacher thought this true of girls.
- Only three of the teachers thought that an understanding of gender differences would be helpful in the development of anti-bullying strategies in primary schools.

The points shown in the above questionnaire results were elaborated on within the interviews. One interviewee stressed the fact that girls were a bit more ready to discuss worries, suggesting that girls were more likely to admit to being bullied.

> I've found that girls are a little more ready to tell you if there is a problem, if there is something going wrong or if they are unhappy or if someone is being picked on.

The interviewee also said that boys are less ready to admit to being bullied.

> I find that it's a bit sort of that they don't like to admit that they could be a victim perhaps, whereas the girls seem more willing to come and tell you about it.

The school had set up a 'School Watch Committee' to help pupils deal with bullying problems and the interviewee noted that within this system, 'there just appears to be a larger queue of girls than boys.'

Discussion and implications

There are two possible reasons for the very low level of girls who reported being a bully and the failure of the teachers to note this. Firstly, the girls simply may have carried out less bullying or secondly, the girls were reluctant to admit to bullying others. The possibility that girls within the sample were reluctant to admit to being involved in bullying is further strengthened by previous research that has shown similar results. Siann *et al.* (1994) showed that girls reported significantly lower levels than boys of carrying out all types of bullying. They found that boys experienced physical bullying and the girls 'mental bullying', but found that girls were reluctant to admit to bullying others. Paradoxically, this present study shows that teachers suggest that girls can be more open about bullying and therefore more likely to admit to being involved in bullying.

A further interesting point shown from this present study suggests that teachers, who are not aware that girls are involved in indirect forms of bullying, perceive bullying to be more typical of boys (the four teachers in the study who said that girls were involved in indirect forms of bullying were the same four teachers who said that bullying was not more typical of boys). In fact, it is not that bullying is more typical of boys, it is just that boys' bullying (i.e. direct types) is easier to identify and therefore teachers perceive bullying to be more typical amongst boys than girls. Furthermore, this has serious implications for the likeliness of intervention by teachers. Since boys' bullying is more direct and more noticeable, teachers are more likely to be able to identify it and consequently intervene in it. A recent study (Craig *et al.* 2000) on prospective teachers' views on bullying showed that physical types of aggression were labelled more often as bullying, were viewed more seriously and were more likely to warrant intervention than verbal aggression. These findings suggest that teachers may require further training in bullying issues, particularly with regard to identifying and dealing with girls' involvement.

This present study implies that the development of anti-bullying policies should take into consideration the gendered nature of bullying issues. Anti-bullying strategies should be particularly focused on girls' experiences of bullying. Interestingly, research has shown that conventional anti-bullying strategies are less effective at reducing rates of bullying amongst girls (Eslea and Smith 1998). Eslea and Smith (1998) conducted research to ascertain the effectiveness of anti-bullying work in primary schools. In the four schools that were involved in their research, all four had reduced bullying among boys, but three experienced a rise in bullying among girls.

Despite being small-scale, the study noted in this paper does highlight some interesting and serious points and areas for further investigation and consideration. The research clearly highlights the need for further extensive research into the gendered nature of bullying in primary schools, particularly with reference to teachers' perceptions and experiences of bullying.

References

Ahmed, Y. and Smith, P.K. (1994) 'Bullying in schools and the issue of sex differences', in: J. Archer, (ed), *Male Violence*. Routledge: London.

Bjorkqvist, K., Lagerspetz, K.M. and Kaukiainen, A. (1992) 'Do girls manipulate and boys fight? Developmental trends in regard to direct and indirect aggression', *Aggressive Behaviour*, **18**, 117–27.

Bjorkqvist, K., Osterman, K. and Kaukiainen, A. (1992) 'The development of direct and indirect aggressive strategies in males and females', in: K. Bjorkqvist and P. Niemala (eds), *Of Mice and Men: Aspects of Female Aggression*. Orlando: Academic Press.

Boulton, M. (1996) 'Bullying in Mixed Sex Groups of Children', *Educational Psychology*, **16** (4), 439–43.

Craig, W.M., Henderson, K. and Murphy, J.G. (2000) Prospective teachers' attitudes toward bullying and victimization', *School Psychology International*, **21** (1), 5–21.

Eslea, M and Smith, P.K. (1998) 'The long term effectiveness of anti-bullying work in primary schools', *Educational Research*, **40** (2), 203–18.

Lagerspetz, K.M., Bjorkqvist, K. and Peltonen, T. (1988) 'Is indirect aggression typical of females? Sex differences in aggressiveness in 11–12 year old children', *Aggressive Behaviour*, **14**, 403–14.

Olweus, D. (1978: original Swedish version 1973) *Aggression in the Schools: Bullies and Whipping Boys*. Washington DC: Hemisphere.

Siann, G. *et al.* (1994) 'Who gets bullied? The effect of school, gender and ethnic group', *Educational Research*, **36** (2), 123–33.

Smith, P.K. *et al.* (ed.), (1999) *The Nature of School Bullying: a Cross-national Perspective*. Routledge: London.

Smith, P.K. and Levan, S. (1995) 'Perceptions and experiences of bullying in younger pupils', *British Journal of Educational Psychology*, **65**, 489–500.

Torrance, D.A. (1997) 'Do you want to be in my gang? A study of the existence and effects of bullying in a primary school class', *British Journal of Special Education*, **24** (4), 158–62.

Whitney, I. and Smith, P.K. (1993) 'A survey of the nature and extent of bullying in junior, middle and secondary schools', *Educational Research*, **35** (1), 3–25.

Chapter 26

Boys don't cry

Pete Johnson

Pete Johnson has written a number of story books about bullying. In this chapter, he discusses reasons why boys may be particularly vulnerable as victims. He cites two reasons: firstly, their tendency to keep things bottled up; and secondly, the concern of being 'shamed up' within their peer group if they draw attention to their plight.

'But why can't boys tell if they're being bullied?' This was the question a teacher asked during a recent class discussion of my novel, *Traitor*. The boys all looked at each other before answering, then one said, quietly. 'It's just too shaming, Miss.'

Another added. 'If he'd been punched in the face he could say something: but not if someone had just been nasty to him.'

In *Traitor*, Tom is regularly intimidated and picked on by a gang on the way home from school. Yet, he cannot bring himself to tell anyone. The overwhelming majority of boys agreed they wouldn't either.

In my new book, *Avenger*, I've explored this theme further. What I've written about here is psychological bullying, or, as boys dub it, 'trying to get inside your head'.

Of course, the myth is that only girls go in for this sort of thing. Boys will settle all their disputes with a swift punch. But that really isn't true. Certainly the boys I interviewed while researching *Avenger* had many stories to tell me of 'mind games'. For instance, how stories are spread about you. Everything from saying you've got fleas, to making up nasty comments about your mum. Others told me of how they'd been deliberately excluded from playing football at lunchtime, or from a party, or from an outing with a group of mates.

We tend to think of girls' friendships as being emotionally charged, while boys' relationships with each other are much more casual. Again, that isn't really true. Boys do have a much keener sense of who their 'best mates' are than might be commonly supposed. And a number spoke of attempts to 'break up' a friendship by 'making up stuff that I'd never actually said'. This aroused especial passion with one boy declaring: 'I swear on my life I never rubbished my mates like he said I did.'

Then there is the silent treatment. This actually happened to me when I started at a new school. A small group of boys decided I was 'big-headed' and all the boys in my year 'sent me to Coventry'. Even boys I'd been quite friendly with had to join in. Each day this went on seemed to last for about five years. Yet, I didn't tell anyone. I just put on a mask and acted as if I wasn't the least bit bothered. But inside, I was seething with hurt and anger. So much has changed since I was at school. Yet, boys still feel they have to suffer in silence and cannot open up about emotional problems.

In *Avenger*, Gareth upsets the charismatic new-boy, Jake. He tells Gareth: 'This is war now' and sets about playing a series of vicious mind games on him. Nevertheless, his form teacher never notices any of it. As Gareth writes: 'It was all smuggled past her. But every day more invisible blows rained down on me. There was never any let-up.'

In the end Gareth barricades himself inside his bedroom. In a blaze of frustration he started pounding his fist against the wall as hard as he could. 'But my anger didn't subside. It grew stronger. It was like some great tornado, whirling and raging about inside me which just had to be released.'

Later he slips under the cover of his bed. 'All I wanted now was to live in this bed forever. My anger was at last ebbing away but I didn't feel calm and peaceful – just totally, totally defeated.' Or, as one boy put it: 'You just want to hide away in your bedroom and never come out again.'

A few boys I interviewed did have a close mate they could completely trust. But the most common person boys seemed able to confide in was a grand-parent. In *Avenger*, Gareth's grandfather becomes his only confidant.

Each night Gareth tells his grandfather what has happened. Only his grandfather is dead. But Gareth still feels he is close-by and says: 'Please come back properly. I need to talk to you urgently. You're my only hope.'

I've already had some interesting discussions in schools about Gareth's feeling of total isolation. 'It's sad,' said one boy, 'that he thinks he can only talk to a ghost about what's happened.' We also talked about Jake and his behaviour. One boy comments: 'People don't act the way he does unless they're feeling bad themselves.'

The really great thing about stories is they enable us to make connections with the characters. And we discover we're not on our own and share much more than we realise.

Can stories also change the culture? I believe they can. And I'd like to think *Avenger* will play a part in challenging the view that boys – if they are to keep their cred – must act as if they're detached from all human emotion. As one boy wrote to me. 'The worst thing of all was not telling anyone how I felt. So the pain inside me just grew and grew.'

Chapter 27

Calm, purposeful, happy

Stephen Lunn

Stephen Lunn, research fellow at The Open University, kept a journal whilst working as a learning support assistant (LSA). This chapter reveals how it is to be at the 'deep end' supporting a child who finds it extremely difficult to comply with the expectations of school. It also identifies some of the dilemmas that confront LSAs when they act as 'intermediaries' building close relationships with children, but also working within the curriculum and behaviour framework which is provided by teachers.

Grant, a jazz aficionado, began singing 'There may be trouble ahead', as his recent friend Matthew went round the class selling 'Hope' ribbons in aid of Dr Barnardo's, at 50p each, during morning registration. What Grant knew that the rest of us didn't, was that Matthew was running a scam – the money was destined for his pocket rather than a good cause. There certainly was trouble ahead, and trouble behind, and the song became Grant's theme tune for much of the school year.

My first day

I started work as a part-time LSA at the school the day before Matthew arrived. Christine, the SENCO (Special Educational Needs Co-ordinator), gave me a brief sketch of his background and explained my duties. Matthew had been assessed as violent, disruptive and low attaining when in Year 2, and in the subsequent four years had been excluded from six schools in five LEA areas. He brought with him a statement of special educational needs made earlier in the term, at the time of his 11th birthday.

My duties included meeting Matthew at the school gates at 8.45 each morning and supporting him through assembly and registration. Matthew would be at school for the mornings only, until he felt ready for more. Christine introduced me to some other LSAs and gave me copies of Matthew's statement and an IEP (Individual Education Plan) that she had drawn up for him. At the time I understood the words but not what they really meant: that would become clearer as the months passed.

Meeting Matthew

Christine and I met with Matthew and his mother in the 'quiet room', a room set aside for individual work. He was a slight, pale, blond boy with hooded, grey eyes. He had chronic asthma, hunched posture and nails bitten to the quick. My first impression was of a small, cowed, frightened child, and a kind but exasperated parent whose resources were all but exhausted. Matthew avoided eye contact and conversation: he was soon ranging round the room looking into drawers and cupboards, but settled down and began to play absorbedly when he found a box of Lego. We discussed how he would get to school: his mother wanted transport provided, but he lived within three miles so would have to walk. He would not be allowed out of school during school hours without written permission.

His mother's plan was that he would leave home at about 7.30 a.m. in order to arrive for registration at 8.45. In practice he often arrived 30 to 60 minutes late, and spending two hours covering two miles gave ample opportunity for mischief en route.

Matthew, being 11, would join a Year 6 class. As Christine and his mother talked, I joined him with the Lego®, and soon we were engrossed in a bridge-building project. From that point on we almost always worked together well on a one-to-one basis in the quiet room, which became a refuge in difficult times, and a daily reward for sustained effort on Matthew's part – on many occasions we gritted out the last twenty minutes of a maths lesson on the understanding that we would spend the half-hour before lunch there.

By the end of his second week Matthew was ready to start full-time. Unsurprisingly, he made friends with three or four boys always in for a laugh with whom he would sit if given the chance. More surprisingly, he also formed a friendship with the popular Laura, an able girl who played for the school soccer and netball teams.

Classroom life

The class teacher, Mr T, was firm and fair, and Matthew got on well with him. Year 6 was 'setted' for English, maths and science: Matthew joined the lower set for each. This meant that for English he was in Mr T's group, which was fine: in maths and science he was with Miss J, a semi-permanent supply teacher, which was not so good. It was in the first science lesson of his second week that we had our first real crisis. Up to this point I had applied gentle but absolutely firm pressure to keep him on task as long as seemed reasonable, negotiating units of work and periods of escape in the quiet room. On this occasion conflict arose between my duty to Matthew and my duty to the teacher.

Pupils were allowed to sit where they wanted, and Matthew gravitated to a table in the back corner, with Grant, Gareth and Simon. Grant, the jazz lover, was bright, with a cruel streak. He was learning to play drums, but was not much interested in learning anything else. He had a great talent for stirring things up, dropping out of sight at the crucial moment, and coming up looking innocent. Gareth watched everything with a broad good-natured grin. He moved slowly, and was often the only one left to carry the can when authority arrived. He never engaged with any work other than the most simple and repetitive tasks. Simon was a bright boy who seemed to be trying to buy street cred with persistent mild naughtiness that never quite came off.

Matthew and I joined this group. The lesson was about nutrition, and the teacher handed out tracing paper and sheets containing pie charts showing what sources contributed what proportions of our energy, protein, calcium, iron, vitamin B1 and vitamin C requirements. The pupils' task for the lesson was to trace these pie charts into their science books.

This task was right up Gareth's street, and his grin widened as he slowly adjusted his tracing paper over the worksheet, and slowly followed the lines underneath with his pencil. Though Matthew rolled his eyes heavenward at Grant, they all made a start. However, this task was anathema to Matthew, involving as it did reading, writing, and close control of eye, hand and pencil. Soon he complained that it was boring, and that he could not see the point of it. He kept making mistakes, rubbing out, starting again, and was getting frustrated. I tried to maintain my 'gentle but firm pressure' to keep him on task, but my heart was not in it. I could not help thinking that, as a Year 6 science activity, tracing pie charts left something to be desired – there was no discussion of the content, before or after the activity, and privately I shared Matthew's view that it was boring.

Eventually Matthew stood up, said: 'I ain't doing it!', and headed for the door. Grant caught him on the back of the head with an eraser, which Miss J did not see. However, she did see Matthew pick it up and throw it back at Grant, before continuing towards the door. Miss J shouted angrily for him to return to his place, and Matthew took one look and bolted. I apologised to Miss J and went to find him and calm him down.

I found him hunched up at the bottom of the stairwell, sobbing. I suggested a visit to the quiet room, but there was a meeting going on, so we climbed back up the stairs to our science lesson. We found the room in modest uproar. Miss J was talking to a group of girls at the front, with her back to the rest of the class. Quite a few things were being thrown to and fro, no one was working. Matthew and I returned to our table to join the three boys. I felt that I was in a difficult position. Did I ignore what was going on, thereby almost sanctioning it? Or did I intervene, thereby undermining the teacher's authority? In the event I did a bit of both: I intervened as far as our table was concerned, and ignored the rest of it.

On our table no one had actually got as far as transferring any part of a pie chart into their science book, and I felt unequal to trying to force them to do so. Instead I tried asking them if they knew what nutrients did, and in particular what would happen to you if you did not get particular nutrients. The gory details of scurvy and rickets kept them interested and engaged until the end of the lesson. I emerged from it feeling confused, feeling that I had not dealt straight with any party, and feeling guilty in several ways: towards the teacher, a professional, for having subverted what I had judged to be a poor lesson, and for having communicated this judgement willy-nilly to the pupils, thus undermining what respect they had for her; and towards the pupils, for having appeared to take their side, while actually engaging them in what I thought was useful learning. Looking back on this now, I still feel guilty, still puzzle about what I could and should have done.

Hearing voices

On a Tuesday morning in early December Matthew arrived looking bruised and battered, with one very black eye. He had missed Monday because of a visit to a psychiatrist at a nearby children's hospital, following what Christine called 'a psychotic episode' over the weekend. As Matthew later described it, the voices that normally only whispered had started shouting and screaming at him about death. His bruises came from punching his head to try to stop the voices. We spent most of Tuesday in the quiet room playing games, listening to music on the radio, playing on the computer. At one point he stopped in the middle of a game and held out his hand, saying 'My hand is shaking'. He seemed more puzzled than disturbed by this. He was very low, humble in his sadness and fear. I was afraid too, and felt that I was being asked to deal with something far beyond my competence.

Christine, the SENCO, joined us to help, later in the morning. She suggested we try to help Matthew develop a strategy for dealing with the screaming voices. Matthew was a Liverpool fan, and the plan we ended up with was that, when the voices threatened, he was to imagine that he was playing up front for Liverpool, at Anfield, in an end-of-season decider for the championship. The score was 1:1 and there were only minutes to go. Matthew received the ball and was through on goal. He ran in, scored in the top corner, and the crowd in the Kop roared. And the roar of the crowd was so loud that it drowned out the voices.

I do not know whether it worked; but the voices were not mentioned again.

One step forward, one step back

In our sessions in the quiet room we worked mostly on reading schemes and literacy workbooks. Working on the computer was Matthew's favourite activity, and tended to be held back as a reward for some less enjoyable achievement. He liked playing games or using a 'paint' programme – until he discovered Logo (a programming language that can be used to control a floor-crawling 'turtle' robot, or to create patterns on screen). I had been a computer programmer in an earlier life, but had never used Logo or anything similar, so we explored together. Matthew enjoyed it, but crossed a threshold of enthusiasm when he discovered 'procedures'.

A procedure is a sub-program that a higher level program can 'call': for example, a program building up a picture of a house and garden could call 'square' and 'flower' procedures to draw these things in appropriate places. A procedure can be called with 'parameters' that tailor its general purpose, for instance, that can say how big, what colour, where to start from. A procedure can call other procedures, to any number of levels. It is a simple, powerful, elegant concept that is tremendously liberating and empowering to the programmer, a bit like learning to fly. Matthew saw this and took off, soon producing magnificent swirling mandalas of colour that grew and morphed on the screen in front of us.

At about the same time, Matthew had a good run of punctuality and better focus in lessons, especially in maths. One morning he rattled through the two worksheets, with almost no help from me. He was the first to finish, and proudly took his book out to Miss J for marking. He had got them all right, and was awarded '1 Merit'.

Later that term a boy called Darren arrived at the school and joined another Year 6 class. His history was not dissimilar to Matthew's, and he too had an LSA, Martina. Darren's arrival coincided with the early retirement of the head and two new appointments. The head of the nearby comprehensive was appointed acting head while continuing in post at the upper school; and Catharine McGivan was appointed deputy head.

Darren was lawlessness personified – Matthew was fascinated. They would meet up on their way to school, and arrive an hour or more late, with an increasingly worrying daily addition to the items that they had 'found' – car keys, a briefcase, bicycle lamps still in their packaging, knives, lighters. Martina and I confiscated anything dangerous, and started to keep a record of 'found' items. Darren and Matthew would get together and get involved in something almost every break-time. Once, when they had an inexhaustible supply of cigarette lighters, they set fire to some waste ground; were seen smoking, and set bales of hay alight in a field beyond the school grounds.

The caretaker's keys

The new deputy, Mrs McGivan, had just redefined the school rules and disciplinary procedures, and these began to bite with Matthew and Darren. Martina and I had to keep one or other in at break so they could not meet; lateness in returning from breaks was to be punished with detention; persistent problems were to be escalated from LSA to class teacher to SENCO to deputy head to head.

One Wednesday morning Matthew arrived before me. He left his bag in the quiet room and told the secretary he was going out to play. He came back half an hour later having 'found' some batteries, of a type kept in the science stock cupboard. This cupboard was usually kept locked. Later that morning we were working in the quiet room when Christine called me aside to say that the caretaker's keys had been taken from his coat in the staff cloakroom, earlier that morning, and asking me to keep a close eye on Matthew. For the rest of the week it was clear that something was going on between Darren and Matthew, which culminated on Friday with Darren threatening Matthew, and chasing him out of school, pursued by several of us until they were lost to sight. They did not return, and parents and police were informed.

The following Monday Matthew arrived on time, with his mother. Christine and I met them in the quiet room. Matthew had 'as good as' told his mother that he had taken the keys to the science cupboard and given them to Darren, who had 'thrown them in a stream'. She asked us if Matthew and Darren could be kept apart. Christine said we would continue to try. Matthew seemed quite light-hearted that day, in lessons. He concentrated well during a maths test. In the library he selected a book and grinned at me as he showed me the title – *Cops and Robbers*. In the afternoon his mother was back again, this time for a progress review. The conclusion was that academically he was progressing. However, his writing and spelling were poor and his behaviour was unpredictable.

His mother added that he liked coming to school, and Matthew's own contribution was: 'My behaviour is improving. I enjoy school. I am improving in reading and writing. I'm good at maths.' It was decided to continue with full-time LSA support; to institute a formal rewards system, including rewards for time-keeping; to keep Matthew away from Darren; and to 'develop strategies to prevent him running away from school'.

The following morning the disciplinary process caught up with Matthew. When we arrived in class for registration, Mr T handed me a note from the deputy head, asking me to take Matthew down to see her immediately. Matthew gave an 'O-oh', and Grant accompanied us out of the door with 'There may be trouble ahead...'

Mrs McGivan told him that it was known with certainty that he was responsible for stealing the caretaker's keys; that as a punishment for that and for running out of school, he would be kept in at break and lunchtime for the rest of the week; and that he was to spend the first lesson in the head's office, writing an account of why he ran away. He continued to deny taking the keys, refused to write anything. Mrs McGivan told him that he could not stay at school if he refused to do as he was asked, and phoned his mother to ask her to come and fetch him.

At that point Mrs McGivan had to teach. She asked me to meet Matthew's mother and explain why he was being sent home. Matthew listened in glum silence.

His mother arrived but Matthew continued to protest his innocence. His mother did not say much, but accepted that Matthew had to go home now, and that the school could not accept him back until he agreed to abide by instructions. Matthew seemed genuinely contrite, apologising for his behaviour, and agreeing that he would come back tomorrow with a genuine attempt to change his attitude. Later that day I phoned Matthew's mother. She said he was genuinely sorry, and would come in tomorrow with a different attitude. She had impressed on him that he would not only be expelled, but might also be taken from her into council care. Thus it was a subdued Matthew who arrived with his mother the following morning. They were asked to see the head and deputy, who reiterated yesterday's messages. Matthew apologised and accepted the conditions of his return. The detentions were to start immediately: I would sit with him in morning break while he worked through maths and English worksheets; the deputy head would look after him at lunchtime.

When we came out of the meeting, Matthew and I had a breather in the quiet room, then rejoined the class for maths. We sat at our table and Matthew got out his worksheet, then leapt up and ran out of the room, coming back moments later eating a large bread roll. I felt that this was a critical period, and told him firmly that he was not to go out without permission; that he was not to eat during lessons; and that he was to do as I asked immediately or he would be sent straight to Mrs McGivan. He shrugged, gave me a tiny smile, put away his lunch, turned to his maths worksheet, and started working intently. I was very relieved.

There but for the grace of God . . .

Later in that lesson the maths test from earlier in the week was handed out. It was a 'mock' national test paper, and Matthew had done well. However, we agreed that he would begin his morning break detentions by working on this paper again, with support, and that we would keep on doing it until he got it completely right.

At break we were sitting outside the staff room near a window working through the test. We were shocked to see a computer monitor fall from a window on the upper floor, hitting the ground not far from us, soon followed by a box full of exercise books and other objects.

Darren had been scheduled for interviews with the head and deputy of a similar nature to Matthew's, and had reacted by running berserk through the school, causing widespread damage. Darren's mother and most of the staff were by now watching with us. Soon we saw a window of the quiet room open and Darren jump out. At the same time a police car drew up and two officers got out. They grabbed Darren and pushed him, struggling, into the back seat of the car. He scuttled across the seat and got out on the other side, running for the school field, pursued by the policemen. He dodged and ducked until he was restrained and driven away with his mother. That was the last we saw of him.

Matthew had watched all this open-mouthed. Afterwards he was subdued. It could easily have been him in the police car but but he was still in the school and had another chance.

A new beginning

Life as Matthew's LSA was never going to be uniformly smooth, but from that moment on he really did seem to change. He would now do as he was told, albeit sometimes reluctantly. He did work hard, and he did keep out of serious trouble. By mid summer term his literacy tests were showing improved ability at reading, writing and spelling. He missed the English Key Stage 2 national tests, but did well in maths and science. He was no longer conspicuously academically inferior to his peers, and this was enormously important to him.

I stayed in touch with Matthew's career when we both moved on at the end of the year. He had full-time LSA support through Year 7 and continued to progress. The following year his support was reduced, and later withdrawn. At the time of writing he had completed his secondary education without any serious trouble, and was employed on the ground staff of the local football club. He may not have become the 'calm, purposeful, happy' person of the school's motto, but he wasn't far off.

Chapter 28

Supporting learning and behaviour

Janet Kay

Given the numbers of children in schools there is always a need to maintain good standards of behaviour so that no one comes to any physical or emotional harm, and moreover, to enable education to proceed. In this chapter, Janet Kay, lecturer in the School of Education and Social Science, University of Derby, examines a sweep of themes of relevance to a productive classroom and school environment.

Introduction

Good standards of behaviour are not just about the actions of individual children or groups of children. Developing good standards of behaviour is part of children's learning, and how effectively this learning takes place depends very much on how behaviour is managed across the whole school.

In this chapter, we will explore the factors that contribute to problems with behaviour across the school, and the ways in which this might affect children's learning. The role of the teaching assistant in contributing to whole school development in this area is discussed. The teaching assistant's responsibilities are discussed in the context of their role within the school and their relationship with the class teacher. Behavioural factors influencing the effectiveness of work with individual children and groups are discussed. The development of a framework of rules and policies within school, which support and promote good standards of behaviour, is discussed. Strategies for dealing with potential and actual conflict are explored, along with limitations on the teaching assistant's role in managing behaviour in school. The various approaches to supporting children in difficulties, dealing with distressed children, and working with children to modify their behaviour are also examined.

A key theme is the development of interpersonal skills for supporting effective behaviour management. These include good communication, responsiveness, developing positive relationships with children and using disciplinary measures appropriately.

Policies and rules

Every school should have a policy on behaviour which clearly outlines the expectations placed on pupils within the school. This policy is drawn up and approved by the governing body, including the headteacher. Parents are usually asked to comment on the policy and contribute to developing it over time. School behaviour policies are important in terms of creating a common standard which can be worked towards by all sectors of the school community. However, like all policies, the value of a behaviour policy can only be measured by the extent to which it is implemented. Put simply, a policy is merely a piece of paper unless action is taken to make sure that the proposals within it are put into practice. Policies on behaviour tend to give an outline of expectations of children's behaviour and when and how disciplinary measures will be taken. These policies are supported by home–school agreements, which are contracts signed by parents and children, stating that they agree to abide by certain rules within school. These include, amongst other things, standards of expected behaviour. Home–school agreements are not compulsory, but are used as a method of stating what the school expects from parents and pupils, and what parents and pupils can expect from the school. Research into home-school agreements, which were introduced in all schools in 1999, has shown, however, that not all schools have found them helpful or influential in improving standards of behaviour (Parker-Jenkins *et al.* 2001). Because they are not compulsory, many do not get signed or returned to school, and the conditions within them are not binding. However, home–school agreements may fulfil an important function in raising the issue of standards and expectations within schools and between schools and parents.

[...]

Children need to know what is expected of them in order to behave well. Learning school rules can take time and children may be worried about breaking rules because they do not really know what the rules are. [...] For young children just entering school, there is a need to explain rules patiently and repeatedly until they start to understand what is expected. Children may not have had previous experiences of having to be quiet and sit still for the length of time school sometimes demands of them. They may have to learn about turn taking, lining up and putting their hands up. They may not remember that it is a good idea to go to the toilet at break time. [...]

School policies are an important starting point for developing a whole school approach to generating good standards of behaviour and positive social attitudes. However, they are not much use unless all school staff, parents and children are aware of the policies and are actively involved in developing them.

[...]

Dealing with conflict

Conflict between individuals or groups within the school community can be a major source of disruption to the smooth and harmonious atmosphere in which children learn best. Dealing with conflict either between children or between you and a child is one of the most important skills for managing behaviour in schools. Conflict is almost inevitable in any situation where there are a lot of children and adults together in an enclosed space. This is not peculiar to schools. Parents will often state that conflict between siblings is a major source of disruption in the home.

However, there are strategies for both reducing the chances of conflict developing, and dealing with conflict effectively when it arises, which can be learned and used with the children you work with. Conflict is not always a negative aspect of any group relationship. It can be used positively to air differing views and ideas and to create and promote debate. However, conflict can be damaging if it is mishandled or someone 'loses' or is hurt physically or emotionally.

What is conflict?

Conflict can be expressed verbally or physically, although sometimes it is not expressed at all. It is about the tension between two or more individuals, based on some form of disagreement. It can be temporary or long term and it can arise for all sorts of major or trivial reasons. Some children are more likely to be involved in open conflict than others. Some may appear never to get involved in conflict at all. The ways in which different children express conflict may depend on what they have learned from the adults around them and their own personality and characteristics. Conflict can be healthy, in terms of the expression of different viewpoints and the ability to express these. However, conflict can be damaging when it is expressed in personal terms, when it goes on over a period of time or when it involves harm to an individual.

Preventing conflict arising

We can never hope to eradicate conflict from the school altogether. However, it is possible to create an environment within school where conflict is reduced, where it is healthy, and where it is resolved quickly without harm to individuals. Where school development is crucial to this process, based on promoting positive relationships between adults and children, founded on mutual respect and consideration. This type of development does not take place overnight but is part of a more general ethos which needs to be constantly renewed and reviewed. Some elements of this whole school ethos could include:

- developing good relationships with children through communication, active listening and an interest in the individual child
- showing respect for all children and adults within the school
- taking action to reduce racism and discrimination within the school
- fostering a climate in which children are encouraged to help and support fellow pupils and adults model this behaviour
- creating and promoting clearly defined standards of behaviour and ensuring that these are part of the high expectations of children in the school
- developing strategies to deal with unacceptable behaviour and applying these in a timely and consistent way
- involving parents in discussions and strategies to develop the whole school ethos.

It is vitally important that you model these types of behaviour in your work with the children, demonstrating good practice in your relationships with others and a calm, problem-solving approach to any difficulties which arise. Receiving respect from others is important in building young children's confidence and their belief in themselves as valued beings; therefore it is important to maintain respectful relationships with the children you work with.

It is also important to consider your self-presentation. Children will respond better to adults around them who behave in authoritative ways and who present themselves as confident and coping. It helps to be firm and calm in your dealings with children and to demonstrate that you do not need to get angry or shout to ensure the children pay attention and respond appropriately to you. Positive, confident body language and open, confident facial expressions can reinforce an effective personal presence. A calm tone and relaxed manner can help children to learn to trust you and to gain respect for your authority.

A positive, problem-solving environment in school, in which opportunities are taken to discuss and explore difficult issues, either one to one or in circle time or assembly, will contribute to reducing the incidence of conflict. However, children bring many worries, problems and difficulties to school, as well as those that develop at school, and inevitably some conflict will arise.

Dealing with conflict in school

Conflict most commonly arises between children, but can arise between teaching assistants and a child or children. Dealing with conflict between children needs patience, sensitivity and tact to ensure that positive solutions are found and implemented. Not all conflict requires adult intervention. Unless a child is becoming distressed or there is physical aggression it may be better on many occasions to let children work out their differences themselves. In this way, children learn about compromise and negotiation, controlling their stronger emotions and altruistic behaviour. It is important that young children have the opportunity to do this, as a significant contribution to their social development. Children of school age often have the skills and maturity to sort out short-term conflicts between themselves. However, adults should always intervene when:

- conflict between the same individuals persists
- there is bullying
- any child is becoming distressed or humiliated
- there is physical aggression
- other children are becoming involved or distressed.

Strategies for intervention will obviously vary, depending on the situation, the age of the children and the type of conflict. Power-assertion techniques, such as shouting at the children, may be successful in the short term, but do not solve the longer-term problems that have caused the conflict in the first place. In order to do this, it is important to consider causes and motivations and to ensure that the outcomes of conflict resolution are going to be positive for all involved. A good solution is one where there are no 'winners' and 'losers' but where all involved gain from behaving in different ways.

There are a number of stages to dealing with conflict, which may include:

- stopping aggressive verbal or physical behaviour and ensuring all children's safety as a priority
- communicating with the children about their behaviour and the reasons for it
- listening to the children and accepting their feelings about the situation
- looking for the underlying problems which are causing the conflict
- seeking solutions that help everyone involved to behave and feel better, and which reduce the chances of further conflict.

[...]

Children and adults may sometimes get into conflict and this may need dealing with in a similar way to conflict between children. If a child is angry or aggressive, it is important to:

- remain calm and in control, never become aggressive
- seek help if necessary
- talk to the child and listen to him/her
- acknowledge that the child is upset and try to encourage him/her to share his/her feelings
- try to remove oneself and the child to a quiet place
- try to get other children to move away.

It may be necessary to involve others in an incident to ensure that it does not escalate and that it is dealt with appropriately and within the law and policy guidelines. Teachers are permitted to restrain children physically in certain limited circumstances, to avoid harm to the child, other children or adults, or property. If a child becomes physically aggressive, it is very important to seek help immediately from the teacher and to ensure that other children are removed from the vicinity as quickly as possible. Any such incident should be recorded and discussed with the teacher and possibly the headteacher so that strategies to avoid a repetition can be developed, and parents informed.

[...]

Dealing with other types of unwanted behaviour

In this section we will explore effective responses to a range of more general unwanted behaviour in children. In order to provide children with an effective learning environment, there needs to be order and discipline in schools. Children should not be fearful or oppressed by rules and disciplinary measures, but should be taught to recognize the benefits of an orderly environment. Children learn positive social values such as self-discipline, concern for others, helpfulness and respect for others from being in a school where values are part of their wider learning. Discussions about values, what is expected and what is unacceptable, are part of the day-to-day learning about good behaviour which young children need.

Inevitably, there will be some unwanted behaviour among children in primary schools. Young children are still learning a great deal about accepted social behaviour at this age. There are many variations in the level of maturity among children in the infant stage. They may know what is expected of them but occasionally forget. They may be testing the boundaries to see if they are firm. They may he bored or tired, or upset about something at school or at home. They may be confused or uncertain about the activity they are supposed to be doing, or unable to understand what is expected of them. They may need help, but not feel confident about asking for it. Or they may want to attract more attention from other children or adults because they feel forgotten or ignored. The sorts of behaviour that are expected of children within the home also vary, So that there may be disparities between what is expected at home and school for some children.

There are many reasons why children behave in unwanted ways. There are also many different possible responses to unwanted behaviour, which may have different outcomes. It is important to recognize that most young children need support and help to behave well, rather than criticism, harsh discipline or condemnation. Some basic principles for dealing with unwanted behaviour include:

- Criticize the behaviour not the child.
- Explain to the child why the behaviour is not acceptable.
- Do not describe the child in negative terms e.g. 'silly girl'.
- Listen to the child's explanation.
- Use firm tones, but do not shout or raise your voice.

- Be clear about the behaviour that is expected.
- Praise and encourage desired behaviour to help children understand what is expected of them and to 'reward' them for meeting those expectations.
- Do not humiliate the child in front of others.
- Make sure the reprimand or punishment is proportionate to the level of unwanted behaviour, and not excessive or unkind.
- Be fair and consistent.
- Deal with the behaviour at the time, not later.

Types of unwanted behaviour

The sorts of behaviour which are unwanted in young children in school are those which:

- are disruptive to the learning process
- threaten the health and safety of children or adults
- distress, embarrass or upset other children or adults
- involve verbal or physical abuse of another child or adult.

Typical examples of some of these are:

- During 'carpet time' Ryan ties his shoelace to that of the child next to him, creating a domino effect so that after twenty minutes four children are shackled together.
- During whole class teaching in literacy hour, Hannah leans forward and starts to twiddle with the hair of the child in front of her, distracting about five other children in the process.
- During silent reading, several boys gather at the shelves to 'change their books', and instead start to chat among themselves about toys.
- Kay and David reach for the same pencil at their table and then start a loud squabble about who should have it, culminating in pushing and shoving each other off their chairs.
- At dinnertime, Dan leaps out of the queue for lunches and entertains the other children by dancing round, pulling faces and blowing 'raspberries', until the queue collapses.
- Karen and Shiraz, both 7, rampage around the playground play-fighting with each other, shouting at the top of their voices, oblivious of others until they flatten a smaller child.
- Supposedly absorbed in completing drawings of different types of dwelling places, Mark entertains his table by drawing pictures of 'willies'.
- Cheryl asks Tom to pass her a rubber, instead he throws, she catches and tosses it back and so on.
- Harry refers to the child next to him as 'you prat'.
- Fauzia and Jane follow the lunchtime supervisor down the playground doing an exaggerated imitation of her walk.

Strategies for dealing with unwanted behaviour

Dealing with unwanted behaviour requires patience, tact, firmness and fairness. The object is to minimize the disruption caused by the behaviour and to discourage the child or children from repeating it. In some cases, the child or children may need to be made aware of the distress they have caused and to make reparation, usually apologies. Children respond best to disciplinary measures from adults who they respect and feel positive about. Possible strategies include:

- verbal reprimands, delivered in a calm, but very firm tone
- ignoring minor incidents of unwanted behaviour, in the context of praising unwanted behaviour
- explaining to the child why their behaviour is unacceptable, dangerous or hurtful to others
- suggesting alternative ways of behaving
- removing the child from an 'audience' or removing the 'audience' from the child
- giving the child additional responsibilities or tasks to do to occupy him/her more.

For more serious incidents, teaching assistants will need to report the behaviour to the teacher for consideration of further sanctions or punishments. However, it is important to be able to deal with incidents as they arise and to do this confidently and with authority.

[…]

Finally, it is important to remember that repeated and possibly escalating unwanted behaviour might be an indication of a deeper problem. Children who are abused or being bullied or who are worried or distressed may behave in unacceptable ways in order to draw attention to their plight. Children who have learning difficulties or special educational needs may be trying to distract others from recognizing their difficulties or gain the status they feel they cannot get through achievements in the classroom. Children going through changes at home, such as divorce or the birth of a new baby, may be expressing their uncertainty and anxiety. Any concerns about the possible causes of patterns of unwanted behaviour should be shared with a teacher who may then discuss these with parents.

[…]

Conclusions

Teaching assistants play an important role in whole school development towards a positive learning environment, both within and outside the classroom. The development of personal skills and strategies to promote good standards of behaviour and to deal with conflict, bullying and racism is important for anyone working within the school community. We know that children learn best in orderly, well-managed environments. Teaching assistants need to be able to support the teacher in creating and maintaining an appropriate learning environment within the classroom. They also need to create and manage a positive learning environment within their own particular remit, working with groups and individual children. Children not only learn best in such an environment, but they also learn about positive social behaviour, consideration and respect for others and anti-discriminatory behaviour. Developing skills to manage behaviour and learning effectively, without the use of power-assertion (shouting, threatening, frightening) techniques, is a significant part of the teaching assistant's learning requirements.

References

David, T. (ed.) (1993) *Educating our Youngest Children: European Perspectives.* London: Paul Chapman.

Kay, J. (2001) *Good Practice in Child Care.* London: Continuum.

Parker-Jenkins, M., Briggs, D., Taylor-Basil, V. and Hartas, D. (2001) *The Implementation and Impact of the Home-School Agreement in Derbyshire Primary Schools.* University of Derby, School of Education and Social Science, Research Centre for Education and Professional Practice Working Papers Series 1: No. 1.

Section 4
Learners' identities

Roger Hancock and Janet Collins

The final section of this Reader contains nine chapters that link learning to issues of class, ethnicity and ability. These chapters examine the identities of learners, the way in which individuals think about their own identities and the ways they are viewed by others.

Chapters 29, 30, and 31 make links between social class and children's school learning. Diane Reay, in Chapter 29, suggests that it is mothers who tend to provide 'emotional support' to children when they are at school. She also highlights the fact that there may be resource inequalities between middle and working class families. In Chapter 30, Gillian Plummer focuses on the childhood experiences of women who describe themselves as coming from a working class background. In particular she highlights some of the ways in which the women's definitions of class are related to changing circumstances and the experiences of other families. The way children speak can cause adults to make inaccurate assumptions about their abilities and their potential to learn. In Chapter 31, Graham Jameson describes a project that served to bring unwarranted linguistic assumptions to the surface.

Chapters 32 and 33 both consider potential impairments to learning. Jonathan Rix, in Chapter 32, describes the work of a teaching assistant as she draws upon the available human and material resources in a classroom to enable Jared, a child diagnosed with autism, to be included in the life and learning of that classroom and the school. In Chapter 33, Gina Gardiner, a headteacher who currently needs to use a wheelchair, reviews the positive and negative sides of her work.

In Chapter 34, Sarah Pearce addresses issues of race and ethnicity and the need for increased understanding between groups. She suggests that white people should examine the taken-for-granted nature of white behaviour and assumptions in order to decentre from a position of 'whiteness'. Developing a multicultural theme, in Chapter 35, Charmian Kenner outlines an approach to fostering a multilingual learning environment. Learning for bilingual children can be greatly enhanced when teaching assistants and teachers enable linguistic and cultural interaction to take place within the school.

Robin Cooley is particularly interested in promoting anti-bias understanding amongst the children she teaches. In Chapter 36 she provides an account of work in her classroom which highlights gender and family stereotypes. Lastly, in Chapter 37, Diane Reay notes a history of concern about boys' behaviour in primary classrooms. She feels that their achievement needs to be viewed against a background of race and class, but that boys (and girls) respond well to teaching that maintains good order but is also fun.

Chapter 29

Family capital, schooling and social class

Diane Reay

> Although we often talk of 'parental' involvement in children's schooling, Diane Reay, professor of education, London Metropolitan University, reminds us in this chapter that it is often mothers who have the most contact with schools. Mothers, she suggests, provide important emotional support to children at school but there are notable inequalities in the resources that can be drawn upon by middle and working-class families respectively.

One of the most surprising findings from my research study of home–school relationships was the recurrence of intense emotions, both positive and negative, permeating mothers' accounts of their children's schooling. I have used the concept of 'emotional capital' to better understand the welter of emotions that mothers both expressed and talked about in relation to their children's schooling.

Emotional involvement did not differ greatly by social class. However, working-class women found it more difficult to supply their children with resources of emotional capital than their middle-class counterparts because they were frequently hampered by poverty, insufficient educational knowledge and lack of confidence. Working-class women were often caught up in a spiral in which low levels of dominant cultural capital, economic capital and social capital all made it relatively difficult to provide their children with the benefits of emotional capital. Class differences also played a part in determining whether mothers could divert their emotional involvement into generating 'academic profits' for their children. Working-class women often lacked the right conditions for provoking either emotional or cultural capital. Contrast:

> When I get in I get them both something to eat, then do whatever needs to be done in the house and that includes getting their clothes ready for school so by the time everything is done I find I never have a minute to sit down until half eight or nine. Then she'll come and sit with me and read and that's every night.
>
> (Lisa, white working-class lone mother)

with:

> I try and make sure that at least twice a week I take my children out to tea somewhere relaxed and leisurely where we can all chat about our day. I've always worked on the

principle of taking my children somewhere nice for tea, for socialising since they were little, that's always been the way I have made space for them to tell me about what's happening to them.

(Linsey, white middle-class married mother)

Lisa, dealing with the pressure of domestic chores after a day's paid work, finds it extremely difficult to focus exclusively on her children's educational needs in the way that Linsey does. This is not an issue of 'good mothering' but of resources. Linsey can afford both a cleaner and an au pair. She talks of being able to concentrate on her children's schooling in a 'relaxed and leisurely' way in contrast to Lisa, on a low income, who describes a frenetic juggling of competing, equally pressing demands. However, that is not the same as saying working-class mothers did not provide emotional capital through their involvement in schooling, rather it did not go hand in hand with cultural capital to anything like the extent middle-class women's did. Lisa, talking about Lucy's reluctance to go swimming, combined powerful feelings of empathy with an incisiveness about what was in Lucy's best interest:

> She had never come up against anything she didn't want to do at school before. I didn't want her as soon as she came up against something she didn't want to do to think she could opt out. I wanted her to develop strategies to deal with it, you know. I mean I did feel for her and so I ended up phoning up the school a few times and went along with Lucy saying she felt unwell, but then I said to her 'You can't keep avoiding it'. Then I went to talk to her teacher first to say, you know, 'this is going to be very hard for Lucy, can you keep a special eye on her'. Then her teacher and I spoke to Lucy together and I said 'You mustn't give in without trying'. She took a lot of helping through the first few weeks she went but it got better. She's passed her first two grades. I've had them framed (pointing to where they hung on the wall), you know, to show her efforts are appreciated because it was hard for her.
>
> (Lisa, white working-class lone mother)

This is just one of many examples of working-class women's sensitivity, emotional support and encouragement all combining to enhance their children's emotional capital. Yet, it was far more difficult for the working-class mothers, often dealing with a personal history of academic failure, to generate the same levels of academic confidence and enthusiasm among their children as their middle-class counterparts. History is key here and I suggest that, in common with other forms of capital, there are generational aspects of emotional capital in that reserves are built up in families over time. While working-class Dawn talks in terms of a mother working long hours in the labour market who 'was never there for her and so I found primary school terrifying', middle-class Linsey talks of a mother who always encouraged and helped her with her school work; 'she was always certain all her daughters could do anything they set their minds to'.

Much of the data demonstrate the costs to mothers of their emotional involvement in their children's schooling. They are using up a lot of time and emotional energy in their support which, as I have demonstrated above, sometimes brings them into conflict rather than harmony with their children. They are often unsupported in this emotional work by male partners (David 1993; Reay 1998).

Involvement in children's schooling generated intense class anxiety, in particular, for some of the middle-class mothers who expressed fears that it was more difficult than in the past for children from middle-class backgrounds to attain appropriate jobs (Jordan *et al.* 1994; Brown 1995).

I suggest that the relationships between educational success, emotional capital and emotional well-being, and the extent of overlap and difference between them, could provide new ways of understanding how a range of disadvantages which cross class barriers are being manufactured in the contemporary educational marketplace.

References

Brown, P. (1995) 'Cultural Capital and Social Exclusion: Some Observations on Recent Trends in Education, Employment and the Labour Market', *Work, Employment and Society*, **9**, 29–51.

David, M. (1993) *Parents, Education and Gender Reform*. Cambridge: Polity Press.

Jordan, B., Redley, M. and James, S. (1994) *Putting the Family First: Identities, Decisions, Citizenship*. London: UCL Press.

Reay, D. (1998) *Class Work: Mothers' Involvement in their Children's Primary Schooling*. London: UCL Press.

Chapter 30

Life in a working-class family

Gillian Plummer

Gillian Plummer, educational consultant and an associate adviser with Essex education authority, has researched the educational failure of working-class girls. In this chapter she draws out some of the distinctive elements of being 'working class' and considers how class is defined and experienced by women.

Most people do not articulate how the sociological category of class has shaped their life. Evidence is there, nevertheless, in the stories we tell – or don't tell – about our lives (Richardson 1990). In this chapter I first identify aspects of class difference and illustrate how concepts of class and class positions are learned through specific experiences and *in relation* to *others* in general.

The women in this study all identified themselves as from a working-class background. In our experience, class position is historical and situational, not fixed or universal – for instance, through our educational achievements we have, or are perceived to have, marginally shifted our class position. Whilst the model of a class continuum with working-class at one end and middle-class, or upper-class, at the other – with a few people moving up and down (Richardson 1990) – may underlie our stories, what we focus on is difference and perceived relational positionings. Using three women's texts, I identify perceived indicators of class position – which are also shifting – and demonstrate that class awareness is a learning process. Class mobility and differences within the working classes become apparent.

Talking about one's own working-class family to others raises notions of potential betrayal. 'You don't let other people know your business.' So I have been careful to protect individual families while still raising important family issues.

Social mobility: becoming aware of difference

[There are] divisions within the working-class itself, between its respectable and upward-striving representatives and the poor...

(Campbell 1984: 46)

Housing areas (and now post codes) have been one crude indicator of people's class. This awareness of housing location as a class indicator is revealed in one woman's description of her family as moving up. 'Up' meant out of a working-class area into a middle-class one and this denotes an awareness of hierarchy. In this instance, housing also symbolises sectarian differences:

> [A] working-class family...with so many kids...I mean I'm sure the neighbours must of...'cause it was very Protestant...I'm sure they must of shit themselves when we arrived. Twelve children all trooping around the streets...which was...like a working-class tradition, but we were in a middle-class area.

Other class indicators emerged. '[It] was only because dad worked in the shipyard that he could afford to buy a house up there.' Male occupations, particularly fathers', have traditionally been the marker of class position. J's father would be classified as a skilled or semi-skilled manual worker according to the textbook definitions, so categorised as working class. J uses different criteria to classify him. While she identifies her mother as coming 'from a very strong working-class background, a Catholic ghetto', she does not feel the same is necessarily true of her father.

> Dad actually lived in quite a nice house...a huge big house...behind and above a sort of butcher's shop...I think they were quite well-off really...so he wasn't really working-class.

Further details in her text suggest that what J identifies as evidence of her father's middle-class origins, others would perceive to be characteristics of the 'respectable' working-class family. This is evident in other aspects of her family history.

> You couldn't really call us working class, not really...We sort of lived out the area ... we were always relatively well-dressed...and education was [important].

In addition to housing location, cultural practices in childhood, father's occupation, parents' family of origin, two more indicators of class positioning arise: dress and education. The phrase 'relatively well-dressed' is interesting. She was, after all, one of twelve children. Her family's only income was her father's wage. In her early teens he lost his job in the shipyard, was unemployed and finally took a low-waged, unskilled job. By then, only one of the children was at work. Money was short. Saying she was well-dressed, her clothes handed on from older sisters, was possibly a reference to cleanliness – a marker of the respectable working-class family (see Bourke 1994). In terms of education she was talking about the importance of making the best of state-funded education, as private education would not have been an option.

Perception of a family's level of poverty touches upon another important indicator of class position, income. Whilst on the one hand J feels, that

> We weren't poor that you didn't ever have any money, but there wasn't a lot of money to go around. You got what you needed to survive sort of thing and that was it.

She adds,

> Money didn't appear to be a problem, although it must have been for my mum...We weren't sort of made aware of it...I think that it's mum sort of like being a wizard.

J put her family's economic survival down to her mother's remarkable money management skills. Yet at the same time she recalls that her mother 'spent a lot of time paying people, borrowing from people', that there was the 'Provident cheque as well' and that a lot of their 'clothes were bought from the shop round the corner...on tick.'

Having only 'what you needed to survive' and yet not perceiving yourself as being poor, is a feature of working-class life, a part of working-class people's social conditioning. Poverty is relative. There is always another family worse off than yours. Furthermore, to acknowledge you were poor in a society that blames poor families for their poverty means blaming your working-class parents. They had not worked hard enough or taken advantage of the opportunities offered to them. If we accepted this, what would it say about them, about us?

The other women interviewed unquestioningly described themselves as coming from working-class backgrounds but there was evidence of social mobility in two families, one upward and one downward. These women's stories, as the first, further illustrate the relativity of poverty and the diversity of those defining themselves as working class.

Upward mobility was identified in terms of father's changing occupations. The one upwardly mobile father, a lift operator and electrician before the war, became a bank messenger after the war and gained bank manager status on retirement. His daughter K talks about him making the switch from blue to white collar worker and infers that the Masons may have been influential in this rise. The younger of two children, born and brought up in a council and later privately rented flat in the east of London, she describes her childhood as a time when her father was poorly paid. She recalls him having to work in the City during the day and clean the bank underneath their rented flat at night. This, she says, was necessary for the family's survival. K describes her father as 'a conventional working-class father', explaining that he would try and do everything for her. 'If I wanted a bike he would work overtime to get me a bike.' Not all the women would see this as characteristic of 'a conventional working-class father'.

What was unique in this story is the part cultural activities play in signalling a person's class position: opera, ballet, piano lessons. K told me her parents, 'used to sing together and...be at amateur dramatics' and that she had ballet and piano lessons. Such pursuits are not generally associated with a working-class life style though they do indicate a desire for upward social mobility, a mirroring of the middle classes. K ascribes these activities to the 'middle-classness' of her Italian mother, her cultural interests, which she acknowledges were unusual in a working-class family. 'We always had good music in the house...we always had opera...We always had that culture bit.'

The upper-classness of opera is a very British notion. While K tells me that she did not think 'I'm poor', she did distinguish her family from others around her:

> There were a lot of people who were wealthy…They lived in a different house to where I lived. They had big houses [laughs]…I became aware of quite a high settlement of…moneyed Jewish people…Becoming aware of those kinds of differences…When you don't live in a house, when you live in a flat…you kind of perceive that difference.

Yet she was conscious of having things others did not. She was also aware of being in rented accommodation, not private, a flat not a house, of having extras but not wealth. Money was, however, spent on sending her brother to private school – although the school was inappropriate for him. She notes the gender difference, a son's education took priority over a daughter's.

I grew up in private rented accommodation, in the east end of London. She tells me her parents came from 'families with money'; dad's relatives had 'loads of money' and mum's were 'very wealthy'. The parameters of this wealth are unclear. She believes that when her parents married they were disinherited, 'they didn't get a penny either of them.' As one of ten children, she described herself as growing up in conditions of extreme poverty, possibly a consequence of downward social mobility.

Looking closer – emerging indicators of social class positioning

Other traditional class indicators are evident in the stories we told of our childhood: parents' levels of education, housing conditions, health. All our parents were educated within the state education system. All but one received an elementary education, one a secondary education. They all left school at the age of fourteen so were restricted to the lowest end of the job market. With the exception of the father who had received three years of secondary education our parents worked in single-sex, unskilled, semi-skilled or skilled manual occupations. These were generally poorly paid dead-end jobs: labouring on building sites, the dockyards, in shipyards, factory work, domestic work, jobs done only by those who are the most financially insecure.

Even the mothers who did well in school were denied secondary education. Severe economic and social constraints forced them into what, traditionally, was seen as 'women's work', summed up by my mother as 'dirty work', 'boring work'. Our mothers cooked, cleaned, worked in factories or for the National Health Service caring for others – jobs only the working classes do, low-paid, often temporary or part-time and with no career opportunities and few employment rights.

In terms of housing, we all began our early childhood in very cheap, privately rented accommodation and then moved into council housing or the lowest end of the private housing market, houses that only the working classes lived in.

Overcrowded conditions, the lack of space and privacy were serious problems, ones which provoked family stress.

Health too is class-related. There is a direct correlation between health and people's level of wealth. At some stage in our childhood our mothers and fathers were highly likely to experience some kind of physical and/or mental breakdown, manifesting itself in serious illnesses, drink problems, emotional withdrawal and depression; an outcome of their hard lives. As medical journals show, breakdowns continue to be a serious threat to health for many working-class people.

References

Bourke, J. (1994) *Working-Class Cultures in Britain,* London: Routledge.

Campbell, B. (1948) *Wigan Pier Revisited,* London: Virago.

Richardson, L. (1990) *Writing Strategies: Reaching Diverse Audiences,* Newbury Park: Sage.

Chapter 31

Three Billy Goats: language, culture and class

Graham Jameson

It is very easy to make unwarranted assumptions about people based on how their speech sounds rather than on what they actually say. Graham Jameson, headteacher at Edmund Waller Primary School, London, uses the story of 'The Three Billy Goats Gruff' to stimulate children's understanding about the relationship between the way we speak and the value of what we say.

About a year ago, one of our infant classes did an assembly based on the story of the *Three Billy Goats Gruff*. Like most fairy stories, the basic structure allows for 'caustic interpretation' and we certainly saw that in vivid and dramatic form – the fight between the Troll and the Great Big Billy Goat Gruff in particular being positively Wagnerian. In the week that followed I asked a group of older children (Year 5) that I was taking for a writing session to recast the story as a television programme. In deciding to call this 'Spotlight', they demonstrated straight away an understanding of the portentousness that attends so many news programmes and this level of sophistication continued throughout the programme. We taped the final production and a group transcribed the result.

The programme started with suitably urgent and arresting music and then Sophia came to the microphone and said: 'Tonight on Spotlight we investigate the case of the three Billy Goats Gruff. They've got a problem. We ask are they entitled to cross the bridge and eat the green grass on the other side? Or do they have to put up with the crusty conditions in their own field? We talk to the Billy Goats. But what about the Troll? What is his opinion? The Billy Goats have a right to decent grass, but doesn't the Troll have a right to be left in peace in his own field? We talk to him as well.'

We went over to the goat field to talk to 'our woman on the spot,' Mary. She was interviewing Rebbekah as the middle-size Billy Goat Gruff who, when asked why the Billy Goats wanted to move fields, replied: 'Because when mi a wak di grass a juk up ina di battam a mi foot and when me eat di grass a eatch up ina mi throat. Dat is why mi waant fi move'. And later said of the Troll that: 'Him is a very selfish monster, mi a go tell fada Billy government an see whaat him a fo say about it.'

Then it was back to the studio for Sophia to say judiciously: 'Of course, there are always two sides to any question. We're going to go over now and talk to Mr Brian Troll'

The exchange between Mr Troll and the reporter casts an unusual light on the story:

'Mr Troll, why won't you let the goats cross the bridge to eat the grass?'

'Because it is my grass and if I let them eat my grass, then a whole family of goats will eat my grass and then there will be no grass for me.'

'But surely, more grass will grow.'

'It will take weeks for it to grow. Do you eat grass? You don't know nothing about eating grass!'

'But there is water and fish.'

'I know there is water and fish but I hate water and fish!'

'Mr Troll, be reasonable, give them a chance. The goats are living in disgusting conditions. What are you going to do about it?'

'Nothing!'

'I think you should let them eat your grass, think about it.'

'Listen mate, this is my grass and those goats have dirty grass because they made all the mess. I am not letting them come to eat my grass.'

'But don't you think they have rights?'

'Yes, I think they should have rights. But what about my rights!'

Then 'back to the studio' and from there to: 'Down here at the goat field things have really moved on. Apparently, the goats got really fed up with the situation and are now in Mr Troll's field. The whereabouts of Mr Troll himself are unknown. I've got two eye-witnesses here, Georgie Porgie and Dave Divhead who saw what happened and I'm going to talk to them.'

Messrs Divhead and Porgie turned out to be a *Brookside*-style Liverpudlian and a Racer-style Geordie who described the expulsion of the Troll from the field and his disappearance into the waters after which event the goats were perhaps a little unsuitably triumphalist:

'He danced about and his brothers came on the bridge with him and they danced about too.'

'Yeh, yeh and then they wrote "Goats Rule OK" on the side of the bridge and then they all went trip-trapping into the new field.'

'That's all we've got time for, terrar.'

The immediate drama over, we were back again to the studio for sage summing-up by the presenter. The moral maze traversed. 'Viewers, what I would really like you to think about is what do you think would happen if it were you in such a situation? Would you 1) fight the battle out or 2) converse with your opponent? Please think positively; when the goats and Mr Troll were fighting it out, has it done them much good? Think to yourselves a moment, what do you think would have happened if they were to talk the matter through? Would they have such a problem? The big problem is - Who is right? Well the correct answer in one sense is that neither of the two sides is right. But in another sense, if one lot of people (or trolls) have too much and another lot of people (or goats) are on the edge of starvation, then I know where I stand on the matter. Personally, I think they should pack in the argument and share the grass between them all.'

A year later

A year elapsed before we went back to the project. This was not intentional, I just got overtaken by events. Anyway a year on, I got these now-Year 6 children to reflect on their programme.

Their reading of the title music and the images over it was that it was about 'News' because it was 'serious' but 'fast'. It was 'direct' and 'straightforward'. The images were 'moving' (in the sense of dynamic) and the people in them were 'action men'. The words and the music were saying to the viewer 'see this', 'hear this', 'this is serious', 'pay attention', 'stop the ironing and look at this'. The positive aspects of such presentation are that 'it gets people to watch the news'. On the other hand such presentation can try to pass off boring subjects as interesting. Following this a more general point was made about why some things were counted as news. They were very clear that it was not the viewers who decide what the news is. It was 'the people who make the programmes'.

I talked to the children about the opening of their programme being the first of many voices. I asked Sophia to read the opening sentences of her transcript as the anchor person/narrator of the piece. As in the original, she enunciated in measured, received pronunciation ('RP') vowels. Why, I wondered. Nobody had told her to talk like that as the presenter. She had chosen this voice in the interests of clarity and because the people who make the news and present it are 'posh'.

I wondered if it were possible to read the same text in a different accent but with equal intelligibility. Mary read it with a West African accent and it was, to be sure, equally clear. However, the group thought that we don't ever hear that voice in that context because 'it isn't British' and the 'posh people' think that the audience won't understand it. They think African people are 'uneducated' and the way they speak is therefore redolent of 'stupidity'. The only way for a black person to become a presenter, like Moira Stuart or Trevor McDonald, is to sound like a posh white person – 'they have to train their voice'. At least two of the group thought this dynamic was an example of racism, but they all thought that the exclusion of all but the prestige dialect of RP from the narrating role in TV was to do with the workings of class. One of the group, for instance, with a now only vestigial Liverpool accent would be unsuitable as a newsreader, as would another white member of staff with a South London accent even though each speaks 'very clearly'. The group thought that programme-makers thought it slightly less important that the reporter should speak with a posh accent but she/he still had to make it sound official.

I wondered how young they were when they first would have known that it would be appropriate to speak like this. The consensus was that you developed this knowledge with the development of language itself. Rebbekah gave the example of her sister who from the age of three showed in her play that an official role was articulated in a 'posh' voice. They all gave examples of older relatives making their own speech 'more posh' in situations such as answering the telephone.

None of the group had been conned by the notion of RP as 'standard' or neutral. 'Everybody' had an accent, they thought. One of them said it beautifully, 'everybody who speaks English is standard English' and 'any language is standard language' and 'language is language'.

Language for them, however, is clearly to do with identity. Rebbekah chose to enunciate the voice of the Billy Goat in Jamaican South London because 'she doesn't really need to put on any accent, she's just herself'. She doesn't bother to change her speech because 'she's fine about the way she is'. Having said that, she can speak to her brothers and sisters in a way that would be unintelligible to the reporter. Jamaican people can, if they choose, have a 'private language'. The historical antecedents of this, they thought, are that the slave owners made the African slaves speak English so that 'they couldn't resist' in their own languages but they can still resist by adapting English to their own purposes and having a common, but 'private', language.

Brian's Troll is 'angry', 'fierce', 'smelly' and 'lower class'. He has a good point, but doesn't help himself by the way he articulates it. People are thus judged – as Mary puts it, 'people think that how you speak shows your character'. The poor Troll is judged as 'rough' and a 'nut-case'. He could make what he says more effective by seeming to be more reasonable but he would be 'less honest'.

George's 'Divhead' and Brian's 'Porgie', are 'dopey'. People believed that all 'scousers' are stupid, drink beer and smoke heavily. We rehearsed the same text using 'posh' accents. Exactly the same words were spoken but this time the two respondents would be judged as intelligent, they would not drink beer nor smoke. Equally, Sophia's final summing-up of the moral issues is attended by a gravitas that is to do with register, not content. If she said exactly the same things in 'an African accent' it wouldn't have anything like the same impact.

It is possible for a person who speaks with an accent like this to become a presenter but only at the price of 'changing who they are'. This was thought by all of the group to be a very high price to pay. I wondered how they thought things might change. They were not optimistic about change, but thought we should make a start in school by valuing the way real people speak, by not 'correcting' 'errors' of accent, only correcting when children 'get words wrong'.

A teacher's reflection

Like the man said, the isle is full of noises. It is the same as it ever was, only more so. This work reflects the multiplicity of voices that children hear, voices which reflect the plethora of cultures they consume. We see them trying to synthesize these voices into a coherent and critical understanding. My head is also full of voices, some of them frameworks or templates for understanding how the world works. It is interesting how much of the children's understanding fits within these. They know about a range of literacies, that different genres have their own grammars that encode weighted meanings. They know about the 'dialogistic' nature of cultures – that one culture feeds and is fed by another, that texts are social artefacts. They know that 'a speech genre is not a typical form of language, but a form of utterance' and that each such utterance has social (political) weight. That, as Bakhtin put it 'any speaker is not the first speaker, the one who disturbs the eternal silence of the universe', that 'an utterance is filled with dialogic overtones' (Bakhtin 1986).

They know about the 'linguistic equivalence' that you can say the same thing in different registers and the meaning, linguistically, is the same. Equally, they know about the power of class. They are well towards the edge of what Vygotsky calls 'a zone of proximal development', they are on the verge of knowing that, as Labov puts it, 'the myth of verbal deprivation is particularly dangerous as it diverts attention from the real defects of our educational system to the imaginary defects of the child' (Labov 1972).

They nearly know that the 'twaddle' articulated by Ministers of Education about 'standard English' is a reflection of their own class positions rather than analysis.

To be sure, it could be said that I have been 'leading the witnesses', but then I am with Jerome Bruner (1986) in that I think it is part of our job as teachers to set up situations where students can extend and develop their own critical ideas, guided by structures and enthusiasms of teachers, occasions where they are led through 'zones of proximal development'.

I am emboldened by this work. In my gloomier moments I think that what Gramsci called 'hegemony' is getting more and more complete (Gramsci 1970). I think of the way that our lives are more and more structured and controlled so that ideas, consumption and education become all of a piece each reinforcing the other and all speaking with one controlling voice. Then I think to myself, what if someone had set up a similar situation for me and my classmates in 1957 and asked us similar questions? Almost certainly we would have said that standard English was that of the strangled, hernia vowels of the chappies who read the news on the radio. We would probably have 'known' that the social order, reflected in such articulation, was contingent with the moral order. That the class system was, in some way, 'natural'. What if...? – the idea is absurd. Nobody would have considered such a thing; in that sense hegemony then was even more complete.

When I hear this word hegemony an image floats into my head from the Eisenstein film, *Alexandr Nevsky*. I see the frozen lake, the ice forming a skin over the water, a smooth meniscus of normality. Later in the scene, the Teutonic knights ride confidently out across that surface but their combined weight is too much for it and it cracks and breaks and they slide desperately and ignominiously into the icy water.

In my gloomier moments, the world feels like the frozen lake. I wouldn't go so far as to wish the fate of the drowning knights on the present order. I lighten up, though, at the prospect of work like this, especially as I know that knowledge about language is being discussed and extended into 'meta-linguistic' and social awareness in classrooms all over the place. The ice may not be breaking up yet, but there are plenty of air-holes in it.

References

Bakhtin, M.N. (1986) *The Problem of Speech Genres.* Texas University Press.
Bruner, J. (1986) *Actual Minds, Possible Words.* Harvard University Press.
Gramsci, A. (1970) *Selections from the Prison Notebooks.* London: Lawrence and Wishart.
Labov, W. (1972) 'Language in the Inner City', in *Studies in the Black English Vernacular.* Philadelphia University Press.
Shakespeare, W. *The Tempest.*
Vygotsky, L. S. (1962) *Thought and Language.* MIT Press.
Vygotsky, L. S. (1978) *Mind and Society.* Harvard University Press.

Chapter 32

A balance of power: observing a teaching assistant

Jonathan Rix with Anna Tan and Susie Moden

Anna Tan is a teaching assistant at a primary school in West Sussex. This chapter describes Anna's morning as she works to include Jared, a child diagnosed as experiencing autism, alongside his peers in their typical class activities. Anna shares this task with the class teacher, Susie, and a classroom assistant, Bridget.

Anna arrives at 8.30 am, earlier than her contract requires. She checks the teaching resource boxes and what is happening today. Susie greets her warmly and says she needs to show her some information from Jared's Statement of Special Educational Needs. The information is at home, and Anna would not normally have access to it since she is not part of the formal assessment process. Anna has little to do with formally assessing Jared's work, although she sometimes passes notes to Susie for assessment purposes.

Anna gathers together her visual timetable for the morning, and Susie asks Anna what she knows of Jared's holiday. They then talk about Jared's desire to do cutting and sticking, computer work and drawing tractors. Anna explains that Jared turned the spiral that they were doing the day before into the wheels of a tractor. Everyone is impressed by some of the patterns that he was producing on cards by himself the day before.

Susie and Bridget tell Anna about the previous afternoon when Anna was not in class. They tell Anna about a disagreement that occurred in the afternoon between Jared and another boy. Jared kept distracting the boy when he wished to listen to the story. Anna feels it is important to find out how Jared gets on when she is not around. She worries that he is not independent enough to get the most out of the learning situation. She is also aware that there are times when he becomes anxious about her leaving. Susie tends to have more open activities when she is working on her own. She often draws upon strategies she has seen Anna using or has discussed with her. She sometimes struggles to cope without Anna there, but feels it is important for her relationship with Jared, so that she gets to see him as a whole person. She is aware that there is a danger of assuming that Anna is the expert on Jared and that she does not have the knowledge or experience to work with him. Susie also thinks that maybe when the sessions have more freedom the children get on better with Jared.

Susie takes Anna around the class, running through the activity tables for the day. On one table is a cut-and-stick activity based around a Guy Fawkes storyline. On the other tables are sewing, drawing opportunities, leaves, picture sequences, alphabets, white boards, shapes and numbers. They discuss the need to read the Guy Fawkes book again so that Jared knows what is going on, and is able to carry out the activity. They both agree that the bad photocopy will make it more difficult for him to relate to the story. This is Anna's first chance to be involved in the planning for the day's work. This is something that frustrates her. Anna explains that she will ask Jared to describe what he sees in the pictures, before cutting and pasting. Susie values Anna's ability to adapt to the situation as she finds it.

At 8.50 am the parents enter. Jared arrives and drops off his bag, crosses to Anna and is welcomed. Anna sits down with Jared and has a brief chat with his mum, then gets Jared involved in an activity so that the mother can leave with minimum disruption.

Susie claps for the children's attention and they sit on the carpet. She takes the register and Anna chats quietly at the back of the group with Jared. She is explaining the activity that will follow. The students are to go into singing practice. As they get up to leave for the hall Anna picks up the visual timetable.

Anna sits at the side of the hall, and then, at Susie's request, goes to check for an absent class. She returns with the class. She sits down again and then notices that there is a boy crying. She crosses to the boy to comfort him. He wants his mum so she gives him a hug and asks him what his favourite song is. The boy is suitably distracted and the singing begins.

Jared is happily positioned in the front row joining in with the singing to a certain degree and copying the hand movements of Susie, who is leading the practice. After a few minutes Jared turns, looking for Anna to ask a question. She slides forward from her position beside the boy who was crying. As the class stand up Anna focuses on Jared again with a reminder that soon they will return to class where he'll be able to blow bubbles before carpet time. Susie is not aware of Anna's intervention, but later says that if Jared had become too distracted, distressed or anxious she would have asked a member of staff to take him out.

At 9.25 am the students return to their classrooms and Anna takes Jared into the adjoining room to re-read the story of Guy Fawkes and to blow a few bubbles. Before beginning, however, she gives Jared a choice of whether to join the others on the carpet or to have this one to one session. Jared wants to have this moment to himself, which Anna sees as a moment to calm and reorient himself after the stress of the singing practice. They agree too on an activity that they can carry out later. This is a tempting prize to keep him on target for the next couple of hours. She is aware though that she is separating him from the rest of the class. She feels that in a few weeks' time she will be able to take out some of the other children too, making this session less segregating and more of an opportunity for social learning.

After reading the story and after a few minutes of playing with the bubbles, Anna gives Jared advance warning that he has two minutes left before they will return to the carpet. When it is time, Jared runs into the classroom and throws himself into a corner, potentially disrupting the focus of the other children. Transition is often tricky. Susie checks with Anna that Jared is joining them and gives him some instructions about coming to join them on the carpet.

Anna feels that Jared usually responds well to instructions from Susie. She feels the buck stops with the teacher, but, on this occasion, Jared shouts at Susie that she can't tell him what to do and begins to talk about not being at home. Anna crosses to Jared with the egg timer and calms him. She and Susie both feel that he is aware that he has got away with behaviour that others in the class would not. But they do not make an issue out of it and neither do the other children. (At the end of the morning Susie wonders if Jared responds this way because he has been singled out and, unlike other children, would respond better to a class-wide request for silence.)

Susie explains to the children the different activities that they can carry out that day. She is aware that Jared and other pupils will benefit from simple language supported by strong visual cues and attempts to build this into her explanation. She points out that they have got some 'join the dots' sheets to do today, because one of the boys had expressed an interest, and a number of parents said children enjoyed doing them at home. On the table Susie finds one of Jared's pictures. She picks it up and hands it to Bridget to file, congratulating Jared on a good piece of work. As Susie demonstrates the different activities, Anna repeats some of the questions that Susie is asking. Jared is too distracted and is not following Susie's description of the Guy Fawkes story. He gets up. Anna goes across to the visual timetable, takes this with her and leaves the class once again with Jared.

Outside they discuss the story of Guy Fawkes, which Anna feels Jared only partially understands. At 9.45 am the class split up. Susie will be working on the letter Y and spelling and handwriting with groups of children. Bridget will be working with groups on number. These are based on ability as defined by the teaching staff. Anna is not a fan of this system. She feels that the group Jared is in does not do him any favours. She feels that being in the bottom group means that he suffers more than most from their being distracted. She feels a more focused group would help him.

Anna positions herself first of all at the cut-and-paste table with Jared but she is regularly approached by pupils from the other tables, particularly the sewing table, for her assistance and her opinions. Susie believes this demonstrates how important Anna is to the whole class, even though they know that she focuses on Jared.

Anna talks to all the pupils on a table, helping to focus them on the work, correcting mistakes and encouraging Jared in his communication with them. Jared is not that taken with the task, but, by giving him small targets, she keeps him focused. After 20 minutes Jared decides he wants to go into the Post Office area so Anna accompanies him after inviting another boy to join them. Some other children join them too. Anna has to gently reprimand one boy for his behaviour, and then Susie gives a stern reminder from her place at the literacy table.

A 10.15 am Jared leaves the Post Office and Anna goes to get the visual timetable again. She crosses to Jared and shows him that he has one activity to do before playtime. At this table a young boy begins to talk to Anna about a leaf that he has, but Anna notices that Jared is standing and spinning in the middle of the classroom and therefore likely to fall over. Anna apologises to this boy and quickly crosses to Jared who has now fallen over. She refocuses Jared, but it's break time, so sends him to get his coat, pointing out two boys who have got their coats. Jared returns with his coat, having inspected his work file on route. When he comes back he pushes into line and is reminded by Anna that he really should have lined up properly like everyone else.

Once Jared has left, Susie apologises to Anna for not having given Jared specific instructions at the start of the day. They agree that something is bothering Jared. They wonder if it is the interruption of going out for the singing. They discuss whether it's more important for him to be involved in an activity and to understand what that activity is or whether it is better for him to be involved in carpet time. This encapsulates much of their concern about how they work with Jared. They are aware that many of Jared's difficulties in learning are due to the curriculum and teaching and learning environment, but that equally he does bring with him unusual sets of skills and ways of thinking that they cannot always be in tune with. They are aware that sharing their ideas at a planning stage may make it easier to overcome their concerns, but to do this they must make time out-of-work.

At 10.35 am, after a quick cup of coffee, Anna goes into the playground to see what Jared is doing. She is aware that he may become too dependent on her, so often leaves him alone at break or just goes to quickly check how things are going. Jared is in the large cubes with other children clamouring around. Anna turns to leave but suddenly Jared is behind her asking her to join him, which she does for a few minutes. Anna sees dependency as a real risk. This is one of the reasons she believes that across the years Jared should work with a variety of support staff. She feels the transitions between staff and year groups need to be carefully handled.

At 10.45 am the class activities start again. Jared is busy doing the joining the dots activity, but using the visual timetable and the temptation of a train-set activity Anna gets Jared to join Bridget at the numeracy table. While she's doing this she congratulates a boy on his strip story.

Bridget is aware that Jared is joining them, so moves a girl to sit next to her so that the two members of staff are not seated together. Jared focuses on the questions being asked of him by Bridget in relation to fireworks, shapes, patterns and numbers. Anna encourages Jared with his answers. She is aware that at times he does not appreciate how much he is achieving. She sees it as important that she helps him to understand his capabilities. After ten minutes

Jared is distracted. Anna and Bridget allow him to make the contextually inappropriate noises for a couple of minutes, and then Anna brings Jared back to complete the task. Jared quickly finishes and then moves off, with Bridget congratulating him as he goes.

Jared wants to work on the computer but there are already other students working there. Anna negotiates the order of computer usage. Jared must wait, but through Anna he becomes involved with the discussion with three other boys about the game one of them is playing.

When Jared begins his activity, Anna discusses what he is doing with another boy. She helps this boy with his own work too, solving a computer problem. She gets him to comment on a picture that Jared has produced on the computer. Jared is enjoying his computer work. He does not wish to move on to the next task despite Anna's negotiation. She explains she will leave him to his work and wait at the next table. She waits for a few minutes and then returns. She reminds him of their agreed plan, and asks him if he wishes to have the computer turned off. Jared is annoyed. He pushes Anna away firmly, touching her on the side of the cheek. Anna repeats her words after another patient explanation and this time Jared joins her at the sewing table.

Jared begins rocking his chair and is clearly distracted. Anna allows him this space. Susie says 'Sh!', automatically, then realises that it is Jared who is making this noise, looks across at Anna and decides to leave the control of the situation in her hands. A boy shows Anna his picture and she points it out to Jared. The boy makes some comments to Jared about the drawing he's just done; Jared makes comments himself and immediately starts to draw a picture. Much to Anna's relief something has come out of the everyday context of the class to help with her problem of how to focus Jared on the next task.

Susie asks Anna whether Jared is ready to do the literacy session. They agree that he will be a couple of moments, so Susie gathers the rest of the group together leisurely in order to give Jared the time to move on happily. It is in informal moments such as these that most of their communications about ideas and situations take place. It is important to both Susie and Anna that they can learn from each other in this way, but they are aware that they lack formal opportunities in the workday to have discussions. Anna would like more formal time allocated for this, but Susie feels that Anna's past experience with the class prepares her for whatever they do.

At 11.15 am Anna negotiates with Jared again about moving on to the next activity. She uses the visual timetable, once more pointing out that if he carries on with the timetable activities as agreed he can play with the train set. Jared joins Susie at the literacy table but once again argues with her about her instructions, saying that she can't tell him to sit. He leaves the table but Anna brings him back. It is clear that Susie now feels awkward and undermined. Susie controls her own sense of frustration, but tells off another distracted boy with more firmness than she might typically. She then starts a story about yoghurts, and when she mimes the eating of yoghurts, and Anna and the other children join in, Jared's attention is grabbed.

Anna is able to leave the table to go to the other group on the ground. She has moved away from Jared but she is keeping her eye upon him, in case she can be of assistance. She is never sure what will happen next. She is always wondering if he is happy doing a task and wondering how she can change the situation to maintain his interest. She sees it as moment-to-moment, trying to work it out as she goes along.

Jared's interest in another boy's name and how it is spelt is evident. So is his desire to make the shape of letters with his hands and then with ribbons on sticks, and then in sand. At the end of the session Jared and a number of others in this group have received a house point for good work.

At 11.30 am Jared leaves the class and Anna follows. There are 15 minutes until the next carpet time. Anna has an egg timer and they go and collect a train set from the toy cupboard and set it up. Anna has also taken the visual timetable with them. Back in the class there's been a disturbance. Susie has to deal with one boy destroying the work of another and the refusal of children to co-operate with this disruptive boy. This is the group that Anna has left to go out with Jared.

At 11.45 am, through precise use of her visual timetable and egg timer, Anna returns with Jared, discussing past activities with the toys he has spotted in the cupboard. Jared begins tidying up. He spends quite some time examining what the other students have built. Susie puts on some music. Jared crosses to this music and begins to play with a car on the table. He does a little clearing up – one book – and then joins the other children on the carpet.

Bridget reads the class a poem and then leads a discussion about rhyme and the pictures in the book. The children leave the classroom and head out to get their lunchboxes. For the last 15 minutes there has been no contact between Anna and Jared.

It has been a good morning, but nothing out of the ordinary.

Conclusion

Watching Anna, Susie and Bridget it is clear to see their awareness of the importance of each other in the creation of a learning and caring environment. Each of them gives way to the other at different times out of respect for their role and because of their different abilities to work with the pupils. There is a considerable scope for role expansion and role overlap. Rather than clearly designated boundaries between three individuals, theirs is a team endeavour and a 'division of labour as an interaction' (Dewar and Clark 1992: 119). At times too, they give way to the pupils, fitting in with them, though it does not always make their professional role any easier. This chapter has been about teamwork in progress. It is not meant to be an ideal example of inclusive practice, but it serves as one example. It reveals differing views about ways of working and organising the class. What is clear, however, is that in attempting to make the most out of their situation, the staff and pupils find themselves constantly shifting their positions and related interactions within the classroom's balance of power.

Reference

Dewar, B. and Clark, J. (1992) 'The role of the paid professional nursing helper: a review of the literature', *Journal of Advanced Nursing*, **17**, 113–20.

Chapter 33

Life as a disabled head

Gina Gardiner

In the last 20 years there has been a concerted move towards the inclusion of children with physical impairments in mainstream primary schools. However, the number of teaching assistants and teachers with such impairments remains conspicuously low. Inclusion, it seems, is not being promoted at the level of the primary school workforce. Gina Gardiner is a headteacher at Parklands Junior School, Romford, Essex. In this chapter she reflects on the negative and positive aspects of her job in the light of her disability.

Manager, organiser, problem solver, are all attributes of successful headship. Being a disabled head teacher simply means you get a tremendous amount of extra practice in these skills. A sense of humour is an absolute necessity; a good staff a godsend, and a school site that is reasonably accessible makes it possible.

I have been a head teacher for 18 years, and have used a wheelchair for 14 years, being in it full-time for the last five. I run a large junior school on the outskirts of North East London. Headship is never easy; being disabled adds another dimension to the position, which has both negative and positive sides to it.

Positive aspects

In good educational style let me identify the positive things created through my disability first. My children have an opportunity to see disability in a constructive way. New pupils will often ask why I am in the chair and are quite satisfied with the explanation. Pupils who have a disability have a positive role model; disability need not mean you can't assume a management position. They know that being in a wheelchair does not mean you are an idiot, unable to speak for yourself. Not so the bar tender at a hotel entirely taken over by a head teacher conference who took the £20 note out of my hand and asked the person pushing me what I would like to drink!

I have learned to be super organised, to use my limited reserve of energy in a more productive way. I have learned to make the most of my time, and where possible give myself space before deadlines just in case. The recent plethora of Government initiatives make it much more difficult for us all to achieve this of course.

I think I have become more patient about some things, and less tolerant of others. I think being disabled has made me more sensitive to the needs of others.

My style of management has changed over the years and professional development of staff is a priority. We achieved Beacon Status in 1997 on the strength of our programme. I believe that the school and the individual staff have gained much from the programme, and developing their skills, confidence and expertise had also ensured that things are covered (many of them outside my physical capacity).

The LEA and Manpower Services have been very supportive and the school has only two classrooms which are not accessible. For example electronic doors have been fitted onto the front door, so that I can now actually get into the building by myself. Many is the time I have sat in the car park waiting for someone to arrive in school, hear me beeping or the phone going. It would be untruthful to say that being disabled is easy. It remains a constant struggle to keep one step ahead, no sooner do you think you have things sussed and something else gets in the way. A bit like being an able bodied head when you think about it.

The downside

Daily life in school as a head in a wheelchair has a number of pitfalls. I cannot negotiate the wheelchair around the classrooms. No it isn't simply that I'm a bad driver, although the doorways have been remodelled somewhat. (I put the really big flakes of paint/plaster in the bin before they are noticed.) This means that monitoring has been organised in a rather different way; my deputy and co-ordinators have received training to enable them to undertake a range of monitoring. Contact with the children has to take a different form, as once through the classroom door furniture moving is the most pressing skill needed. Whilst the children are super about moving things and being helpful it is not conducive to slipping in and out without making a grand entrance.

When I became completely wheelchair bound I was unable to access any toilet within the school. It was a circus act trying to get into the loo until a wall could be knocked down. Discussing personal needs with LEA officers, was not a comfortable experience – my problem not theirs; they were very sympathetic. I find no difficulty in fighting for my staff, pupils or their parents but fighting for yourself is a very different thing. Eventually a new building project included a loo suitable for me and the wheelchair. On one morning we played my version of 'how many people you can get into a Mini' as the site manager, caretaker, surveyor, builder, sanitary ware inspector and I were all squeezed into the new loo space discussing what height the loo needed to be.

When I first found my mobility getting difficult I delayed using a wheelchair longer than was good for me as I was very worried about the response from others, particularly parents. The school site is very large and spread out. I have nearly half the school in outside classrooms, which are situated right across a large playground. For a couple of years I struggled to manage movement around the site and had to plan my movements very carefully. When things deteriorated to the point that I really had no choice I broached the subject with my governors and the LEA first and I was extremely concerned about their reaction. There was no problem. The children took it in their stride; they are much better than adults I find in simply accepting you as you are. They were actually far less bothered about it than I was. The parents made very little comment to me, but I know the talk at the gate has given me most conditions found in a medical encyclopaedia. At times I think it helps parents, particularly those who have children with special needs. Now as an established head it is accepted by everyone that I am in a wheelchair. New parents are occasionally surprised when they meet me for the first time but the school's reputation is the reason they have come so they seem confident to leave their children in our care.

Reliance on the wheelchair is fine until it goes wrong. My electric wheelchair has been known to die in the middle of the corridor much to the amusement of staff. I provide much opportunity for humour. Still when one or two staff have asked for a go in the chair their appreciation for my driving expands hugely; usually great squeals of mirth emitted as they make their higgledy piggledy way down the corridor. One lass has been banned since she ran my secretary over at speed! The children are happy to push me in the manual chair when necessary. (More chips in the paintwork.) Machines I believe are very sensitive to your mood and level of stress. It is quite apparent that computers always go wrong when you have the least time and temper to deal with their games. My electric chair is no exception: it has died on the first day of both the Ofsted Inspections, four years and a term apart!...creepy.

I now have a chair which rises until you are at standing height. It gave the children such a shock when I rose majestically in assembly the first time. Not quite so impressive when I failed to get it back down into the right position the first time. I use the facility sparingly but it has its uses.

School is actually the place where my disability has the least effect. I have a super staff, a deputy, secretary, site manager and chair of governors who are all very supportive and whose roles are somewhat modified so that each of us contributes the best of their skills and where the effect of my inability to walk is minimised. There are usually people about to lift things I find too heavy. School is where I feel most effective, in fact far more than when I am in a social capacity as I am very limited in those things I can access when I have no electric chair.

Off site

Life as a head becomes far more complicated and frustrating when I leave the site.

Local meetings require prior organisation. I have to arrange for someone to meet me in the car park as once I leave school I use a manual chair. Timing for head teachers meetings is critical, too early you cannot get into the playground of the school in question and you sit and wait, too late and the kind head teacher colleague you have asked to meet you is left standing – usually in the rain! I have arrived and beeped the horn to let people in the office know I am there and watched whilst they scratch their head, wondering who was making all that row. The advent of mobile phones is a boon – until they go wrong.

Gatherings are complicated as once I'm in the manual chair I am dependent on people approaching me rather than being able to network. Neck ache usually follows from looking up at those standing. Some kneel as they are trying to be sensitive or perhaps their feet or their back are killing them. On one occasion I was on stage in front of several hundred people, being handed our Investors in People award, the dignitary in question knelt to present me ours. My then deputy was a little too keen to get out of the limelight and dragged the poor fellow right across the stage on his knees...

Accessibility is a word which means entirely different things to different people. The gap in the translation becomes greatest when attending courses and conferences. Please bear in mind that I always take great trouble to contact the providers to check how wheelchair friendly places are and only go if I'm told things are possible.

Some examples

Our local Education Offices are built on a nightmare site. The main corridor has a flight of steps half way along; if I have to visit both ends, or indeed wish to access the one disabled loo and am at the other side of the steps, I have to be pushed outside the entire length and width of half the building. On those days the weather always seems to be awful. The main hall has a flight of steps down into it that can be accessed from outside but I am unable to join colleagues at the coffee area. I tend to limit my intake of liquids on these occasions because I hate having to ask if someone will wheel me to the toilet but it also limits the opportunity for informal chat with colleagues. I have to wait for people to approach me in those situations, which is a pain. I have a super network of close friends who are brilliant about helping me. I still hate being dependent upon others. The building has an upstairs, in two halves. When the LEA moved to these premises it took them three years to have a lift fitted to one half of the building. I'm still waiting for them to make the curriculum side accessible. As they are now talking about moving again I expect the lift will remain as a plan on a drawing. No venue has been decided upon so it could be a long wait. I have to check that every meeting, course, workshop etc has been sited in a room I can access. Occasionally I turn up and communications have broken down. I am allowed to know the combination for the security system as I can only access the side door. Fine until they change the number.

I attended a local course, run by Social Services. It was held at a site completely unknown to me. I phoned to check that it was accessible and was told, 'no problem.' When I arrived I was told that I would have to be carried up three flights of stairs, that it was all arranged. In these situations I have a real dilemma – do I make a scene, go straight home or put up with it. Particularly in the early years I didn't want to make a fuss or draw attention to myself so often put up with things, which made me cry inside. I was hauled up the stairs, an embarrassing and uncomfortable experience for me and positively dangerous for the two unfortunate volunteers. After the second session on the first day (Titled – 'Inclusion, all about dealing sensitively with people's needs') I was told I should not return for the second day as I constituted a fire risk. In those days I didn't want to make a fuss. Today I'm much less prepared to accept the indignity.

Last year I attended a training session where I sat downstairs whilst the other ninety-nine delegates ate upstairs.

Buildings are often said to be perfectly accessible – once you negotiate the steep flight of steps to the front door. I have been left in a busy London street whilst the taxi driver tried to sort things out and it was raining, of course.

I have been to hotels for training or a conference where access has been up a plank of wood through a window.

In another hotel last year, I was unable to get to the room where the introductory session was held, and probably more importantly, the bar. The same hotel required a journey through the car park, onto the road, along the pavement and in through another door every time I needed to get from the conference area or my bedroom to the restaurant. Guess what the weather did for the three days of the course? They offered to bring me a tray to the conference area, where I would have eaten in total isolation. This was a course run to train Threshold Assessors.

I was invited to speak at a conference. After a long drive I arrived to find the site quite impossible, flights of stairs between each of the rooms, some with temporary ramps which were so steep you needed crampons. Some rooms totally inaccessible including the room designated for me to give my talk.

I could go on...at length...

The teaching profession, which takes equal opportunities for its pupils very seriously, often pays far less attention to the needs of the adults who work within it. I feel strongly that all venues used by educational organisations putting on conferences and courses should only use appropriate venues. An added pressure is created because often the organisers both private and governmental are unprepared to take responsibility. As a disabled head it is left to me to check every time. It is common to be passed from person to person when trying to get information about the venue. The record stands at seventeen different phone calls for one event. That information is often incomplete or incorrect. When things don't go to plan people are always apologetic but that doesn't really help very much.

I get great satisfaction from my job but I have been determined that school should not be adversely affected by my disability. This has been an added pressure, entirely self inflicted but nevertheless uncomfortable. To run any school well takes enormous commitment and leaves little time for a life outside. Being a disabled head adds an extra dimension to planning and organisation.

Chapter 34

The practice of 'whiteness'

Sarah Pearce

In this chapter, Sarah Pearce, a lecturer in teacher education at Goldsmiths, College, explores her own thinking and practice as a white primary school teacher in a multi-ethnic primary school. She draws on recent research in the field of 'whiteness studies' to explore attitudes to race. She invites white staff to consider how this approach could inform the way they work with children and staff from diverse cultural and linguistic backgrounds.

Introduction

For those working in education over the past 30 years, approaches to 'race' have been dominated by two competing philosophies. The approach of multi-culturalism, familiar in many schools, is that racial harmony can be achieved through a deeper experience and understanding of other cultures. Anti-racists, on the other hand, deride gestures such as 'samosa-making' as meaningless in the face of institutionalised racism. Yet over the past decade both schools of thought have been criticised. The superficiality of much of the work which has passed for multicultural education is rightly condemned, but the refusal of anti-racists to recognise the importance of culture as a marker is also now seen as misguided by many (Donald and Rattansi 1992; May 1999). Further, the dualism which underpins the approach of some strands of anti-racism, in which whites are depicted as always and inevitably the oppressors, and blacks as passive victims, has also been called into question. How, then, are teachers and teaching assistants to think about 'race' and ethnicity?

In the first place, primary school staff need to examine their own ethnicity. Given that the vast majority in Britain are white, this is likely to be an unfamiliar notion. Most white people are not accustomed to thinking of themselves as members of an ethnic group. But paradoxically, in order to begin to get beyond the black/white dualism, I propose that white staff need to examine their own 'whiteness'. We need to consider how far our preconceptions and assumptions derive from our membership of the dominant group in society, conceiving of whiteness not as a biological fact, but as a social construction. It is on this point that ideas about whiteness offer a more positive message to practitioners than anti-racism, while carrying forward that movement's commitment to challenge institutionalised racism. If we can learn to see how being white influences our behaviour and attitudes toward others, both white and non-white, then we can begin to 'unlearn' that behaviour, to disown the 'practice' of whiteness.

[...]

The implications of whiteness studies for teachers and teaching assistants are enormous. They are inevitably the mediators of the dominant discourse, and middle-class white staff are also successful products of the dominant culture. It is not difficult to read the many studies (e.g. Wright 1992, Basit 1997; Haw 1998) that suggest that white teachers sometimes adversely affect the education of ethnic minority students as a result of the practice of whiteness. The issues are immensely complex, and Levine-Rasky (2000) fears that elitist theoreticians of whiteness are moving too fast for white educators. She advocates that theoretical work on whiteness be integrated with work on teacher education, and this is beginning, though the work on both sides of the Atlantic has focused on trainee teachers, and, again, work in Britain appears very limited (see Gaine 2001). In the following section I seek to apply the force of this theoretical work to my own practice as a white primary school teacher.

The practice of whiteness

I examine the data from my practitioner enquiry under four organisational headings. In doing so I wish to add to the catalogue of work being done on how the practice of whiteness works on a day-to-day basis.

The problem is how people cope with difference, not that whites dominate

My initial perception of the problem was that the curriculum I taught excluded the history and culture of the vast majority of the children in my class. Thus I was initially drawn to the multi-culturalist project of adapting the curriculum to include material from other cultures. Early work on the project was concerned with finding out more about Islamic history and philosophy. This locates my thinking at the time among those who feel that racial conflict and discrimination are a result of the difficulties individuals have in coming to terms with ethnic and cultural differences. Later, I became interested in the development of identity among young Muslims, and recorded my interests in my journal thus:

> I want to examine first the extent to which Muslim schoolchildren perceive a conflict between the liberal western culture of the school and the Islamic culture of the home, and then the part which I as a (white) teacher have to play in that process.

Later still, I saw my project as an attempt to answer the question: 'how do Muslim children reconcile their experiences of schooling with the very different values and traditions they bring from home?'

Though the first quote shows that I acknowledge the need to explore my own role, this is very explicitly a secondary goal. The bracketed reference to my own ethnicity reveals a dawning realisation that this may be fundamental. In the second, formulated for a more formal purpose, I have removed an examination of my own part in the process, and in particular the role of my whiteness. I chose to move away from the influence of my own ethnicity and to focus instead on to the behaviour of the non-white group. In conversation, a few teachers appeared to articulate a similar attitude. One colleague was concerned that: 'African-Caribbean children had problems with identity, and that their problems with aggression were a direct outcome of this. She felt the difficulties came from their own search for a place, rather than other children's hostility.' This view locates the 'problem' very explicitly with the African-Caribbean children themselves. The idea that racism has any part to play is rejected – both explicitly, in relation to other children, and implicitly, in the exclusion of the role of teachers from the discussion. Thus the problem is conceptualised as residing with ethnic minority groups, rather than with white hegemony. But a comment from another colleague who also saw children struggling with problems with identity suggests a more complex picture: 'They've got people at the National Curriculum whose job it is to say "do this and this". They could organise this – if we could be given links...'. I asked why she thought this didn't happen: 'because England is predominantly white and what do they care?'.

This teacher was explicit in identifying white hegemony as the root of the problem. Comments such as this serve to underline the fact that it is not always and only a lack of awareness that prevents teachers from providing a more equitable education.

Whiteness is never referred to – whiteness is invisible, normalised

In the classroom, the normalisation of whiteness can take many forms: discouragement of the use of minority languages; the use of 'multicultural' literature only when required by the National Literacy Strategy; disapproval expressed of other cultural norms such as large families. In my journal I recorded a belated understanding of the importance of the choice of classroom materials. The children I refer to have Bengali, Pakistani or mixed white and African-Caribbean backgrounds.

> The stimulus for the story was a photo I'd selected of a white boy lying on what was clearly a classroom floor. They named the boy Tom, and then created a story in which his arch rival was a boy named Robert. Though the photo required a white name, it reminded me of the discussion about the way the mostly Asian and African-Caribbean children in the school invariably choose white names for their characters. On the other hand, what was I doing providing a photo of a white boy, if I'm so concerned about this phenomenon?

A similar inability to challenge the invisibility of whiteness can be seen in the following exchange between myself and a group of nine-year-olds. I had brought in a series of photographs of people as a stimulus for some descriptive writing. I recorded the response:

> The one which excited the most comment was a photo of a group of men in graduation garb. They were all black, and were smiling against a blurred background which looked like trees in the sunshine. L said, 'oh, it's the Zulus' and laughed as I put it up. They all placed the men as being from Jamaica at first, and then decided on Africa. I asked if the photo might have been taken here, and they said, 'no', and when I asked why, said, 'because they're black'. There then followed a discussion about why some people are black:
>
>   'My uncle says people are black because they drink too much coffee and then go out in the sun.'
>
>   'People are black because they haven't got enough to eat.'
>
>   L's reference to the Zulus reveals a popular racist conflation of a black skin with an aboriginal African identity, one which conjures up images of cannibalism, war paint and other strange exotic practices. The other children's refusal to consider the possibility that the men were British, or even that they were in Britain at the time 'because they're black' is mystifying in the context of the school in which there were a number of different races, including several families from African or African-Caribbean backgrounds, including L's mother.

There is much to consider here in terms of the children's attitudes to race. Here I wish to focus on the influence of whiteness on my way of seeing. By permitting this deconstruction of blackness as a strange exotic property while failing to see the obvious potential for a parallel discussion on why people are white I unwittingly reinforced the notion of blackness as a departure from whiteness, the norm that does not need to be examined or deconstructed. Crucially, it was not until much later that I even saw that I could have challenged the invisibility and power of whiteness by initiating such a conversation.

Racism is a personal failing, not a structural issue

I noted above that whites tend to view racism as an individual character defect, and often do not understand the notion of the racism of social structures. Linked to this is a belief among many whites that one can only be guilty of a racist act if that act was intentionally racist. This conceptualisation of racism can be seen in my ambivalence as I compare two incidents in which a child had been referred to as having 'slanty eyes':

> A similar thing happened in another class, recounted to me by the teacher. D, who is Vietnamese, was attacked by A, a Pakistani boy, who called him 'slanty eyes, and flat face', reducing him to tears. I remember an incident in which someone referred to his eyes as 'slanty' earlier in my diary. On that occasion he cried too, and I did nothing more than have a 'serious talk' with the group. On that occasion, it seemed clear that no offence had been intended (does it matter?). But here it seemed obvious that the intent was malicious.

The earlier incident caused much hurt, but I did not feel it warranted anything more than a 'serious talk' because it had seemed clear to me, from the offending child's reaction to D's tears, that she was not in her mind making a racist remark. But my parenthetic question, 'does it matter?', reveals my own questioning of the offending child's point of view as the appropriate place from which to start. D clearly saw the remark as racist, and that is the more significant point of view. Again, I reveal a tendency to excuse apparently racist incidents in conversation with a colleague about the nature of young children's racism:

> Small children had sometimes used racist names but she [the colleague] didn't feel they were being deliberately racist. I asked whether she thought they used it as a way of retaliating when they were upset about something else, and she agreed this was probably true.

What links these two incidents is my conception of 'deliberate racism' as the sole problem. Other conversations with colleagues revealed a similar pattern. Asked if they had witnessed any racism in school several replied that they had not seen anything they regarded as 'blatantly', 'really' or 'specifically' racist. The use of these qualifiers may reveal a distinction similar to my own between intentional and unintentional acts. That there is a distinction to be made is not at issue. My concern is that rejecting the significance of the casual use of racist insults and the unintentional hurt caused by stereotypical racial references is concomitant to ejecting the significance and power of structural racism. The MacPherson report into the murder of Stephen Lawrence was explicit in defining 'unwitting' racism. Exchange the words 'police' and 'traditional' for 'teaching' and 'white' and the description may be said to apply equally to the education system:

> Unwitting racism can arise because of lack of understanding, ignorance or mistaken beliefs. It can arise from well intentioned but patronising words or actions. It can arise from unfamiliarity with the behaviour or cultural traditions of people or families from minority ethnic communities. It can arise from racist stereotyping of black people as potential criminals or troublemakers. Often this arises out of uncritical self-understanding born out of an inflexible police ethos of the 'traditional' way of doing things.
> (MacPherson 1999: 22)

Even when white teachers do perceive an incident as racist, some research suggests that they do not respond effectively. Troyna and Hatcher (1991) consider that the absence of an anti-racism policy in many schools is due to a belief among many teachers that racist incidents are neither sufficiently common nor serious to demand the introduction of such a policy. This leads to an ad hoc approach to individual incidents. This entry in my journal records my initial reluctance to tackle racist remarks from children:

> I had a session with three children who are learning English. We were looking at a book in the Oxford Reading Tree series, which concerns a white family this group is familiar with. The book we were looking at introduces Wilf and Wilma, two African-Caribbean characters, for the first time. F, who came from Bangladesh about a year and a half ago, looked at the picture in the book, pointed to Wilf and Wilma:

F: I don't like them.

SP: why not?

F: I like him, and him and her and her (pointing to the white characters), but I don't like them.

SP: why not, F?

F: their hair...it's (he touched his hair with his fingers, in a spiral motion) I don't like it.

I did not know what to say. Should I have challenged him? How?

It is difficult now to explain or understand why I did not respond to this remark in any way. My final comments suggest that I knew that I should have said something, but even after a period of reflection I did not know what an appropriate response would have been. By allowing F to make such a remark without challenging it I colluded with him.

'We don't know what to say'

A few colleagues admitted to sharing their fears, variously describing situations of uncertainty as 'a minefield', getting into 'deep water', and worries over 'saying the wrong thing'. The fear here was often of unconsciously saying something that others would construe as racist:

R talked about the issue of talking about Pakistan as the children's home country – 'am I being racist when I say that? I feel as though I am saying the wrong thing when some of the children have never been to Pakistan, for example'.

Another colleague noted during this conversation that 'even though the three of us were colleagues and had socialised together, we were still pussyfooting around because we don't want to be seen as racist'. Some commentators suggest that the fear whites feel when forced to confront racism, and the dominance of their group in general, is the fear of ultimately losing their status, and their material and psychological advantages (see, for example, Sleeter 1996). In contrast Frankenberg (1993) suggests that well-intentioned white people often feel deeply insecure about whether they have the credibility to talk about racism. This issue looms large in my later attempts to address the under-representation of non-white groups in the curriculum. This entry in my journal records my feelings when I learned I was to be joined in the classroom by T, a supply teacher. The lesson concerned immigration and emigration in Britain in the 1950s and 60s:

I have no opportunity to discuss the lesson with her before the day, and I feel very self-conscious about talking about issues of migration and the ill-treatment received by immigrants in front of a Pakistani-born woman who is given no role in the proceedings. What is this, liberal white guilt, or is it OK to think that there is something odd about a white woman talking about migration while a Pakistani woman stands by?

After the lesson I recorded:

I discussed my plan for the lesson very briefly with T at lunchtime, and she agreed to take a group, but did not comment on the material. I didn't say anything of how I felt either. We spoke about how difficult the class is, and how hard it is to get them to listen to each other. During the lesson the children were quite interested in the texts, and I tried to highlight the main issues, which were that people were invited to come to Britain, and the racism they encountered. The children...did not seem inclined to discuss it, and I did not press very hard for them to do so. Why? Because T was there. Why did that make such a difference? Because I was afraid of saying the wrong thing. After the children had gone we had a chat about the children, and agreed it was a shame there had not been more of a discussion. We were both content to blame the children for that...it was very friendly, and yet I had not been able to say what was on my mind. Had she?

My analysis of these extracts identifies two apparently common features of the practice of whiteness. In the first place I note the complete lack of communication between us. I complained that I would have no opportunity to discuss the lesson with her, but took no steps to try to contact her. I discussed the plan 'very briefly' but did not mention how I felt about it. At the end of the lesson we spoke about how it had gone in terms of classroom management, but again said nothing about the real issues. It seems I could not bring myself to admit my fear that I was not sufficiently experienced in approaching sensitive issues with children, and in particular that, as a white woman, I would not be able to deal appropriately with the material. Was I unwilling to surrender my superior position, or was I simply reluctant to make myself vulnerable to someone I did not know?

The second feature of whiteness this incident exemplifies is my desire to allocate roles in the lesson on the basis of 'race'. Being white, I felt I did not have as much right to talk about issues of racism as T, my Asian colleague, who, by virtue of her 'race', was the expert. Such feelings may be traced back to the legacy of 'moral anti-racism' (MacDonald *et al.* 1989) which over-simplified racism as only ever white-on-black oppression. This simplistic model essentialises the experience of both whites and blacks, offering whites no escape from the role of racist, and forcing blacks into the role of passive victim. Such a dualistic conception of the problem also traps blacks in the unasked-for role of experts on racism and spokespeople for all ethnic minorities. Nayak records the disappointment of a black teacher who felt she had been appointed partly because of her ethnicity: 'I objected to her seeing me as having a specific role because I was different to any other teachers. I was the only Black teacher on the staff, therefore I had this particular role' (1997: 64).

Discussion and conclusion

One way out of the debilitating conception of whiteness I have described in this chapter is to conceive of it as an abstract and socially constructed process, rather than an inescapable biological fact (Levine-Rasky 2000). In this way, individuals are not asked to bear the burden of personal guilt: they are able to see whiteness as a political and historical artefact, and one that can eventually be rejected. This model offers whites the possibility of moving beyond guilt: and fear towards positive action for greater social justice. The first step is to identify what, among whites, has for so long remained unidentified: whiteness as a cultural identity that defines the way we behave, speak and look at the world. When we know what it is we are talking about we can begin to change that way of seeing, to decentre whiteness, to take its place alongside, not pre-eminent among, other cultural and ethnic norms.

However, while there is much useful work that could be done in terms of initial teacher education the curriculum and INSET, there is no escaping the responsibility of the individual practitioner to recognise the myriad ways in which the practice of whiteness has skewed perceptions of self and others. There is much that stands in the way of such a personal project: lack of intellectual, moral and financial support; fear of controversy; and an already almost intolerable workload. I have been fortunate to find the necessary support structure to begin such a project, the progress of which I have attempted to chart in this chapter. In it I have attempted to document some of the ways in which I have behaved and thought because of my whiteness:

- a tendency to see conflicts between white and non-white groups as a 'natural' result of the difficulties of living in a multicultural society, rather than sometimes the result of non-white groups resisting the dominance of whites
- a habit of seeing whiteness as a neutral, core entity, and ethnicity as belonging to other, more marginal groups
- ignorance about the nature and extent of racism in society
- a willingness to excuse racist acts and comments for fear of causing a scene and 'saying the wrong thing'.

A reluctance to discuss issues of race with people of other ethnic.backgrounds because of guilt and fear. None of these facets of my whiteness is true for all whites, and none of them is fixed and immutable. They are ways of behaving that I have learned, and I have now begun the process of 'unlearning'. In these times of increased anti-immigration activity and heightened racial tension there is a need for those who see education as a vehicle for social justice to resist the new paranoia and assertiveness among some whites, and to communicate a more just way of thinking about 'race' to the next generation. But we cannot hope to do that until we have taken a long hard look at our own prejudices and preconceptions.

What is required is a teaching profession which is aware of the issues and not afraid to confront them wherever they arise: be it in the curriculum, the corridor or the staff room.

References

Basit, T. (1997) *Eastern Values, Western Milieu: identities and aspirations of adolescent British Muslim girls.* Aldershot: Ashgate.

Donald, J. and Rattansi, A. (eds) (1992) *'Race', Culture and Difference.* London: Sage/Open University Press.

Frankenberg, R. (1993) *White Women, Race Matters.* Minneapolis, MN: Routledge.

Gaine, C. (2001) '"If it's not hurting it's not working": teaching teachers about race', *Research Papers in Education,* **16** (1), 93–113.

Haw, K. (1998) *Educating Muslim Girls: shifting discourses.* Buckingham: Open University Press.

Levine-Rasky, C. (2000) 'Framing whiteness: working through the tensions in introducing whiteness to educators', *Race, Ethnicity and Education,* **3** (3), 271–92.

MacDonald, I., Bhavnani, R., Khan, L. and John, G. (1989) *Murder in the Playground. The report of the Macdonald Inquiry into Racism and Racial Violence in Manchester Schools.* London: Longsight Press.

MacPherson, W. (1999) *The Stephen Lawrence Inquiry.* London: HMSO.

May, S. (1999) *Critical Multiculturalism.* London: Falmer.

Nayak, A. (1997) 'Tales from the dark side: negotiating whiteness in school arenas', *International Studies in Sociology of Education,* **7** (1), 57–9.

Sleeter, C. (1996) 'White silence, white solidarity', in: N. Ignatiev and J. Garvey (eds) *Race Traitor.* New York: Routledge.

Troyna, B. and Hatcher, R. (1991) 'Racist incidents in schools: a framework for analysis', *Journal of Educational Policy,* **6** (1), 20–31.

Wright, C. (1992) 'Multiracial primary school classrooms', in: D. Gill, B. Mayor and M. Blair (eds), *Racism and Education – Structures and Strategies.* London: Sage.

Chapter 35

An interactive pedagogy for bilingual children

Charmian Kenner

Many people in the world regard their ability to speak and understand more than one language to be an integral part of their cultural identity. In this chapter, Charmian Kenner examines the knowledge and understanding that bilingual children bring with them to school. She also explores the ways in which children can draw on their awareness of different languages in developing literacy and learning in more than one language.

Would you like to do more Gujarati at school?

Yes, write things in Gujarati, draw things and write the words, and make things.

(Meera, aged 7)

In this statement, Meera expresses her hope and belief that her home language, Gujarati, could be integrated into the everyday activities of her primary school class. For bilingual children, interaction between a rich variety of linguistic and cultural experiences is an ever present feature of their lives. If schools can build on these interactions, the potential contribution to children's learning is huge. To do so requires a commitment to developing education for a multilingual and multicultural society, with the all round benefits which this will entail for children from both monolingual and bilingual backgrounds. Whilst the need for a national educational policy is clear, practitioners also have a key part to play. This chapter will discuss how teachers and teaching assistants can enhance children's educational experiences by enabling linguistic and cultural interaction to take place within the classroom, and between school and community life.

As teachers and teaching assistants know, the quality of their relationships with children is key, and depends on a recognition of the 'whole child' as a complex and multifunctional person with an already established history in their home and community. In the case of bilingual children, an important element is the recognition of their bilingual and bicultural knowledge, which is a fundamental part of their identities as learners. I shall first look at what kind of knowledge children might have, based on the findings of research with young bilingual learners in London, England.

The next step is to make links with children's knowledge in curriculum activities, and I shall discuss how this might be accomplished, drawing on the experience of an action research project which created a multilingual literacy environment in a nursery classroom. While my own experience is with young learners, a stage when it is particularly possible – and crucially important – to build links with children and families, a multilingual approach can be used with any age group and I shall suggest how this can be done.

Bilingual children's knowledge and capabilities

The majority of children in the world are bilingual. Growing up with more than one language and literacy is part of life in many countries which operate multilingually (Datta 2000), and also occurs through the increasingly common experience of families moving to a new country. From birth, children have the potential to become proficient users of any language met within their daily environment (Baker 2000). By opening our minds to these possibilities, we can discover what children have already learned in the world outside the classroom.

By the age of 3 or 4, when they begin to enter the school system, many young bilingual children will have encountered literacy materials in different languages at home, ranging from a newspaper being read by a grandparent in Turkish, to an airletter being written by a parent in Gujarati, to a Chinese calendar on the kitchen wall. As part of their continual curiosity about graphic symbols, children start to interpret the potential meanings of these texts. In some cases, they are able to combine their interpretations with ideas derived from direct instruction in their home literacy, because family members may have begun teaching them some initial reading and writing.

For example, 4-year-old Mohammed, growing up in south London, was being taught by his mother how to recognize the letters of the Arabic alphabet in preparation for joining Qur'anic classes at the age of 5 (Kenner 2000). Mohammed's older siblings already had their own copy of the Qur'an, and Mohammed would receive his when he had learned sufficient Arabic – a strong motive for literacy acquisition. When Mohammed's mother prepared a poster showing the Arabic alphabet for use in his nursery class at primary school, Mohammed proceeded to demonstrate his knowledge of the letters. As well as being able to name some of the letters for his nursery classmates, he worked by himself to produce his own version of his mother's poster in which each letter was accurately written. His mother was astonished to see Mohammed's work because she had so far only taught him to read: 'He's never written any Arabic before!' The detail of the letters was a considerable accomplishment for a 4-year-old, and showed Mohammed's desire to become a writer in Arabic.

In contrast, 3-year-old Meera (who attended the same nursery class) was being taught to write only in English by her mother because her parents thought it would be easier for her to learn one literacy first. However, Meera herself had other ideas. As well as speaking Gujarati at home, she had participated in literacy events involving Gujarati script, such as sitting next to her mother while letters were being written to her grandparents in India and writing her own 'letter', or observing her mother filling in crosswords in Gujarati newspapers. When she saw her mother writing in Gujarati for a multilingual display in the nursery, Meera climbed on a chair to do her own emergent writing underneath. She stated 'I want my Gujarati' and 'I write like my mum'. Meera's determination to find out more about Gujarati writing, fuelled by its significance in her home life, continued during the school year with a series of spontaneous versions of a poster made by her mother about Meera's favourite 'Bollywood' film video.

Comments by Meera as she was making these posters in the nursery showed how, at the age of 4, she was able to think about different aspects of literacy and enhance her learning by comparisons between her two writing systems. Like Mohammed, she looked closely at the detail of letters, noting that her mother's version of the English 'a' looked different, rather like an inverted 'p' ('my mummy done a "p" – never mind'), and considering in what order she produced the different elements of a Gujarati letter (asking herself as she wrote it for the second time 'Did I do the line first? Yes I did'). Noticing that her mother had written three groups of letters representing the names of the film heroes in Gujarati, but that only two groups of letters appeared in English underneath, she asked 'Why three?' She had realized that there should be a correspondence between equivalent items in the two languages, and indeed it turned out that Meera's mother had not been sure how to transliterate the third hero's name.

Some children, like Mohammed, begin to attend community language classes at the age of 5 or 6, while also learning to read and write in English at primary school. A recent research project (Kenner *et al.* 2004) showed that young children are very capable of dealing simultaneously with more than one language and script. Case studies of 6-year-olds attending Saturday school classes in Chinese, Arabic or Spanish produced striking evidence of their ideas about different writing systems. This knowledge was demonstrated when the children were engaged in 'peer teaching sessions', showing their primary school classmates how to write in their home literacy.

Selina, for example, who had been attending Chinese school since the age of 5, was already proficient at writing Chinese characters. A page from her first year exercise book showed the process of building up a character through the correct stroke sequence, and then practising it for several columns. Each stroke needed to be executed precisely, to achieve a character which was both correct and aesthetically pleasing. Selina was proud of her writing, demonstrating characters of considerable complexity to her primary school peers. She also understood that the Chinese writing system operated very differently from English. Chinese does not have an alphabet; rather, most Chinese characters correspond to an English word. Selina's mother was teaching her about the meaning of different elements within a character, for example, the symbol for 'fire' appears in a number of associated characters such as 'lamp'. Selina would point out the symbols she found within characters, such as 'fire' in 'autumn'.

Tala, learning Arabic, emphasized that her 'pupils' in peer teaching sessions must start from the right-hand side of the page when doing Arabic writing, and she provided a helpful arrow to remind them. She also commented on grammatical features of Arabic such as male and female verb endings, writing an explanation to emphasize (in case her audience was unsure) that 'femail is a girl' and 'mail is a boy'.

Brian showed his primary school class the typical way of learning to write in Spanish, by forming syllables which combined a consonant with a vowel. Using the example of the letter 'm', and translating his Spanish teacher's explanation into English, he told his classmates 'the M on her own doesn't say anything, just "mmm" - you have to put it together... with "a" it makes "ma"'. He also showed his 'pupils' how to write and pronounce the Spanish letter 'ñ' (as in the word 'España'), saying 'It's a different N'.

We can see that these children – all of whom were also making steady progress in English – were deriving considerable benefit from the experience of biliteracy. As a result of their participation in the research project, their knowledge became evident to their primary school teachers, just as Mohammed and Meera's understandings had become visible in the nursery class. I will now discuss how the teachers' responses enabled children's bilingual knowledge to become more closely woven into their primary school learning.

Developing multilingual learning environments in the classroom

An interactive pedagogy for bilingual children involves several elements. The first of these is a teacher who sees bilingualism as a *resource* rather than a problematic condition, and wishes to expand her knowledge about her pupils' home and community learning. It is not necessary to be an expert on what happens in children's homes – indeed, this is not even possible, given the huge variety of linguistic and cultural experiences which would be relevant to any multilingual group of pupils. What is important, and will be sensed by children and families, is a clearly stated support for bilingualism and an open-minded interest in how children are achieving this.

Support and interest are most strongly demonstrated by the second element of the pedagogy, which is a *direct engagement* with children's bilingual learning in the classroom. In the research project in Meera and Mohammed's nursery class, I worked collaboratively with the teacher to find out in what ways it was possible to create a multilingual literacy environment. We began by informally talking with parents about literacy materials and events in different languages which children enjoyed at home. In this way we found out that, for example, Mohammed liked listening to a tape of a children's song about the Arabic alphabet. We invited Mohammed to bring this tape into the nursery so that the whole nursery group could hear it, and asked his mother to make a poster showing the alphabet letters (with a transliteration in English) so that we could sing along with the tape.

The third step is to *integrate* bilingual material into curriculum activities. In the case of the Arabic tape and poster, these became part of the nursery's investigation of how graphic symbols relate to meaning – an essential building block for early literacy. As well as the English alphabet, we now had a new set of different looking symbols which related to a different set of sounds. The teacher talked about this with the whole class, and, whether bilingual or monolingual, the children were intrigued. Extra impetus was given to their understanding of the concept of sound–symbol relationships. Mohammed's own Arabic alphabet poster was displayed alongside an English poster, next to a cassette player into which children could place different tapes. Over the next few weeks, the children were observed to select the English alphabet song, or the Arabic one, and to dance to the music while pointing to various letters on the posters, showing that they were thinking about the possible connections. Children also made their own alphabet posters, using the English and Arabic posters as a resource. Again, this extended the range of their investigations into literacy.

The fourth element of the pedagogy is to give *institutional support* to children's home and community learning activities. In the nursery, this was happening directly through the important place being given to bilingual learning in the classroom. For Mohammed, it meant that he gained the opportunity to further explore and reflect on his home experiences of the Arabic alphabet. A few weeks after making his first poster, he decided to make a similar one, again based on his mother's example. He also wrote some of the Arabic alphabet letters as part of a text which included a drawing of 'a snake in the garden'. The interest of his teacher and classmates legitimized Mohammed's Arabic learning, which would otherwise have occurred at the margins of officially recognized education rather than in the mainstream, and this had a positive effect on his involvement at home; his mother reported that she heard him singing the Arabic alphabet song more often.

Over the school year, many bilingual texts were produced by children in the nursery, and, by engaging with material which interested them from home, the multilingual work proved motivating to several who otherwise seemed to be 'reluctant writers'. Billy's main enthusiasm for writing at home, according to his mother, was shown when he sat alongside her as she wrote letters to Thailand, talking about what she would say to the family and doing his own writing at the same time. When Billy's mother wrote an airletter in Thai in the nursery, this led him to write some symbols of which he said 'Mu-ang Thai' ('Thailand') and 'I write like my mum'. This was the gateway to a spate of texts produced by Billy at home, including both English and Thai symbols as well as drawings of people, and to an increase in his writing at nursery. When his mother brought a birthday card to Billy from his aunt in Thailand to show us, she placed it in the nursery book bag which was designed to carry his school reading books. Her action symbolized the links built between home and school literacy.

In the pedagogy just described, each element of the process interacts with the others, leading to the development of a 'virtuous circle' which recognizes, sustains and extends children's learning. When we engaged with Meera's home language in the nursery by asking her mother to join in a multilingual activity for parents, we discovered more about Meera's interest in home literacy events; while she did her emergent Gujarati below her mother's writing, Meera began to talk about films and TV. By asking her mother more about this, we discovered that Meera loved watching Indian films with her family. Thus the second step of the pedagogic process linked back to the first, expanding our knowledge about Meera's home experiences. The third step, integrating the film material into the curriculum, owed its success to the centrality of film watching in Meera's family life. When Meera brought her film video into the nursery, we showed one of her favourite extracts during the nursery's weekly 'video time'. Her mother's poster about the film, written rapidly at our request in the nursery one morning before she left to go to work, then provided Meera with a link between home and school which inspired her to create five related texts over the next three months adding to her learning in both English and Gujarati.

The third element of the pedagogy, integrating bilingual learning into curriculum activities, has a direct effect on the fourth, because it is the strongest form of support for bilingualism from an institution which ethnic minority families perceive as particularly powerful – the school. It also links back to the first and second elements, because as parents and children see that home literacy materials are being used as part of the curriculum, rather than as temporary decoration, they are motivated to bring more materials and to participate in writing events in the classroom. When Billy's mother and other parents were asked to write airletters in different languages in the nursery, as if they were writing to relatives at home, they agreed to participate in this role play activity because they knew that their texts would be used for the children's further learning.

Another way of taking the fourth step – giving institutional support to children's home learning activities – is to initiate direct contact with community language schools. During the research project with biliterate 6-year-olds, the children's primary school teachers began to see evidence of their community school learning. The teachers were keen to meet their pupils' Saturday school teachers to find out more about this other educational setting. At a specially organized seminar, the two groups met together, with the primary teachers expressly stating that they were coming in order to learn. As the community teachers explained how they went about their work each Saturday, the mainstream teachers realized that these were colleagues with professional knowledge, whose commitment to their pupils was total despite their low paid voluntary status.

The seminar had a profound effect on the primary teachers' understanding of bilingual learning, giving them a much fuller idea of how such learning was both possible and productive. When the biliterate children taught their whole primary school class as part of the research project, the teachers used this new information to support the activity. Ming's teacher decided to give him the opportunity to teach Chinese in one of the periods assigned daily to reading and writing work, the Literacy Hour, and drew on what she had learned from the seminar to make suggestions about the kind of issues he could talk about. These suggestions linked in with Ming's own ideas; he had spontaneously set about planning his lesson at home the night before, and arrived with a set of activities already on paper. The lesson lasted for an hour and a half, with Ming's classmates thoroughly engaged in the challenge of writing Chinese characters on their Literacy Hour whiteboards. As soon as he arrived home from school that afternoon, Ming phoned me (I had also been present at the session) to ask 'Charmian, when can I teach Chinese again – the whole class?' He had already evaluated his lesson and decided which characters would be most appropriate to teach next time; the experience of teaching in mainstream school had thus validated and added to his Saturday school learning.

Maintaining an interactive pedagogy

Once having begun to make links with bilingual pupils' educational experiences outside the mainstream classroom, teachers can conduct an ongoing dialogue with children and families which enriches learning This dialogue can include remaining aware of children's current home and community interests, and celebrating Saturday school work, for example, by making a photo display of children who attend community language classes and noting their achievements. In Britain, children can now be encouraged to record their knowledge in the European Language Portfolio designed for use in schools (CILT 2002).

Where multilingual activities have been incorporated into the curriculum, teachers can direct parents' attention to the texts made by children and what has been learnt from them, and this discussion can take place with monolingual as well as bilingual parents. The learning may involve general issues about language, such as how alphabets work, or specific content, such as how to write particular Chinese characters. In either case, teachers do not need to know the languages involved in order to facilitate learning; in the nursery there were at least ten different languages, of which we only knew one. We were able to draw on the knowledge of children, their siblings and other family members.

This interactive pedagogy can also be pursued with children in the upper primary years and with young people in secondary school. They may have had the opportunity to further develop their biliteracy knowledge at community language school, or they may have come directly from another country where they have been educated in a different language. As well as demonstrating their knowledge in activities which raise language awareness for the whole class, pupils can make use of their other literacies to write subject-based material. A project in a London secondary school involved producing web pages in English and Bengali (Anderson 2001) with a potential worldwide audience; this experience enabled the pupils to extend their range of writing in both languages. In this kind of work, texts brought from home can again be a point of reference; newspapers in different languages, for example, provide a resource for a vast number of culturally related topics.

Expanding multilingual pedagogies

Multilingual work in schools can flourish more widely if there is institutional support. At the level of the individual school, this is aided by a whole-school language policy which states that home languages are an integral part of learning. This, in turn, is given weight if national policies take a similar view. Taking England as an example, it seems that the tide which has been running against multilingualism in education since the 1980s may be beginning to turn. Although bilingual children's knowledge has been little recognized in educational initiatives of recent years – the national curriculum of 1989 was set up on an entirely monolingual and monocultural basis – there are signs of change at a national policy level which can potentially support work in home languages in schools.

Both in England and elsewhere, as increasing numbers of children live multilingual lives, teachers need to engage with this variety of experience and explore its potential to enhance learning. A multilingual pedagogy engages children positively by integrating their home and community knowledge into mainstream classroom work. The impact on children's self-esteem is considerable and supports further learning both inside and outside school. Classrooms become sites where, as 7-year-old Meera envisaged, children can 'write things...draw things and write the words, and make things' in more than one language. Teachers and teaching assistants become the active facilitators of this linguistic and cultural creativity.

References

Anderson, J. (2001) 'Web publishing in non-Roman scripts: effects on the writing process', *Language and Education*, **15** (4), 229–49.

Baker, C. (2000) *A Parents' and Teachers' Guide to Bilingualism*. Clevedon: Multilingual Matters.

CILT (Centre for Information on Language Teaching and Research) (2002) *European Language Portfolio*. London: CILT.

Datta, M. (2000) *Bilinguality and Literacy: Principles and Practice*. London: Continuum.

Kenner, C. (2000) *Home Pages: Literacy Links for Bilingual Children*. Stoke-on-Trent: Trentham Books.

Kenner, C., Kress, G., Al-Khatib, H., Kam, R. and Tsai, K-C. (2004) Finding the keys to biliteracy: how young children interpret different writing systems, *Language and Education*, **18** (2), 124–44.

Reproduced from Kenner, C. (2003) 'An interactive pedagogy for bilingual children', in: E. Bearne, H. Dombey and T. Grainger (eds), *Classroom Interactions in Literacy*, pages 90–102 with the kind permission of the Open University Press/McGraw-Hill Publishing Company.

Chapter 36

Beyond pink and blue

Robin Cooley

Robin Cooley, a teacher in Newton, Massachusetts, has worked to increase children's understanding of the way in which advertising and commercial products reinforce gender, race and family stereotypes. In this chapter she tells how she used stories to break gender stereotypes and how this led her fourth grade class (9-year-olds) to influence the advertising approach of a toy company.

'Pink, pink, pink! Everything for girls in this catalogue is pink' exclaimed Kate, one of my fourth graders, as she walked into the classroom one morning, angrily waving the latest 'Pottery Barn Kids' catalogue in the air,

'I hate the colour pink. This catalogue is reinforcing too many stereotypes, Ms Cooley, and we need to do something about it!'

I knew she was right. And I was glad to see that our classroom work on stereotypes resulted in my students taking action: As we finished up the school year, my students initiated a letter-writing campaign to Pottery Barn, one of the country's most popular home furnishings catalogues.

Newton Public Schools is actively working to create an anti-bias/anti-racist school environment. In fact, beginning in fourth grade, we teach all students about the cycle of oppression that creates and reinforces stereotypes. I wove discussion of the cycle of oppression throughout my curriculum to help my students understand how stereotypes are created and reinforced, and more important, how we can unlearn them.

Anti-bias literature

I began the year's anti-bias work in my multiracial classroom by looking at gender stereotypes. As a dialogue trigger, I read aloud the picturebook *William's Doll*, by Charlotte Zolotow. This is a wonderful story about a little boy who is teased and misunderstood by his friends and family because he wants a doll. When I finished the book, I asked the students the following discussion questions: 'Why was William teased? What did William's father expect him to be good at because he was a boy?' I explained that the fact that William was expected to like sports and play with trains were examples of stereotypes, oversimplified pictures or opinions of a person or group that are not true.

Next, I asked the class, 'Why did William's family and friends tease him because he wanted a doll? Why should only girls play with dolls? Where did this idea come from?' The students immediately said, 'Family!' Through discussion, the students began to understand that they are surrounded by messages that reinforce these stereotypes. We brainstormed some ideas of where these messages come from, such as television shows, advertisements, and books.

Next, I asked the class, 'Why didn't William's father listen to his son when he said he wanted a doll?' One student exclaimed, 'Because William's father believed only girls played with dolls!' I explained that the father believed this stereotype was true.

One boy in my class complained, 'I don't get it. I like dolls and stuffed animals. Why did William's dad care? Why didn't he buy his son what he wanted? That doesn't seem fair. Someday, I'm going to buy my kid whatever he wants!'

Finally, I asked the class, 'In the story, who was William's ally? Who did not believe the stereotype and helped William get what he wanted?' The students knew that William's grandmother was the one who stood up for him. She was an example of an ally. William's grandmother bought William the doll, and she taught the father that it is okay for boys to want to hold dolls, the same way he held and cared for William when he was a baby.

Each week during the fall semester, I read a picture book that defied gender stereotypes, and we had discussions like the one on *William's Doll*. Tomie dePaola's *Oliver Button Is a Sissy* is another excellent book about a boy who wants to be accepted for who he is. Oliver really wanted to be a dancer, and all the kids at school teased him about this. Despite great adversity and risk, Oliver had the courage to do what he wanted to do, not what others expected him to do or be. After reading the book, students in my class were able to share personal stories of what their parents expected them to do, or when they were teased for doing something 'different'.

A few more tales that helped to break gender stereotypes were *Amazing Grace*, by Mary Hoffman and *Horace and Morris but Mostly Dolores*, by James Howe. In *Amazing Grace*, Grace loves to act in plays and has been taught that you can be anything you want if you put your mind to it. When she wants to audition for the part of Peter Pan, her classmates say she can't. But she pursues her dream and gets the part.

Horace and Morris, but Mostly Dolores is about three mice that are best friends. One day, the two boy mice decide to join the Mega-Mice Club, but no girls are allowed. Dolores pins the Cheese Puffs Club for girls. She is unhappy and bored because all the girls want to do is make crafts and discuss ways to 'get a fella using mozarella'. One day, the three friends decide to quit their clubs and build a clubhouse of their own where everyone is allowed, and you can do whatever you want, whether you're a boy or a girl.

Looking at families

Next we explored stereotypes about families. The students were aware of the messages they've absorbed from our culture about what a family is supposed to look like. Ben, who is adopted, said he was upset when people asked him who his 'real' mom was. 'I hate that I have to explain that I have a birth mother who I don't know, and my mom lives with me at home!' he said. We discussed some different family structures and talked about how some families might have two moms or two dads, a single parent, or a guardian. *Heather Has Two Mommies*, by Leslie Newman, is a great picture book that illustrates this point.

After two months of eye-opening discussions, the last anti-bias picture book I read to my class was *King and King*, by Linda De Haan. This picture book does not have the typical Disney ending. In this story, the queen is tired and wants to marry off her son so he can become king and she can retire. One by one, princesses come, hoping the prince will fall in love with them. Each time, the prince tells his queen mother that he doesn't feel any connection. Is not until the last princess arrives with her brother that the prince feels something – but it's not for the princess. He falls in love with her brother. The queen approves, and they get married and become 'king and king'. My students loved this story because the ending is *not* what they expected at all! They also appreciated hearing a picture book that has gay characters because they know gay people exist. They wondered why there aren't more gays and lesbians in picture books.

Since my students were so excited about their anti-bias work, I decided we should do a project with our first-grade buddies and teach them about breaking stereotypes. We created a big book called 'What Everyone Needs to Know'. This became a coffee-table book that we left on the table at the school's entrance waiting area. The first and fourth graders brainstormed all the stereotypes that we knew about boys, girls, and families. Then each pair picked a stereotype to illustrate on two different pages. On one page, the heading was, 'Some people think that…' with a drawing portraying the stereotype. On the next page, the heading would say, 'but everyone needs to know that…' with a drawing breaking the stereotype. For example, one pair came up with, 'Some people think that all families have a mom and a dad, but everyone needs to know that all families are different. Some families have two moms or two dads. Some families have one grandparent All families are different.'

Another pair came up with, 'Some people think that only girls wear jewellery but everyone needs to know that both boys and girls wear jewellery'.

I knew our work on stereotypes was sinking in because my students would continually share with the class examples of how they tried to speak up when they saw people acting on stereotypical beliefs. One day, a student told the class about how she spoke up to a nurse at the hospital where her baby brother was just born. 'I couldn't believe the nurses wrapped him in a blue blanket and the baby girls in pink!' she said. 'I asked the nurse why the hospital did that and she said it was their policy. I don't think I can change the hospital's policy, but maybe I at least made that nurse stop and think.'

Making a difference

The day my class decided that they wanted to write individual letters to 'Pottery Barn Kids' catalogue was the day I knew my students felt they could make a difference in this world. They wrote letters that told the truth about how they felt and why they thought the catalogue was so hurtful to them. I was so proud that my students were able to explain specific examples of gender stereotypes in the catalogue and why they thought the images should change. The students analysed the catalogue front to back, and picked out things I hadn't noticed. One student wrote:

> Dear Pottery Barn Kids,
> I do not like the way you put together your catalogue because it reinforces too many stereotypes about boys and girls. For instance, in a picture of the boys' room, there are only two books and the rest of the stuff are trophies. This shows boys and girls who look at your catalogue that boys should be good at sports and girls should be very smart. I am a boy and I love to read.

The boys in my classroom felt comfortable enough to admit out loud and in writing that they wished they saw more images of boys playing with dolls and stuffed animals. Another boy wrote:

> Dear Pottery Barn Kids,
> I am writing this letter because I am mad that you have so many stereotypes in your magazine. You're making me feel uncomfortable because I'm a boy and I like pink, reading, and stuffed animals. All I saw in the boys' pages were dinosaurs and a lot of blue and sports.
> Also, it's not just that your stereotypes make me mad but you're also sending messages to kids that this is what they should be. If it doesn't stop soon, then there will be a boys world and a girls world. I'd really like it if (and I bet other kids would too) you had girls playing sports stuff and boys playing with stuffed animals and dolls.
> Thank you for taking the time to read this letter. I hope I made you stop and think.
> – From a Newton student

The day we received a letter from the president of Pottery Barn, my students were ecstatic. The president, Laura Alber, thanked the students for 'taking time to write and express your opinions on our catalogue. We'll try to incorporate your feedback into the propping and staging of our future catalogues and we hope that you continue to see improvement in our depiction of boys and girls.'

I knew the students would expect the fall 2003 Pottery Barn Kids catalogue to be completely void of pink and blue and I reminded them that change is slow. The most important thing is that they made the president of a large corporation stop and think. I pointed to two of the quotes I have hanging in my classroom, and we read them out loud together

> Never doubt that a small group of thoughtful, committed citizens can change the world. Indeed, it's the only thing that ever has.
> – Margaret Mead

Each of us influences someone else, often without realizing it. It is within our power to make a difference.

– Deval Patrick

Epilogue

The fall 2003 Pottery Barn Kids catalogue arrived in my mailbox in late August, and the first thing I noticed was the cover. There's a picture of a boy, sitting at a desk, doing his homework. Another picture shows a boy talking on the phone, not just a girl, which was something one of my students had suggested. The boy is also looking at a *Power Puff* magazine, something that is typically targeted for girls. When I asked one of my former students what she thought, she said, 'Well, the catalogue sort of improved the boys, but not really the girls. They still have a lot of changes to make.'

One thing I know for sure is that my students now look at advertisements with a critical eye, and I hope they have learned that they do have the power to make a difference in this world.

References

De Haan, L. (2002) *King and King*. Berkeley: Tricycle Press.

dePaola, T. (1990) *Oliver Button Is a Sissy* . New York: Voyager Books.

Hoffman, M. (1991) *Amazing Grace*. New York: Scott Foreman.

Howe, J. (2003) *Horace and Morris, but Mostly Dolores*. New York: Aladdin Library.

Newman, L. (2000) *Heather Has Two Mommies*. Los Angeles: Alyson Publications.

Zolotow, C. (1985) *Willam's Doll*. New York: HarperTrophy.

Chapter 37

Working with boys

Diane Reay

Boys' achievement in schools is a cause for concern. In this chapter Diane Reay, professor of education at London Metropolitan University, looks back over her career and suggests that this is not a new phenomenon. Boys' achievement, she believes, cannot be separated from a discussion of class, race, or an understanding of how these different factors impact on boys' self perceptions and group identity.

Introduction

There is a long history of concern in relation to boys' behaviour in primary classrooms. My own career has been inextricably entangled with, and defined by, that concern. After becoming a Gender Equality Advisory Teacher in Ealing, London, even more of my energies went into boys. Despite my own desire to work on gender projects that involved girls, the pressing concerns of the primary school teachers I was working with dictated that the vast majority of the projects that I initiated focused on boys. As I wrote in the article describing my work on gender in Ealing:

> In the last two years over a dozen teachers, all female, have approached me to discuss boys in their class who were presenting problems by demanding an excessively high proportion of teacher time and attention; in terms of discipline in both the classroom and playground; and through lower levels of engagement with the English curriculum resulting in lower levels of achievement than the girls.
>
> (Reay 1993: 13)

The inevitable consequence was that gender work became work with boys. So, in the mid-1990s, after 17 years as a primary practitioner whose main tasks had been variously motivating, 'rescuing' and 'reforming' boys, I was amused by the allegedly new discovery of boys' underachievement and disaffection. Where had everyone been for the past two decades? Certainly not in any of the inner London schools that I had been working in. This concern about boys' disaffection has continued into the millennium.

The first key point to make is that it is primarily, although not exclusively, a class phenomenon. The research by Frosh *et al.* (2002) is very useful here. It demonstrates how challenging the teacher is an integral component of popularity among male peer groups across social class, although the middle-class boys, and particularly those attending private schools, also recognise the needs to work hard academically. The second key point to make about boys and disaffection is that it has a long history.

Classed and racialized masculinities

The educational context of boys' disaffection is very different now to what it was in the late 1980s. The tensions have both increased and intensified. There has been a widening of social class inequalities, an increasing privatisation of education, the implementation of the National Curriculum and an intensification of both selection and testing (Reay 2003). As David Jackson (1998: 79) points out, these processes have resulted in many boys feeling 'brushed aside by dominant definitions of school knowledge – their home and community languages, their often raw but direct insights and their everyday, street knowledges have all been experienced as invalid' as a limited, exclusive definition of school knowledge has gained dominance.

Competitive grading, testing and streaming have instituted a steep academic hierarchy which has emphasised differences between masculinities and has widened the gap between 'failing and disruptive boys' (particularly white working-class and African Caribbean boys) and successful boys (predominantly white and middle class). Paul Connolly (1997) captures the radicalization of disaffection in his account of the overdisciplining of Black boys in primary schools, a process which sets up a vicious cycle of stereotyping. Connolly describes how the overdisciplining of 'the bad boys', four African Caribbean boys in the primary school he studied, generated a peer group context in which they were more likely to be physically and verbally abused. Connolly (1997: 114) concludes that as a consequence they were more likely to be drawn into fights and to develop 'hardened' identities which then meant they were more likely to be noticed by teachers and disciplined for being aggressive.

The current educational climate has exacerbated an entrenched culture of winners and losers broadly along social class and ethnic lines, and in doing so, increased the already existing working-class and racialized alienation from schooling. Willis (1997) captured the powerful, and often explosive, combination of anger, fatalism, alienation and resistance that characterised white working-class male relationships to schooling in the 1970s but in the 2000s the conditions that generated such disaffection are even more pervasive. And, in primary classrooms across the UK, the resulting social exclusion and academic rejection that such conditions generate entice failing boys 'into a compensatory culture of aggressive laddism' (Jackson 1998: 80). Lucey and Walkerdine attribute this 'aggressive laddism' and the anti-reading and anti-school position that underpins it to 'a defence against fear. They act against study for fear of the loss of masculinity'; a masculinity that, they go on to argue, 'is already seriously under threat in terms of the disappearance of the jobs which require it' (Lucey and Walkerdine 2000: 49). However, it is important to recognise that there are other losers from boys' disruptive behaviour – girls and teachers – and we need to explore how they are affected by boys' disaffection.

At the receiving end?: the impact of boys' behaviour on girls and women teachers

Women teachers, classroom assistants and female pupils can be dominated and oppressed by certain boys in primary classrooms. A classic study by Valerie Walkerdine (1981) describes the humiliation of a female nursery teacher by a 4-year-old boy. Almost all women teachers can recite low level incidents of rudeness and abuse by a small number of boys who have been in their charge.

In many classrooms I have worked and researched in, it is girls who are at the bottom of the male peer group hierarchies! It is easy to forget when responding to the pressure to change boys' behaviour, and the media hype that 'the future is female', that it is still necessary to engage in work that focuses on girls' learning as well. What boys and girls need are gender equality programmes which privilege both sexes rather than focus on the needs of one at the expense of the other (Skelton 2001b).

Practicalities: what can teachers and teaching assistants do?

So how can school staff work productively on changing peer group hierarchies rather than either challenging or accommodating them? And how do they improve the classroom environment for the girls and the majority of boys who, as Connell (2000: 162) points out, 'learn to negotiate school discipline with only a little friction'? It is important to remember that in spite of popular scare stories about underachieving and uncontrollable boys, the majority of boys in primary schools relate perfectly well to their female teachers and girls. I still believe that paradoxically bringing the concerns of the pupil peer group into the classroom is important in reducing and addressing disaffection. There is an even greater temptation now with the National Curriculum and the relentless testing and auditing to leave those concerns at the classroom door but I strongly believe that they will flood in anyway, impacting on behaviour and learning, creating at best divisions amongst children, at worst major disruption. This is particularly so in relation to bullying.

A great deal of my work with boys in the 1980s focused on bullying because that was an issue that all the boys' groups identified as a major problem for them. Writing about the boys' group I ran in 1988/9 I stated:

The sessions we had on bullying were amongst the most productive of the year. First there was genuine relief amongst the boys that the subject was being tackled directly. Everyone, including myself, recalled an incident in which they had been bullied, while just over a third of the boys admitted to having bullied on at least one occasion. It was obviously a very emotive issue, and one that for the year six boys was inextricably bound up with their fantasies and fears about moving on to secondary school. We spent two sessions attempting to work through such fears and fantasies, focusing on how to use humour, peer group support and adult authority to prevent bullying.

(Reay 1990: 276–7)

Of course now there would not be the space for such sessions among the contemporary preoccupation with Standardised Assessment Tasks (SATs) but perhaps what I did with the Year 5 (9–10-year-old) boys would be more of a possibility. I integrated a focus on bullying into their maths and information communication technology (ICT) curriculum. We designed a questionnaire for a whole school survey on bullying, worked out a representative sample and then the boys carried it out. An integral part of their task was to impart the strategies for dealing with bullying we had discussed and agreed in the group sessions to any younger child who disclosed that they had been bullied. As only two children in the sample claimed never to have been bullied, the boys had lots of opportunities to rehearse preventative strategies. Since this work on bullying, my own more recent research and that of others (Reay and William 1999; Frosh *et al.* 2002) has revealed that working hard at school can lead to boys being bullied. Frosh *et al.* (2002) found a polarisation of popularity and schoolwork in which popular masculinities are pervasively constructed as antithetical to being seen to work hard academically, leading to hardworking 'clever' boys being demonised within the male peer group.

Recent research has uncovered disturbingly high levels of bullying in primary schools. Whitney and Smith (1993) revealed that over 25 per cent of primary school pupils were being bullied in Sheffield, while according to MacLeod and Morris (1996) 50 per cent of primary pupils in London and the South-East reported being bullied in school during the previous year.

A further continuing concern for primary school teachers is boys' literacy practices. In my own work with boys I tried to combine 'doing' with writing activities through book making projects involving both mixed and boys only groups. Setting the groups the task of producing book proposals that appeal to the widest possible class readership both challenges and modifies existing stereotypes, and if supported by whole class surveys, generates useful information for the teachers as well as the children (Reay 1993). The subsequent process of designing layout, working out the graphics, producing publicity and marketing materials, as well as writing the text, meets the requirements of English, maths, art and ICT curricula at the same time as helping to change preconceived ideas about gendered preferences.

In addition to concerted work on bullying and literacy a lot of my time in the sessions was spent helping the boys to question conventional gendered characterisations. Any work with boys needs to recognise gender as relational elements (Francis 1998; Skelton 2001a) and focus on the images of femininity as well as those of masculinity that boys bring with them and construct in the context of schooling. Relatedly, I would argue that such work also needs to recognise the relationships between gender, class and ethnicity. The other curriculum interventions I developed were rooted in this belief that gender cannot be explored in isolation from other powerful aspects of identity. The anti-racist work on Black history was enjoyed by all the boys and even prompted the most writing phobic boys in the group to commit pen to paper. One of my main worries about the National Curriculum is that it has marginalised any notion of 'really useful knowledge' (Johnson 1979) for the working classes but anti-racist work that looks at the lives of 'ordinary but heroic' black people like Rosa Parks is clearly both useful and inspiring. So was the work on the franchise and working-class histories I covered. At the time I wrote that the primary-aged boys I was working with suffered the fate of all low status groups in society, be they black, female or working class: 'They had had no access to a meaningful history which explained why they and others like them came to be situated in a particular social location' (Reay 1990: 279). Today the literacy and numeracy hours and the obsession with 'the basics' have left even less space for curriculum initiatives that I still see as vital in predominantly working-class schools like those I was working in.

Devolving power to pupils and instituting more collaborative, reflexive and democratic ways of working are also simultaneously ways of tackling disaffection. It is good to see the 'new-found' enthusiasm for formative assessment (Black *et al.* 2002) as that underpinned learning in the boys' groups that I was teaching in the 1980s. The self and peer evaluation with its focus on pupil discussion and responsibility for learning that has become fashionable in the late 1990s was a pivotal part of the boys' groups I ran in the late 1980s:

> From the beginning I instituted a process of self-evaluation where boys evaluated their ability to work co-operatively on a scale of one to ten. They then made a group assessment which involved evaluating the input of other members of their group in addition to their own contribution. I fed back my own observations and we negotiated a final score. Initially, their contributions were brief to the point of curtness but by the summer term they seemed to have a much better grasp of what self and group evaluation entailed, giving far more detailed comments.
>
> (Reay 1990: 273)

Black *et al.* (2002) argue that both self and peer assessment are valuable but that peer assessment is especially valuable because pupils accept from one another criticisms of their work – and I would add behaviour – which they would not take seriously from their teacher. As is implicit in the quote above, peer assessment also allows the teacher space to observe and reflect on what is happening and to frame useful interventions.

Implicit in all the above is the view that the issue of tackling boys' disaffection and disruption in primary classrooms needs to be intrinsically, irrevocably linked to a project of social class, gender and racial justice in education. This does not mean suspending the National Curriculum and instituting a series of boys-only discussion groups. Rather, the curriculum and attainment targets need to be creatively rethought. A good starting point is to find out 'the gender state-of-play' in your classroom and cover mathematics, ICT and English curricula at the same time by getting the children to research what ideas pupils hold about men and women and how they differ by sex (see Francis 1998). When I attempted something similar I was pleasantly surprised:

> I came to the boys' group with a set of preconceived ideas about boys not being able to express their feelings and expecting female servicing. I was not entirely wrong but like all stereotypes my preconceptions were far too simplistic. It transpired that I was drawing on more traditional notions of masculinity in the spheres of domestic labour and tears than were the boys.
>
> (Reay 1990: 274)

However. as Christine Skelton (2001b) points out, work on the images of masculinity and femininity children bring with them into school and act out in the classroom and playground needs to be accompanied by parallel work on the dominant images of masculinity and femininity schools reflect to their pupils. Reflecting on and questioning dominant gender categories is something the staff need to do as much as the boys and girls in their classes.

The bigger picture: contextualizing boys' disaffection

In Shaun's story (Reay 2002) I write about a white, working-class boy, who, in spite of a contradictory, ambivalent relationship to schooling (that, I would argue, characterises almost all, and especially white, working-class relationships to education) desperately wants to achieve educationally. The article raises questions about the possibilities of bringing together white working-class masculinities with educational success in inner-city working-class schooling. Lucey and Walkerdine (2000: 43) argue that 'to be both academically successful and acceptably male requires a considerable amount of careful negotiation on the part of working class boys'. I argue that to combine the two generates heavy psychic costs, involving boys and young men not only in an enormous amount of academic labour but also an intolerable burden of psychic reparative work. Shaun's situation reveals the tenuousness of working-class, and in particular male, working-class relationships to schooling. In the article I describe how he is caught between two untenable positions, continually engaged in a balancing act that requires superhuman effort; on the one hand ensuring his masculinity is kept intact and on the other endeavouring to maintain his academic success. Inner-city schools and their wider contexts are often spaces in which success is in short supply and, as a consequence, it is frequently resented and undermined in those who have it. Below we see both the enormous effort Shaun puts into reconciling two contradictory aspects of self, and also the ways in which they are beginning to come apart:

It's getting harder because like some boys, like a couple of my friends, yeah, they go 'Oh, you are teacher's pet and all that'. Right? What? Am I a teacher's pet because I do my work and tell you lot to shut up when you are talking and miss is trying to talk? And they go, yeah so you're still a teacher's pet. Well, if you don't like it go away, innit.

(Reay 2002: 228)

Shaun's ambitions are created under and against conditions of adversity. Reputations in his school comes not through academic achievements but is the outcome of jockeying for position among a male peer group culture, in which boys are 'routinely reproducing versions of themselves and their peers as valued because of their hardness, appearance or capacity to subvert schooling' (Phoenix and Frosh 2001) Shaun's narrative suggests that the problem of 'failing boys' cannot be solved alone through school based initiatives. How can Shaun both set himself apart from and remain part of the wider working-class male collectivity? That is the task he has set himself and the dilemma it raises lies at the very heart of the class differentials in attainment within education. I conclude that until social processes of male gender socialization move away from the imperative of privileging the masculine and allow boys to stay in touch with their feminine qualities the problem of 'failing boys' will remain despite the best efforts of teachers, teaching assistants and researchers.

Frosh and his colleagues (2002) offer further helpful insights into male peer group cultures in school in their delineation of popular and unpopular masculinities and the classroom behaviours that underpin them. They found that 'an important part of being "cool" and popular entailed the resisting and challenging of adult authority in the classroom' (Frosh *et al.* 2002: 200).

Popular boys were expected to 'backchat' teachers, while boys who were seen as too conscientious were made fun of. As Christine Skelton (2001b) demonstrates through her case study of Shane, primary school boys who consistently challenge the teacher's authority earn themselves not only significant amounts of teacher attention but also the attention and tacit approval of their male peers. Here we can see a frightening correlation between popularity among the male peer group and getting into trouble in primary classrooms.

So have I moved from a counsel of hope to a counsel of despair? At times the research and literature in the area appears overwhelming, giving the impression that the male peer group is so dominant there is little teachers can do. However, as I've tried to show in the section on practicalities, teachers can make a significant difference and not just in terms of curriculum offer which is the area I have concentrated on, but also in terms of ethos and culture. Boys (and girls) respond best to teachers who can keep order and have fun with pupils. All children have a keen sense of unfairness: for example, they resent being punished collectively when only one or two boys have misbehaved. Frosh *et al.* (2002) found in their interviews with boys that many reported that their teachers treated boys unfairly with some also saying that teachers particularly picked on black boys. They conclude that

While this does not necessarily indicate that most teachers are unfair in these ways – particularly since, from their own accounts boys can make life difficult for teachers – the pervasiveness of this narrative from boys is important to considerations of boys' educational attainment.

(Frosh *et al.* 2002:224)

Conclusion

I am certainly not advocating my ways of working as the answer. What I have tried to do in this chapter is give some indication of which strategies worked best in the educational contexts that I was working in during the 1970s and 1980s. I have also tried to map out how 'the problem' of boys has changed since the late 1980s and suggested, through recounting some of Shaun's story, that only partial solutions can ever lie with teachers and schools. Wider constructions of both masculinities and femininities need to change and while teachers have a part to play, it is ultimately a challenge that the whole of society needs to face up to.

References

Black, P., Harrison, C., Lee, C., Marshall, B. and Wiliam, D. (2002) *Working Inside the Black Box: Assessment for Learning in the Classroom*. London: King's College Publications.

Connell, R.W. (2000) *The Men and the Boys*. Cambridge: Polity Press.

Connolly, P. (1997) *Racism, Gender Identities and Young Children*. London: Routledge.

Francis, B. (1998) *Power Plays: Primary School Children's Constructions of Gender, Power and Adult Work*. Stoke-on-Trent: Trentham Books.

Frosh, S., Phoenix, A. and Pattman, R. (2002) *Young Masculinities*. London: Palgrave.

Jackson, D. (1998) 'Breaking out of the binary trap: boys' underachievement, schooling and gender relations', in: D. Epstein, J. Elwood, V. Hey and J. Maw (eds), *Failing Boys: Issues in Gender and Achievement*. Buckingham: Open University Press.

Johnson, R. (1979) 'Really useful knowledge: radical education and working-class culture 1790–1948', in: J. Clarke, C. Critcher and R. Johnson (eds), *Working Class Culture: Studies in History and Theory*. New York: St Martin's Press.

Lucey, H. and Walkerdine, V. (2000) 'Boys' underachievement: social class and changing masculinities', in: T. Cox (ed), *Combating Educational Disadvantage*. London: Falmer Press.

MacLeod, M. and Morris, S. (1996) *Why Me? Children Talking to ChildLine About Bullying*. London: ChildLine.

Phoenix, A. and Frosh, S. (2001) 'Positioned by "hegomonic" masculinities: a study of London boys' narratives of identity', *Australian Psychologist,* **36** (1):27–35.

Reay, D. (1990) 'Working with boys', *Gender and Education,* **12** (3):269–82.

Reay, D. (1993) '"Miss, he says he doesn't like you", working with boys in the infant classroom', in: H. Claire, J. Maybin and J. Swann (eds), *Equality Matters: Case Studies from the Primary School.* Clevedon: Multilingual Matters.

Reay, D. (2002) 'Shaun's story: troubling discourses of white working class masculinities', *Gender and Education,* **14** (3):221–34.

Reay, D. (2003) 'Reproduction, reproduction, reproduction: troubling dominant discourses on education and social class in the UK', in: J. Freeman-Moir and A. Scott (eds), *Yesterday's Dreams: International and Critical Perspectives on Education and Social Class.* New Zealand: University of Canterbury Press.

Reay, D. and Wiliam, D. (1999) '"I'll be a nothing": structure, agency and the construction of identity through assessment', *British Educational Research Journal,* **25** (3):343–54.

Skelton, C. (2001a) 'Typical boys? Theorising masculinity in educational settings', in: B. Francis and C. Skelton (eds), *Investigating Gender: Contemporary Perspectives in Education.* Buckingham: Open University Press.

Skelton, C. (2001b) *Schooling the Boys: Masculinities and Primary Education.* Buckingham: Open University Press.

Walkerdine, V. (1981) 'Sex, power and pedagogy', *Screen Education,* **38**:14–25.

Whitney, I. and Smith, P.K. (1993) 'A survey of the nature and extent of bullying in junior and secondary schools', *Educational Research,* **35** (1): 3–25.

Willis, P. (1977) *Learning to Labour.* Aldershot: Saxon House.

Reproduced from Reay, D. (2003) 'Troubling, troubled and troublesome? Working with boys in the primary classroom', in: C. Skelton and B. Francis (eds), *Boys and Girls in the Primary Classroom,* pages 151–166 with the kind permission of the Open University Press/McGraw-Hill Publishing company.

Index